Literature Lost

Yale University Press New Haven & London

Literature

Lost

Social Agendas
and the
Corruption of
the Humanities

John M. Ellis

Published with assistance from the Charles A. Coffin Fund. Copyright
© 1997 by Yale University. All rights reserved. This book may not be
reproduced, in whole or in part, including illustrations, in any form
(beyond that copying permitted by Sections 107 and 108 of the U.S.
Copyright Law and except by reviewers for the public press), without
written permission from the publishers.

Designed by Nancy Ovedovitz and set in Adobe Garamond type by
Keystone Typesetting, Inc. Printed in the United States of America by Vail-
Ballou Press, Binghamton, New York.

Library of Congress Cataloging-in-Publication Data
Ellis, John M. (John Martin), 1936–
Literature lost : social agendas and the corruption of the
humanities / John M. Ellis.
p.   cm.
Includes bibliographical references and index.
ISBN 0-300-06920-0 (cl.)
    0-300-07579-0 (pbk.)
1. Humanities—Study and teaching (Higher)—United States—
Evaluation.   2.Humanities—Political aspects—United States.   3. Political
correctness—United States.   4. Humanities—United States—History.
I. Title.
AZ183.U5E45   1997
001.3'071'173—dc21   96-37680
                    CIP

A catalogue record for this book is available from the British Library.

The paper in this book meets the guidelines for permanence and
durability of the Committee on Production Guidelines for Book Longevity
of the Council on Library Resources.

   10   9   8   7   6   5   4   3   2

Contents

Acknowledgments

I am indebted to many friends and colleagues for their helpful suggestions on all or part of the manuscript, including the comments I received following presentation of parts of the book at various conferences and universities. I wish to thank especially Stephen Balch, Paul Cantor, Peter Collier, Barbara Ellis, Richard Ellis, Norman Fruman, John Hollander, Siegfried Puknat, Peter Shaw, Christina Sommers, and Fred Sommers. Gary Saul Morson gave the entire manuscript a particularly thorough reading; his suggestions improved it considerably.

I am proud and grateful to have had this work generously supported by the Lynde and Harry Bradley Foundation, the Carthage Foundation, the John M. Olin Foundation, and the Smith Richardson Foundation.

Introduction

This book is about the great changes that have taken place—and are still proceeding—in humanistic education and learning throughout the English-speaking world, though they are most advanced in America. This is a matter of great social importance. From elementary school through university, literature and history are two of the most significant aspects of the education of young people. The effect of a profound change in the way these subjects are taught and in what teachers are trying to achieve in teaching them is therefore far from trivial—especially when part of the purpose of this change is to transform students' attitudes toward the society in which they live.

Although I am concerned with what is happening to humanistic education and learning in general, I focus mainly on one area of the humanities: literature. There are good reasons to do so. First, literature has been affected more than any other field; and, second, insofar as these same changes have occurred in other fields, they have done so in large part through the influence of literary studies, for that is where the most influential advocates of the new approach are concentrated. Paradoxically, however, even this narrowing of focus will take us well beyond literature itself, because the new approach to literature is heavily involved in political and historical matters.

These changes have already provoked much discussion, both on the college and university campuses where they originated and among the wider public. Interestingly, the questioning has been reasonably open and direct in the public sphere, whereas on campuses it has been much more inhibited. At first, much of the argument was about whether the changes were being exaggerated by those who objected to them. Defenders insisted that accounts of political correctness in classrooms, and of a transformation in curricula to accommodate race, gender, and class perspectives, were nothing more than a few unrepresentative anecdotes. By now, however, it is clear from the sheer persistence of these reports that such is not the case. Nor was it ever a plausible contention in view of a strange discrepancy that was apparent from the beginning: the same people who reassured the public with the explanation of unrepresentative anecdotes told a different story on campus.[1] There they claimed that the changes were revolutionary and that they had already experienced considerable success in implementing them.[2] I have no doubt that the story told on campus was the correct one.

My concern in this book, however, is not to establish what is happening—others have done this well enough already[3]—but, rather, to examine the forces behind these changes and the arguments that are made to persuade others to accept them. My aim, in other words, is to interpret the situation. In the process, I hope to give my reader an analysis of the coherence of the arguments that are used to justify the installation of race, gender, and class perspectives at the center of the college curriculum, so that he or she will be in a better position to decide whether they are sound and, if they are not, to understand what is wrong with them.

The present is so compelling that it soon crowds out thoughts of how things were even a short time ago; so completely do present problems command our attention that even when a rapid and startling change takes place, we soon adjust to it, as the situation that preceded the change begins to fade away. Already it requires some effort to recall what the typical attitudes toward the study of the humanities were just a short while ago. It is worth making that effort. Looking back has nothing to do with a nostalgia for the way things were or a conservative resistance to change. The point is that to grasp the character of what is happening now we must contrast it with what it has replaced.

Just a few years ago, we were accustomed to a standard set of arguments about the place of the humanities in an education. People with a utilitarian cast of mind were typically lukewarm to the humanities: they were wary of letting too much time be taken up by subjects that had no relevance to a career and a future livelihood. Law, politics, economics, science, and technology were all practical things to study, and although some literature, history, or philosophy might make life a bit more interesting, too much would be an indulgence. The standard defense of the humanities, on the other hand, was that humanistic education provided all kinds of rewards, but the least important was the enrichment of our leisure through great literature and the arts. The most weighty arguments were that the humanities enabled us to see ourselves in perspective, to become more enlightened citizens, and to think more deeply about important issues in our lives. A society of people educated not just for a vocation but for full and intelligent participation in a modern democracy would be a far better and happier society—so ran the argument—and this overriding social usefulness of humanistic education compensated for its not leading directly to a means of earning one's living.

These two opposing viewpoints could be heard over and over again, and while all kinds of people *might* voice one or the other, a stereotypical distribution of them was also part of our common experience. People in the world of business were more likely to voice the first, whereas teachers of the humanities were—naturally enough—advocates of the second. And so we heard people who taught difficult but unique books for a living—books like Dante's *Inferno,* Goethe's *Faust,* or Homer's *Iliad*—arguing passionately for the power of Dante's or Goethe's or Homer's understanding of human existence and the profundity of the questions they raised. If there was unquestionably a self-serving edge to these arguments, this logic nonetheless proved sufficient to convince even most businessmen that the humanities should be part of their children's education. These were, after all, writers of such quality that, by common consent, they towered above their fellows; their thought was so arresting that few who were exposed to them resisted their spell.

Some now seriously misrepresent this attitude toward the great writers and thinkers by referring to it contemptuously as a passive, uncritical swallowing of "eternal verities."[4] Nothing could be further from the truth: these writers were more apt to present eternal dilemmas and challenges than dogmas, and insofar as there could be said to be doctrines or lessons in Shakespeare or Dante, Plato or Hume, the development of thought and the unfolding of different sides of issues and problems was always far more visible than this caricature allowed. The body of enduring literary and philosophical books of the Western tradition is not a collection of ideas demanding to be believed but a remarkable set of fascinating struggles with problems and issues. Always prominent is the conflict and competition between the ideas and vision of one writer and those of others, and there is often a high degree of self-criticism.

If we could use a time machine to go back to the scene of this classic set of arguments for and against the humanities in education, we would likely not find a single person willing to believe that within a few years the participants in these arguments would have changed sides: those who had formerly made the case for Dante, Goethe, and Homer and against narrowly utilitarian attitudes would now be making the case for those same attitudes and against the great writers, whereas those who had formerly been skeptical would constitute the most vocal lobby for them. Yet this is indeed what has happened: professors of literature now argue against the Western tradition in thought and literature, and in this new-found role they go even further than their predecessors. They argue not that studying Shakespeare and Plato is a superfluous diversion from more serious pursuits but that such study can be positively harmful. High culture is full of pernicious ideas and influences—even Shakespeare's plays reflect reactionary attitudes: jingoistic imperialism, racism, sexism, homophobia. And because high culture embodies these attitudes, the argument goes, it plays a leading role in reinforcing them in the general public and is therefore a means by which the socially, racially, and sexually privileged maintain their power. High culture is part of the ruling elite's apparatus for social control. And for that reason we were mistaken—according to this newer view—to think that study of the great books of the West opened our minds and trained us to think critically. It is just the reverse: these books close our minds, get us to believe unquestioningly in a reactionary ideology, and make us conform to the ideas of a privileged class of white upper-class European males. Consequently, the former teachers and defenders of the great works of Western thought and literature now scorn them, leaving the defense of these works to those who do *not* teach them.

This strange reversal has been accompanied by another. People outside the university, impatient with academia's independence, used to urge that higher education preach the values of our society so as to further, in a direct way, its cohesion and internal strength. The threat of communism was most frequently the spur for this kind of pressure. Universities, it was said, should teach the virtues of our way of life and not employ Marxists to present the case for our bitter ideological enemies. In response to this pressure, professors would argue that universities served society in a nonpartisan way; the outside world could call on them for expert knowledge and advanced teaching, but to make this possible colleges had to remain politically neutral. Direct involvement in everyday life was to be avoided so that professors and students could reflect on it, analyze it, and see it in broader perspective from a distance. Requiring them to preach would destroy this inquiring spirit. Academics reasoned that it was dangerous to know but one side of an argument; those who understood the case for communism as well as its own partisans were really best equipped to oppose it, not those who knew nothing of it.

Although some inside the academy spoke as if this attempt to politicize the universities was an imminent danger, the argument for independence made by the overwhelming majority of professors easily prevailed, because it seemed obvious to nearly everyone that this was the one reason for the success of our universities. The alternative of the politically and ideologically correct universities of totalitarian regimes, both Marxist and fascist, had resulted in such absurdities as Lysenkoism, the genetic doctrine of Soviet biologist Trofim Lysenko which held that acquired characteristics could be inherited. Because of the direct political interference of Stalin, Lysenko was allowed to corrupt Soviet biological research with his ideas for several decades. Stalin had good political reasons for liking the idea that the blacksmith could pass on to his children not just the fine physique that had made blacksmithing a good choice of occupation but also the enlarged muscles that had resulted from that work. If that were so, then the new Soviet man and woman might pass on to their children the characteristics that Stalin had instilled in them during their lifetime. If Lysenko was right, then Stalin could control the next generation as well as this one. An even more important point was that the realities of biology could not impede social change. The lesson of episodes like this seemed clear: once political considerations, rather than a disinterested search for truth, were allowed to dictate the course of university research, any crackpot theory that a country's rulers found useful could dominate a whole field.

Again, twenty years ago no one would have believed it possible that professors, of all people, would one day argue that the universities should have an overtly political function, work directly for social and political change, and inculcate a particular political viewpoint in their students.[5] It seemed obvious that a nonpolitical stance was their only protection against governmental interference with their academic freedom. Everyone knew that once professors took on the role of instilling correct political thinking, it would not be long before a newly elected government of a different political persuasion used its mandate to fire them all and appoint its own partisans. (And only the more fastidious governments would even require an election to justify their actions.)

Yet once more, the same bizarre reversal has occurred. Now it is the professors who say that they should be political. In fact, a quite different conception of academic life has gained ground recently, one that is not content with merely reflecting and analyzing but instead wants the academy to get into the day-to-day jostling of the real world and pursue direct political action to transform it.

Now when we see a demand that politics be given a more important place in the academy, it would be natural to assume that professors and students of politics were behind it, perhaps intent on maximizing the importance of their field of study. And yet—even more strangely—they are not the source of this demand. It is humanists, but especially teachers of literature, who press for this new centrality of politics to everything, not those who are the academic specialists in that field. How, one might wonder, can literature professors claim to know more about the scope of politics than specialists in political science do? But professors of literature are now experts on everything. They write authoritatively on sociological topics like racism and race relations; political and historical topics like imperialism and socialism; psychological topics such as sex, both straight and gay; and topics in criminology such as rape, pornography, and pedophilia. Some even express themselves trenchantly on economics. And it is plain that in all these cases, far from feeling insecure about their lack of professional training and breadth of knowledge, they believe they have the edge by virtue of a superior conceptual framework that they bring to these tasks.

Given these changes, it is not surprising that there have been changes in the way literature is taught. These changes are, in fact, the most visible sign of the overall change in the climate of university life. In a comparatively short time, academic literary criticism has been transformed. Many now regard social activism as the major purpose of literary criticism, and social activism of a very specific kind: the primary issue in all literary texts is the question of oppression by virtue of race, gender, and class. They view the very idea of a canon of great works as an elitist notion and even question whether there should be a distinction between literature and other kinds of writing; that, too, is elitism.

Their new view of human motivation must also astonish anyone who remembers the way humanists used to talk: for them power is now the most basic factor in human motivation. In this grim view of humanity, one central factor displaces and undermines the multiplicity of other motivations that we used to think so important: love, loyalty, fulfillment, ambition, achievement, friendship, intellectual curiosity, and so on.

Humanists used to be rather cheerfully disorganized people whose immersion in very particular, one-of-a-kind human situations—like those in *Hamlet* or *Crime and Punishment*—made them, on the whole, dislike abstract generalizations. Yet now, for the first time, a majority seem to accept the fact that a definite theory should be the one indispensable tool of a critic. But what kind of theory? In the period before this new mood overtook literary studies, a minority of critics—of which I was one[6]—tried to persuade others that critics ought to think about the general theory of their field, that is, to reflect in general terms about what made for good criticism. The more recent success of theory, however, is not in the same spirit. Instead, what has triumphed is not greater openness to general reflection but a narrowing of perspective to a rigid prescription for criticism that insists it be of a certain character and have a specific content and concern. This represents not an opening up but a shutting down of theoretical reflection.

Another departure from the past can be seen in the quality of writing in present-day literary criticism. As was fitting for people whose professional lives were devoted to studying outstanding examples of language use, critics (and more generally, humanists) prided themselves on using their language well. Here, too, the new wave has produced a startling change: people who write about literature now write in a prose thick with impenetrable jargon.

These new attitudes and ideas gained ground so quickly that no full-scale discussion and analysis of them took place before they were already widely accepted; there seems never to have been an intervening stage in which to test their intellectual force in the marketplace of ideas. They became accepted dogma quite suddenly, and quite unusual pressures have built up to make dissent from them seem perilous. This is not just a matter of the rapid conversion of the leaders of the profession or of control of bodies such as the Modern Language Association of America, now squarely behind the new orthodoxy. What is especially intimidating to dissenters—especially young people who are trying to get their first job at a difficult time—is an odd but highly effective blend of two currents, each of which supports the other and neutralizes what would otherwise be serious weaknesses.

One ingredient is a moral appeal: the concern with race, gender, and class makes this new mode seem a just cause, one that no decent person would want to oppose. The second is an arcane language derived in large measure from sophisticated Parisian intellectuals. To understand why this is a uniquely effective combination we need only look at the weaknesses of each factor by itself. Moral sermons easily seem priggish and unsophisticated, which is one reason the literary intelligentsia have usually despised the prevailing morality of their times. On the other hand, when the pursuits of intellectuals become too rarefied, they easily seem out of touch with the real world. Combining race, gender, and class criticism with the language of deconstruction takes care of both problems at once. Politicized criticism gives deconstruction an apparent seriousness of purpose, and in return deconstruction makes a rigidly moralistic position seem avant-garde and sophisticated.

The result is an institutionally entrenched orthodoxy armed with intimidating twin defenses and enforced by what has become known as political correctness, or PC; dissenters can expect to be not only criticized, as dissenters always are, but denounced as both moral outcasts and unsophisticated simpletons. Yet this is done on the basis of a viewpoint that coalesced far too quickly for it to have been properly thought through, one that seemed to advance not by its intellectual force but instead by a kind of tidal action that suddenly surged over everyone. It is time to retrace our steps, to do what should have been done initially: we must take a hard look at what this position really amounts to and see whether it is sound enough to deserve the commanding position it now has. The aim of this book is to give this new orthodoxy the systematic scrutiny it did not get on its way to the top.

Chapter 1 sets political correctness in wider perspective, showing that it represents a recurring impulse of Western society—one with a discouraging history. Chapter 2 examines the current orthodoxy about literature and criticism and argues that it has everything upside down in discussions of the canon and diversity. Chapters 3, 4, and 5 focus on how the issues of gender, race, and class function in this controversy. Chapter 6 considers the arguments advanced for social activism in scholarship. Chapter 7 looks at the typical thought process that results in race-gender-class criticism. Chapter 8 measures the contributions of race-gender-class critics to theory against those of prior critics. Finally, chapter 9 considers where we are now, what factors have produced this result, and what we ought to do about it.

1 The Origins
of Political
Correctness

What we now call "political correctness" may seem to be nothing more than a modern fad, and one that will pass, but to see it only this way is to misunderstand it.[1] Its particular shape may be specific to our time, but its basic impulse is one that recurs regularly in the history of Western society. Herein lies a deep irony. Those in the grip of this impulse are critical of the Western tradition and define themselves by their opposition to it, yet the impulse itself is so much a part of the Western tradition that the attitudes it generates can be said to be quintessentially Western. One reason for studying the Western tradition is to learn some important lessons about this recurring phenomenon and so avoid mistakes that have been made many times before. In this chapter I shall look at some prior episodes to show more clearly what kind of thing this impulse is, what produces it, and what its dangers are. Rather than carp at the absurdities of the current scene, we can understand them more fully as part of the history of Western civilization.

Those who study German culture, as I do, usually get their first account of the early Germanic peoples from the Roman historian Tacitus, who wrote a short treatise entitled *Germania* in the first century A.D.[2] By the standards of civilized Rome, the Germans were barbarians, which is what Tacitus calls them; in modern terminology, they were part of the Third World of their day. But in Tacitus' eyes they were quite remarkable people. They seemed to be instinctively democratic; all major affairs were discussed by the entire community, and only minor matters were delegated to chieftains. Even the views of a king were heeded, Tacitus tells us, "more because his advice carries weight than because he has the power to command." Similarly, in war, commanders relied on example rather than on the authority of their rank. These natural egalitarians were apparently not bothered by questions of social standing and power. And if they seemed to have the sin of pride well under control, the sin of greed seemed to give them no problems either: Tacitus notes that "the employment of capital in order to increase it by usury is unknown in Germany."

Nor was sexism one of their vices, for they had a high regard for the opinions of women and treated them with the utmost respect: "They do not scorn to ask their advice, or lightly disregard their replies." In fact, these Germanic tribes, though primitive, exhibited high moral character, a point Tacitus stresses repeatedly, with remarks such as "They live uncorrupted by the temptations of public shows or the excitements of banquets" or "No one in Germany finds vice amusing, or calls it 'up to date' to seduce and be seduced" or "Clandestine love letters are unknown to men and women alike. Adultery is extremely rare." Tacitus' Germans were also brave, honest . . . and just about anything else one could wish.

Tacitus sums up his idyllic picture by saying that "good morality is more effective in Germany than good laws are elsewhere." That is, of course, because the Germans were a naturally good people who did not need laws to keep their behavior in check. If Tacitus had been speaking about a tribe that had vanished without a trace, we might simply regret that we had never encountered such a splendid and admirable people. Unfortunately, we actually know a great deal more about those Germans than Tacitus did, and they do not seem so admirable in other recorded accounts. Moreover, Tacitus never actually traveled among them. What is going on here?

That vague word *elsewhere* in Tacitus' summary, suggesting as it does an unspecified place where people must be governed by laws to keep their depravity in check, gives the game away. It refers, of course, to Tacitus' own society, to the first world of the time: imperial Rome. What Tacitus really has on his mind is less the virtue of Germans than the corruptness of civilized Rome—its sexual depravity, greed, and obsession with rank and conquest.

We are surely familiar with this situation in our own time. A sophisticated man of letters, disillusioned and even embittered by the flaws, inconsistencies, and retrogressions of a great civilization, deludes himself that a world of primitive innocence and natural goodness exists in peoples who are untouched by the advances of that civilization. So intense are his hostile feelings toward his own society that he is unable to see the one he compares it to with any degree of realism: whatever its actual qualities, it is endowed with all of the human values that he misses in his own. Consequently, he sees his own culture not as an improvement on brutish natural human behavior but as a departure from a state of natural goodness. This recurring Western fantasy runs from Tacitus' idealized Germans all the way to such twentieth-century versions as Margaret Mead's sentimentalized Samoans and ultimately to one of the most far-reaching outbreaks of this illusion—the political correctness of our own day.[3]

Anyone reasonably knowledgeable about the history of Western culture knows that some of these episodes were major factors in the historical development of Europe. Both Jean-Jacques Rousseau's adulation of the Noble Savage and the nineteenth-century German Romantics' glorification of the German *Volk* had serious repercussions. Karl Marx was perhaps in a similar frame of mind when he imagined the end point of his transformation of society to be the withering away of the state. He must have fantasized, just as Tacitus did, that morality could substitute for good laws.

John Searle recently defended Western thought against the criticisms of the politically correct by pointing out that it is uniquely self-critical.[4] But an even stronger point can be made: political correctness itself is a thoroughly Western phenomenon. From earliest times, Western society has been prone to recurring fits of this self-doubt. Those who are seized by this mood may imagine that they are taking an anti-Western stance, but that is all part of the same pattern of self-delusion.

Tacitus was using these imagined noble Germans as a standard against which to judge the Romans, but that was as far as he went; his concern was simply with the particular historical situation he was in. Rousseau went further, however. Instead of being content to think that eighteenth-century French society and its institutions were corrupt and corrupting, and to imagine another people that was morally superior because their natural goodness had remained intact, Rousseau generalized: man in his natural state was naturally good, and all corruptness sprang from society and its institutions.[5] His Noble Savage was not just a particular group of Germanic tribesmen but simply man in his naturally good state before the degradation brought by the institutions of society—any society.

Rousseau had gone beyond Tacitus' local irritation to formulate a general theory of society and human nature, one heavily pessimistic about the former and blithely optimistic about the latter. Tacitus' quarrel was with Roman society, but Rousseau's was with civilization itself, which, he said, had ruined the human race. For Rousseau, the first person who enclosed a piece of land and said "this is mine" started civil society; and, he tells us, if only someone had objected to that first step, "what crimes, wars, murders, what miseries and horrors" he would have saved the human race.[6]

Whether because of the direct influence of Rousseau or through the spontaneous eruption of the politically correct impulse, this dark view of civilization has been revisited often since Rousseau wrote. Yet history has been most unkind to these illusions. Tacitus wanted to see in the Germans the answer to everything that bothered him about his own society, just as the campus radicals of our own time are tempted to see in the contemporary Third World an absence of rank consciousness and hierarchy, of capitalism and greed, of the strong coercing the weak, and of men lording it over women and treating them as playthings. Alas, Tacitus did not live to see his noble Germans run amok in the centuries that followed. One tribe, the Vandals, instituted a legendary reign of terror that gave us the word *vandalism*. We can be sure their victims did not see the sweetness and natural goodness Tacitus attributed to them. The Goths and the Vikings, too, committed more than their share of rape and plunder, and we can be confident that when the Visigoths sacked Rome in A.D. 410, the female inhabitants of the city did not experience the respect for women that Tacitus had described.

Had the Germanic tribes changed in the intervening years? They had not. Tacitus recorded a curious detail in his account of one tribe that might have revealed the truth of the situation, if only he had been receptive to the bad news it contained. He tells us of a tribe called the Suiones, who lived beyond the mainland and built ships in a peculiar way: "The shape of their ships differs from the normal in having a prow at each end, so that they are always facing the right way to put in to shore. The rowlocks . . . can be reversed, as circumstances require, for rowing in either direction."[7] The word *Suiones* is, of course, our modern word *Swedes,* and those ships were already recognizable as Viking raiding ships. There was nothing peculiar about them if one understood the purpose of their design. They were built for what Gwyn Jones calls the "quick-in quick-out Viking raids."[8] In remarking that they always face the right way to put in to shore Tacitus misses the point, which is that they always face the right way for putting out to sea. Just as a bank robber will leave a car idling outside the bank, the Vikings had a ship waiting that did not have to be turned around to get under way. This Germanic tribe was already not what Tacitus imagined it to be.

History has treated Rousseau's theories just as roughly. The French Revolution was Rousseauist in nature: the old institutions were swept away and what was left was simply citizens—an apparently egalitarian society without institutions that would corrupt them. But contrary to Rousseau, the very worst in human nature was about to be unleashed: cruelty, bloodlust, vengefulness, envy, greed. What the institutions of monarchic France had done to its citizens was nothing compared to what they now did to themselves.[9] The atmosphere of fear in Paris is what has most captured the historical imagination, but the loss of life in provincial areas was far worse.[10] (The same pattern was repeated in the Russian Revolution.) The vacuum left by the recently destroyed social institutions was filled not by the resplendent goodness of human beings but, quite the reverse, by the cruel tyrant Robespierre and his minions.

The period is now known to historians as "the Terror." And Stalin's "Great Terror," though on a much larger scale, is a close parallel.[11]

Rousseau died just before the Revolution and so escaped seeing what natural human qualities emerged during the Terror and having to face the fact that society's institutions are there precisely to restrain those qualities. Marx, too, never had to experience the consequences of his views: he was buried long before his romanticized future society turned out to be one in which proletarian leaders proved yet again to be all too human—greedy, corruptible, cruel, and much too fond of the state apparatuses they controlled to let them wither away. A system of thought that never envisaged the need for any check on natural human qualities proved powerless to check the savagery of a Stalin or a Pol Pot.

There is more than a broadbrush similarity between today's political correctness and these recurring fantasies of the primitive innocence to be found outside a corrupt Western society. Many of the views that are currently cherished as the sophisticated products of modern theory are in fact neither modern nor derived from theory; they are instead a replay of earlier episodes in the history of Western culture. Take, for example, the view that the Western canon of great books reflects ruling class values and that when deconstructed it reveals hidden power relations that have the repressive function of social control of the lower classes. This sounds like the very latest thought of those among us who have absorbed the teachings of Michel Foucault, Jacques Derrida, and Antonio Gramsci. But now look at the same point, made in a more felicitous style over two hundred years ago: "Princes always view with pleasure the spread among their subjects of a taste for the arts. . . . The sciences, letters and arts . . . cover with garlands of flowers the iron chains that bind them, stifle in them the feeling of that original liberty for which they seemed to have been born, make them love their slavery, and turn them into what is called civilized people."[12]

This is again Rousseau, and here he presents all the essential elements of the avant-garde thought of our daring modern theorists: both the literary canon and scientific inquiry are really about social control and serve the interests of rulers by brainwashing the lower classes. Terry Eagleton is evidently much too intent on the iconoclasm of what he imagines to be bold new thought to understand that he is merely parroting Rousseau when he tells us that literature in England was designed to inculcate in the masses the viewpoint of their masters and "impress upon them a reverence for middle-class achievements, and . . . curb in them any disruptive tendency to collective political action."[13] There is not a single reference to Rousseau in the entire book from which this citation is taken.

In looking back at Rousseau's version of his thought we have one great advantage: we know what happened next—and we know that Rousseau could not have been more wrong. Nothing proved more dangerous to the rulers of his time than the free expression of ideas by the creative writers and philosophers of the Enlightenment. Unlike Rousseau, those princes correctly saw writers as dangerous subversives, censored them, and generally had strained relations with them. Rousseau's idea turned out to be foolish in his time, and there is no reason to believe that it is any less so in ours. The behavior of modern princes, whether they rule in Baghdad or Havana, tells us that they have no such illusions.

Rousseau obviously did not need modern literary theory to reach his view; to use the jargon of our day, he did not have to deconstruct the canon to reveal a "repressed politics" or to "bring political, psychological and institutional contexts into interpretive practices," as an advocate of this view puts it.[14] He simply fell victim to a crude and unrealistic conspiracy theory—for that is what it is, whether as formulated by Rousseau or in its chic modern formulation.

All the major elements of modern political correctness can be found in the Western tradition, and in every case we can learn something from the way they have played out. One worth a careful look is the currently fashionable theory of cultural relativism.

In the modern context, what has become known as political correctness has two distinct strands. The first consists of people who are rather like Tacitus—intellectuals who are alienated from their own society and who in their disgust with its imperfections imagine a primitive society full of sweetness and light. The second reaches the same conclusion as the first but by a different route. We might call the two groups the alienated insiders and the resentful outsiders. The outsider denigrates the dominant culture not because of his disgust with its imperfections but because he does not feel part of it. Resentment is the reason for his adulation of primitive cultures. The alienated insider is motivated by self-disgust, the outsider by self-defense; and that defensiveness takes the form of cultural relativism.

Faced with a large disparity between the cultural influence and technological development of the West and Third World, the outsider tries to equalize matters with the notion that all cultures are unique—which in some sense must be true—and that consequently no one culture is better than any other. But the conclusion does not follow from the premise, and it is clearly false. Yet even this is not really enough to satisfy the animus against the dominant culture, and so the outsider still rails against it with an inconsistency that betrays irrationality. Because Western high culture is snobbish and elitist, for example, more popular or primitive cultures are preferable, and so some cultures are better than others after all. The end result is that the alienated insider and the envious outsider can agree: both are hostile to the stronger and more developed society and both idealize primitive cultures. Yet this synthesis of the two different strands is also not uniquely of our time.

The convergence of these mutually supportive views is well attested in the Western tradition.

If Rousseau gives us an example of the alienated insider, the German Romantics serve as the example of the envious outsiders. By the middle of the eighteenth century, a number of European cultures were well advanced. The situation will have a familiar ring if we say that the dominance (the correct word today is *hegemony*) of countries like France was much resented in countries like Germany, whose renaissance, for various historical reasons, occurred quite late. Compared to the leading European nations of the day, Germany was culturally undeveloped.

The French often spoke disparagingly of the Germans, a fact that Germans perceived as cultural arrogance. Some German intellectuals began to question the right of French cultural imperialists to regard Germany as culturally primitive based on French standards. Johann Gottfried Herder, the major ideologist of the German Sturm und Drang movement, now invented multicultural theory—or rather cultural relativism, according to which cultures can be judged only by their own standards. No one culture can be said to be better than another—they are just different. And as might be said today, we should celebrate the difference.

Herder used another equally familiar argument to bolster Germany's case: he disparaged high culture as artificial and praised low culture (the culture of the common German Volk) as genuine, thereby breaking the cultural truce that relativism was supposed to offer. Here, too, modern multiculturalists unwittingly follow Herder to the letter, first by asking us to celebrate difference, then by denouncing Western culture as elitist.

Again, the advantage of locating a particular aspect of modern political correctness in its historical birthplace is that we can see how it fared. The fate of Germany's cultural relativism was partly amusing and partly tragic. The amusing part was that almost immediately German culture began to produce in quick succession a dazzling series of artists and philosophers: Mozart, Haydn, Beethoven, Schubert, Kant, Hegel, Schopenhauer, Goethe, Schiller, Kleist, Hölderlin, the Grimms, and a host of others. Suddenly it was the Germans who dominated European culture. Not surprisingly, cultural relativism began to seem less attractive to them.

Now for the tragedy: the European Enlightenment had had a general, humanitarian focus. It espoused the rights of mankind rather than the special rights or virtues of particular nations. But thinkers like Herder would have none of that. What mattered for him was not a general European culture of the Enlightenment but the specifically German character of German culture and thought. He might well have said, consistent with his general position but in the language of today's multiculturalists, that the generalized notion of mankind prevalent among the French was a cover for Frenchmen foisting their values onto everyone else.

This turn away from the Enlightenment's emphasis on a common humanity was a fateful step, however, as was Herder's advocacy of the primitive culture of the German people. His celebration of the special character of the Volk as a more important value than European notions of mankind sowed the seeds of a virulent and persistent German nationalism, one based on blood and soil that echoes throughout the nineteenth century and eventually becomes an unmistakable ingredient in Nazi ideology. Germany was to fight many bitter wars with France in the century and a half after Herder wrote, and one must wonder how much his influence contributed to those wars.

There is a lesson to be learned from this sad sequence of events, and it is one that can be discerned in many comparable situations throughout the world, both before and since, the latest examples being Sri Lanka and the former Yugoslavia. Anyone who thinks that cultural relativism and the celebration of ethnicity will ensure democracy and egalitarianism is sadly mistaken: history has shown us, to the contrary, that these attitudes are more likely to unleash the dangerous forces of tribal chauvinism and resentment. Encouraging people to think of themselves first and foremost as members of a tribe is a perilous undertaking. If Serbs and Sinhalese could have thought of themselves as human beings first and Serbs or Sinhalese second—the Enlightenment's way—much bloodshed might have been avoided.

When some scholars argue that we should pay less attention to the history of the Western tradition and more to both our own age and Third World peoples, we should be aware that this is a very Western thing to say. The Third World cultures so favored by these scholars are generally far more insistent on their own traditions that we are.

As to the other element in Herder's theory—the disparagement of high culture and praise for the culture of the common people—here, too, there is a lesson for us in what followed. Herder had extolled the natural eloquence of illiterate German country folk (especially women) who were unspoiled by books and philosophizing. The brothers Jacob and Wilhelm Grimm liked the idea and set out to show the richness of German popular culture by collecting folktales and fairy tales. The result was their famous *Grimms' Fairy Tales*. Although the brothers insisted in the first edition that they had faithfully represented their peasant sources, we now know that they gathered their material almost exclusively from their literate middle-class friends or simply from other books—even French books—and that whatever the source, they re-wrote everything extensively. The folksy tone and style of the collection is their own creation. When their sentimental preconceptions clashed with the reality of what real peasants said, the brothers chose to lie rather than to admit that their theory had turned out to be wishful thinking.

The trouble was that Herder and the Grimms believed they would find among simple peasants the modern equivalent of the oral traditions that resulted in Homer, not understanding that there was a world of difference between the uneducated, illiterate members of a modern literate society and the elite among the storytellers of a preliterate age. The real equivalent of the elite of that earlier time was to be found in people like the Grimms themselves, a fact that their (unacknowledged) authorship of the *Tales* demonstrates.

This episode shows that two theoretical advocates of the eloquence of low culture understood only too well that the only way to make low culture competitive with high culture was to have two high-cultural writers intervene to make the result appear authentically folklike. And they succeeded: such was their skill that they were able to create a carefully crafted and deceptively simple language that could not have been achieved through any other means. And so this enduring monument of low culture is actually a fraud created by two upper middle class scholars.[15]

At this point we ought to entertain a plea of mitigation for Tacitus and some of his successors. We must remember that, by our modern standards, they had a very limited experience of the world, whereas we have that world brought to us on CNN, in newspapers, through travel, and in countless other ways. Given his limited experience of the world, we ought not criticize Tacitus too severely for a lack of perspective on his Roman society, nor should we fault him for failing to foresee the brutal exploits of the Vandals and Goths. Neither can we blame Rousseau for not foreseeing Robespierre, or Herder and the Grimms for failing to see where celebrating the ethnicity of the German Volk would lead. But we surely can ask that literate people of the modern age who want to take us through all of this yet again first consider the lessons of history that show how disastrous these ideas have proved to be.

Because of modern communications, there is no longer any excuse for ignorance of the violent racial clashes and tribal conflicts of the Third World or for sentimentalizing the often appalling treatment of women there. The list of horrors visited upon women is extraordinary: in India, suttee (the ritual suicide expected of widows and often forced on them if they demur) and bride burning; in China, not too long ago, foot binding; in Africa, to this day, severe genital mutilation; in Islamic countries, the veil (*chador*), draconian restrictions on employment, and a prohibition on driving; and in many parts of the world, widespread killing of female infants. In a recent newspaper article entitled "Stark Data on Women: 100 Million Are Missing," Nicholas D. Kristof reported that census data from Asian countries indicate that "at least 60 million females in Asia are missing and feared dead," based on evidence such as "the number of boy births and the ratio that should exist between them."[16] Worldwide, Kristof guesses that "the number of missing females may top 100 million."

Equally absurd is the idea that where racial harmony or freedom from imperialism is concerned, the Third World is to be admired more than the West. Indeed, in these matters the Third World is politically incorrect to a shocking degree. Ethnic clashes abound, frequently escalating to the level of genocide. During the recent history of Nigeria, for example, tribal warfare resulted in genocidal massacre. Ethnic majorities routinely persecute minorities, and wars of the stronger against the weaker are constrained not by moral considerations alone but rather by military feasibility.[17] Only intellectuals blinded by alienation from their own society could fail to see these clear differences or similarly striking examples of the extent to which state power is commonly abused; for example, the routine use of torture by police is common only outside the West. And the historical record leaves us in no doubt that this behavior predated the arrival of Western colonialism and imperialism—it could not have been learned from the West.

Given our knowledge of the world through modern communications, it takes an extraordinary act of self-deception not to see that it is the developed countries that are slowly leading the world away from racism and male dominance. To demand an end to racism and sexism is not to reject Western society but, on the contrary, to ally oneself with certain Western values. "Enlightened" attitudes toward the relations between men and women; social justice; torture, rape,[18] and other forms of physical brutality; tribalism; and even imperialism have slowly coalesced in Western societies. Only someone who reads history blindfold could think that the absence of these evils is a normal state of humankind from which the West deviates. In denouncing any deviation from their own value system as "oppression," race-gender-class scholars by implication denounce non-Western cultures and measure them rigidly by Western standards, the reverse of what they think they are doing.

What does it mean when not simply individuals but whole groups of people maintain a view that is contradicted by facts too obvious to be ignored? This question takes us to the heart of the politically correct impulse and what it means. Of the two groups—the alienated insiders and the envious outsiders—the motivation of the second is straightforward enough. Their natural insecurity as outsiders, reinforced as it is by encouragement from the alienated insiders, produces a result that is not difficult to understand. The behavior of the first group, however, is less simple. Self-interest helps the outsider to his conclusion, but all that stands in the way of the alienated insider's seeing what is obvious to everyone else is his own determination to see the opposite. Where does this determination come from?

Some degree of dissatisfaction with one's society, or more specifically with one's place in it, is normal and rational. We all think that the society in which we live has room for improvement; a high school teacher, for example, might easily reach the conclusion that he or she was underpaid given the social importance of the work teachers do. Even so, such criticism need not interfere with an ability to form realistic judgments about how this society compares to others in terms of its overall fairness, racial tolerance, standard of living, protection of individuals from governmental abuse, and so on. Experience shows, however, that when these feelings reach a certain level of intensity, all perspective is lost. Antagonism toward one's own society then becomes so great that nothing can be conceded to it. Its imperfections can no longer be compared to those of other societies, yet it is the imperfect implementation of its own values that has caused the anger. The alienated insider is so much a creature of his own society that the values that are the basis of his criticism are uniquely *its* values.

The reasons for this intense alienation probably vary. Intellectuals often develop feelings of isolation, and some groups—for example, homosexuals—may have a good reason to feel left out of the mainstream. In the case of Foucault, the most influential figure among race-gender-class scholars, we know that this was a factor in his feelings of alienation. There is, however, more variety in the causes than in the result, which is not a general loss of the ability to think cogently but a disposition to think along specific lines.

When most of us reflect on the shortcomings of our society, we are likely to remember that the frailty of human nature is always the biggest problem. There is no institution, whether it be the Chrysler

Corporation, the local high school, the Red Cross, or the U.S. Congress, that is immune from the problems of poor leadership, complacency, intellectual laziness, or zealotry—all permanent features of the human condition. Alienated intellectuals are unable to entertain such a thought, however, for that would be to let the society around them off the hook. They must therefore attribute all blame to society and none to humanity.

It is this critical step that determines the nature of politically correct thinking, because from this beginning it must follow that people are not responsible for, since they are inherently better than, what the alienated insider complains about. They are dragged down by this society, and their current state of degradation need not have happened. The politically correct impulse thus leads inexorably to thoughts of a place where people are simply allowed to be what they can be. And this, in turn, leads to the idea of a primitive harmony and Rousseau's idyllic state of nature.

Primitive harmony is therefore not simply a daydream that arises through fantasy but a result that follows with ironclad logic from the premises of the initial impulse. That is why so many different people reach this same point regardless of how many times it has led to ruin. For some, the disparagement of Western culture has had the effect of impoverishing their education so that they have been protected from any knowledge of Rousseau's thought and of the disasters that it has helped bring about. But even for those whose education was not deficient in this respect, the force of the impulse is still strong enough to make them dream of the elusive primitive harmony that allows them to denounce their own society. It is there in the idyllic life of the American Indians, according to Annette Kolodny, before the white man raped the country;[19] or it was there in the Americas before Columbus brought the evils of European society;[20] or it was there throughout the world, before

Western civilization destroyed the reign of the "Goddess," a benign deity who presided over human life just before recorded history began;[21] or it was there in Africa before colonization by Europeans brought misery with it;[22] or it was there before capitalism.[23] In each case we are told of lives of great beauty and simplicity, without exploitation of people or abuse of the environment; in short, these were ecological and human paradises. But they all appear to have existed before we could actually witness them and, in most cases, before recorded history began. In such settings, imaginative fantasy and wishful thinking encounter fewer obstacles.

It would be an understatement to say that arguments can be mounted against all these imagined conditions and more to the point to say that it is embarrassingly easy to show that none really existed. Our knowledge of pre-Columbian society, of North American Indians, or of precolonial Africa establishes that all the Western vices that race-gender-class scholars complain of were there, and more: human sacrifice, cannibalism, slavery, ethnic hatreds, rigidly hierarchical societies, and even a taste for cruelty and torture that would have put medieval Europe to shame.[24]

By now, the notion of a primitive harmony has been ridiculed as wishful thinking so often that race-gender-class scholars seem on occasion embarrassed and defensive about their continued belief in it; yet they cling to it still. Annette Kolodny paints her picture of the idyllic life of the North American Indians—"a harmonious society governed by seasonal change and unburdened either by toil or material wealth"—but at the same time enters a caveat that this is not an invocation of the "noble savage."[25] Yet that is exactly what it is. Fredric Jameson, no less in the grip of the fantasy of primitive harmony both in the contemporary Third World and more generally in the world before capitalism undid it, also mocks unreal "Western Third-Worldism," as if to suggest that there are indeed people who romanticize the Third World but that he is not one of them.[26] But of course he is. The trouble is that Kolodny, Jameson, and others like them have no real choice: the fantasy of original harmony is what they must inevitably reach for when their resentment against their own society reaches an uncontrollable level.

There is another consequence of the belief of these alienated intellectuals that their society's corruption is the source of its problems. They are unable to grasp the fundamental truth that Robert Edgerton sets out in his book *Sick Societies,* namely, that all sociocultural systems must attempt to restrain weaknesses in human nature—traits like greed, envy, cowardice, dishonesty, selfishness—but that none has had complete success in doing so. "Nowhere," says Edgerton, "have adults found it necessary to teach their children to be selfish, greedy, angry, stubborn, envious, or disobedient; instead they search everywhere for means to limit or eliminate these characteristics in their children."[27]

Although societies try to do this in different ways, their common task is to find a way to keep human nastiness in check, not to avoid interfering with the natural occurrence of human sweetness. One judges societies by many criteria, but one of the most important is: How well does a society protect its members from one another? This thought is not accessible to the mind-set we have been discussing, for it has things the other way around—it attributes nastiness to society, not to human nature.

Because the problems of society cannot be attributed in any serious degree to the human nature that it imperfectly restrains, it follows that some faction or force within the society must be to blame. Race-gender-class scholars are therefore predisposed to conspiracy thinking. The conspiracy will usually be run by a group that they can identify and resent: the rich, the patriarchy or, more generally, an "establishment." The chosen group will be imagined as uniquely successful in getting things arranged the way it wants. That our society is what we imperfect human beings collectively make it will not do as an explanation. But the most fateful part of this mind-set is its urge to destroy in order to rebuild. If our society is corrupt, it must be remade from the ground up. To reach the desired state of harmony, we must start again. *And that would sweep away all the progress that we have made so far.*

Most would agree that Western society, though far from perfect, has made very real progress: compared with the rest of the world, its system of laws keeps cruelty and torture in check, its people live longer and are healthier than those in other societies, it feeds its people comparatively well, it manages to change governments without civil war or bloody coups, and so on. But to say this simply angers alienated intellectuals, who know that the core of Western society is rotten, however rosy its surface appearance. Starting again will not return us to natural goodness, however, but only to a natural chaos where all kinds of natural human nastiness flourish; that would mean both undoing the progress made by the Enlightenment and abandoning much practical experience about the calamity of naive utopian political thought.

The cruel paradox of the politically correct impulse is that it is impatient with imperfection and wants something better, but its actual results are always destructive. As Marxism is to the economic sphere, so cultural political correctness is to the cultural sphere. Marxism promised a utopian economic abundance to be shared equally by all—if only we would dismantle the existing bad economic structure. But only the dismantling was ever realized, with the result that the formerly socialist countries must now suffer severe hardships during the long process of rebuilding their economies. In just the same way, cultural political correctness now promises cultural abundance for everyone in a new egalitarian culture if only we are willing to reject our elitist Western culture. The result is just as predictable: we shall all be culturally poorer as, once again, the destruction succeeds but the promised state of cultural utopia that is to replace it never materializes. Our Western cultural inheritance is not perfect, but it has succeeded in raising us from the barbarism of a state of nature. It has managed to abolish many forms of human cruelty, has given us forms of democratic government that actually work, and has a record of human thought in literature and philosophy that offers extraordinary range, depth, and complexity. Far from debasing human beings, it has enhanced their dignity in a thousand different ways. We can build on it, extend it, modify it; but if we allow the politically correct to pull it down with their characteristic utopian promises about what they can replace it with, we have only ourselves to blame. We can be sure that if we allow their destructive resentment to destroy yet again so that they can create perfection, we shall witness the destruction but never see the benefits promised. We shall soon be faced with cultural ruin and a painful period of rebuilding—a cultural disaster analogous to the economic disaster that has befallen eastern Europe.

2 The Diversity
of Literature

The most striking thing about the new prescription for the study of literature is how very specific it is. Traditionally, literature has been considered to have an educative social function, though one conceived in general terms: it has been thought to help develop a richer understanding of human life and to train the mind. But critics who have determined views about what is wrong with our society—namely, its oppressiveness with regard to race, gender, and class—believe that readers should be concerned with those three aspects of society above all others. They are convinced that their triad of issues is fundamental and that anything else is superficial. What is true for criticism must also be true for literature, which is therefore also about problems of race, gender, and class.

Two questions arise immediately: first, how can one know what a book is about before reading it? And second, why must all literature be about the same thing? What reason could be found for reducing the content of seemingly different works to one issue? How could this severe narrowing of content be justified? Ordinarily, when we pick up a book we have not read, we assume we are about to become familiar with its content. Race-gender-class critics, however, seem to know in advance. And if criticism is to be reduced to results that are largely predictable before we even begin, what is the point of it?

It follows from the race-gender-class program that criticism should not be concerned primarily with the content of a literary work—its unique stamp, the individual meaning that makes it unlike any other work, the specific qualities that make readers return to it again and again. But it is puzzling to think that any valid form of literary criticism would not be centrally concerned with such things. What, then, can the point of race-gender-class criticism be?

Peter Washington's answer to this question is that race-gender-class criticism essentially puts works of literature on ideological trial; they are measured against "correct" attitudes toward race, gender, and class and found wanting or not.[1] An example will show how this works: a race-gender-class critic looked at gender roles in *Grimms' Fairy Tales* and found that the boys and girls reflect the sexual stereotypes of the time—which are of course bad.[2] What has been achieved by doing this? Certainly, nothing very surprising; if the Grimms' *Tales* reflect the sexual stereotypes of their age, then presumably one could find those same stereotypes just about anywhere. That is what stereotypical means. What the critic has done here surely fails the test of significance, because it amounts to saying nothing more than that the Grimms wrote in the early nineteenth century. Because the critic has said noth-ing that could not have been said about virtually everything else written at the time, nothing has been said specifically about the stories. It is as if we were asked to say something about Einstein and responded: "He has two legs." True enough, but obviously not worth saying. To be significant, a statement about a man or a poem needs to say something that focuses on the particular qualities of each: it is not enough that the statement be true.

Race-gender-class critics are by no means the first to have made the mistake of thinking that if a statement about a literary work is true, it must, by the same token, also be relevant and useful.[3] One can easily show that this assumption cannot be so. We might use a play, for example, as part of the evidence for a study of the history of handwriting or of printing or of the English language. We might just as easily use it for what it tells us about clothing fashions in the eighteenth century or for information about any number of other historical developments—attitudes toward smoking, dueling, traveling, eating, making love, Christianity, marriage, sodomy, hunting, and so on.

Suppose that we find a scholar going through one medieval poem after another to find out all he or she can about hunting in the Middle Ages. As he reads each poem he has a preconceived idea of the content he is looking for—any reference to hunting—and pays no attention to anything else. If such a person told us he was doing literary criticism, we would be surprised: it would be obvious that he had no interest in the poems as literature. If he could find the evidence that he wanted set out systematically somewhere else, he would clearly use the more convenient source. We can make sense of what he is doing if we call him a social historian, but if we call him a student or critic of literature, what he is doing *in that framework* is absurd: he would have decided in advance of seeing each poem that the most important aspect of its content will be hunting, regardless of how important or trivial hunting turns out to be to the meaning of the particular poem. The same would be true for someone whose concern was, say, marriage: a social historian can legitimately use literature for his evidence, but a critic who decided that the emphasis of every work of literature must be on marriage would be regarded as strange. Literary critics must take the emphasis of each text where they find it, one text at a time, or they cease being critics.

It is worth remembering that there have always been critics who judged the content of each piece of literature in advance: in effect, they had a favorite idea and were determined to make it the favorite idea of every author they read, whether or not it was so. That is the essence of bad reading, but it has been the way of Freudians, Marxists, and some religious critics, and it was just as much the sin of that subset of the New Critics that looked primarily for (and found) ambiguity in every literary text. But for critics with rigid attitudes of this kind, the sheer diversity of literary texts has always been an insuperable problem. Given such diversity, to decide in advance what is going to be the emphasis of every text can only be reductive and distorting. It is not necessary to refute Marx or Freud to reach this conclusion; all that is needed is to remember the obvious fact that literary texts are all different. Once we accept that fact, the determination of race-gender-class critics to see race, gender, and class as the central issues in every work must be regarded as a serious mistake.

If we simply set aside these restrictive theories that tell us all literature is about this or that and look instead at literature itself, we find an enormous variety of theme, content, and outlook. What we call literature is a collection of very different texts written by all kinds of people of differing temperaments and viewpoints. These texts represent a great range of opinion on social and political questions, as well as on every other kind of question. They are written at different times, in different places, about different issues, and in different moods. People write, and read, for many, fundamentally dissimilar reasons. This is the diversity of life itself. How ironic that *diversity* has become a buzzword of race-gender-class criticism when that criticism is committed to ignoring the true diversity of literature.

It is not enough to say that these critics are right some but not all of the time. If we are determined to take from literature only the attitudes that we bring to it, it ceases to have any point. Why, after all, do we read literature? A large part of the answer to this question is surely that although in the course of a life one encounters only a limited number of the people, situations, and problems that exist, literature expands those limits dramatically. The result is both a broadening and a deepening of experience. The new situations and people we are exposed to are not simply those that we might have known had we more than one life to lead; rather, they are created by writers who give us a distillation of real life and an interpretation of it that often takes us beyond anything that everyday life offers.

No other writer has quite the ability of Charles Dickens to create a world full of unique characters, but the remarkable thing is that although we had never met Uriah Heep or Mr. Micawber before reading *David Copperfield,* or Scrooge before reading *A Christmas Carol,* we seem to recognize them instantly. For all their unforgettable individuality, they are distilled from more fragmentary versions found in the real world. We never see anyone quite like them, though we see many who are similar, and we understand these individuals better because Dickens was able to discern the fundamental shape of certain human traits so clearly that he could show them in heightened form. Once we have seen that heightened profile, we are able to recognize and understand more easily the paler versions around us.

Almost everyone knows someone who paints, for example, but the painter of Robert Browning's poem "Andrea del Sarto" gives us much to think about. This is a man known as a faultless painter, a perfect technician who can execute any idea flawlessly but who lacks one crucial thing—a compelling style or vision of his own. Browning focuses the issue for us with the much quoted

> Ah, but a man's reach should exceed his grasp,
> Or what's a Heaven for?

Browning's painter raises in a peculiarly sharp way an issue that everyone struggles with sooner or later: the need to have goals that will stretch but not overwhelm us.[4] Unlike the painter, whose reach *is* his grasp, we need to grasp for something not quite within our reach to give our lives a challenge and a meaning. If the goal is so beyond reach that we have no chance of attaining it, we end up disillusioned and bitter; if it is so close that it is easily reached, it will have no meaning. Browning uses his painter as a means of examining a central principle in human life. Once we encounter his poem, it becomes a permanent part of the way we think about ambition. No philosopher could have captured the principle so vividly, because abstract formulae will not do the job. What is needed is a concrete expression, and that is why the great poets are more often quoted to illuminate human situations than are philosophers.

It is no accident that quotations from Shakespeare have become part of everyday life. If someone seems paralyzed by indecision, we say that he is "thinking too precisely on the event"; if there is an argument as to what to call something, we are likely to hear "a rose by any other name"; and someone who finds that a dear friend has sided with adversaries will likely think of Julius Caesar: "Et tu Brute." Yet this happens not because Shakespeare had a unique ability to turn a pretty phrase but because he comments on central issues in human life with such devastating accuracy, giving us in the process a unique way of grasping and understanding them.

It is the precision of his thought, the sharpness of his observation, and his power to abstract the essence of events that keeps Shakespeare's language so influential hundreds of years after his death. When we begin to worry about the way a commitment to a particular goal makes us simplify issues and so distort them, Hamlet's thinking too precisely on the event enables us to understand this recurring dilemma. Even Macbeth's phony alibi for killing the servants who are to be the scape-goats for Duncan's murder becomes a concise principle that we may recall and use many times over as we wrestle with the same issue ourselves:

> Who can be wise, amazed, temperate and furious,
> Loyal and neutral in a moment? No man.

Hamlet would have found that one useful.

The great writers to whom we return again and again are a limitless source of inspired commentary on the endless puzzles of human exis-tence, and even when two of them look at the same problem, each has a unique interpretation of it. Goethe's *Faust*, like Browning's "Andrea del Sarto," also deals with the struggle to achieve yet dwells on a quite different aspect of it. Goethe examines how creating and destroying are so closely related that the ambition to know and experience more becomes a pact with the devil. Everyday German is as full of quotations from *Faust* as English is from *Hamlet*, and for the same reason; both plays are the work of writers who had the gift of making us see things as we had not seen them before.

Writers whose works are compelling enough to survive after their death and be read and reread by future generations have seen the essence of human situations so clearly that even profound changes in human life cannot obscure their meaning. Take, for example, the question of what it means to be exceptionally talented or to be in the company of those who are. We usually think that great talent is a blessing—something that should enable one to lead a successful life. But three great writers from different epochs saw much more in the situation. The heroic figures in Homer's *The Iliad*, in the German medieval *Nibelungenlied*, or in Tolstoy's *War and Peace* show us that exceptional talent does not make a successful life. Andrei Bolkonsky is a glittering figure for whom there is, surprisingly, no real place in the world: it is his more ordinary friend, Pierre, who survives and lives out a contented and useful life. Siegfried's extraordinary natural ability and strength allow him to get by without ever having to develop an understanding of the people round him; he is therefore surprised when those for whom he has done so much do not admire him (as he thinks they should) but instead plot to kill him at the first opportunity, using fair means or foul. In *The Iliad* the link between brilliance and unfitness for life is strongest of all, so strong that Achilles is already aware of the prophesy that one so gifted will have a short life. The three cases differ in so many ways that one can never be substituted for another, yet on occasion one illuminates the others. Coming from the *Nibelungenlied* to *The Iliad*, for example, we see immediately that the prophesy of Achilles' early death is not simply an arbitrary act of cruel gods; rather, the prophesy is about the distortion that exceptional talent inevitably brings with it.

In works of literature that have been able to grip the human imagination continually for nearly three thousand years, issues must have been abstracted, focused, sharpened, heightened; no one quite like its larger-than-life figures is seen every day. Still, when the remarkable swimmer Mark Spitz won a record seven Olympic gold medals and then proceeded to destroy his enormous popularity through boorish behavior, no one who had reflected upon *The Iliad* or the *Nibelungenlied* could have been surprised. The shadow of Achilles and Siegfried was again visible, and even if Spitz was only a pale shadow of them, he was recognizably part of the human behavior that had inspired their creation.

The literature of remote times and places frequently offers thought and commentary on human life that surprise us with its continuing relevance. There is a German poem that gives powerful expression to a mood we all know well. The poet sees a world in which every value seems to be slipping away from him: taste and style are deteriorating, integrity is a forgotten virtue, modern music is a cacophony, people no longer know how to dress properly, good manners are a thing of the past, and standards in all things no longer exist. It is as if he has slept for a long time and awakened to an alien world.

Most people have felt that their world was disintegrating at one time or other, and so one might ask: What does *this* poem really do for us? It is certainly the most magnificent and sonorous expression of this lament that one could imagine, and that is the result of the focusing and heightening of experience found only in the best writers. But beyond this, the really interesting thing about this poem is that although it seems as if it could have been written yesterday, it dates from the high Middle Ages, around the year 1200. The author is Walther von der Vogelweide.[5] It is a sobering thought that people have been expressing the same kind of lament about their own generation's integrity and its betrayal by the next for a very long time, though, to be sure, without Walther's eloquence. If the world really is disintegrating, it is taking a very long time to do it. And so Walther's poem offers us a wonderful chance to indulge this mood grandly and at the same time a perspective on it that will never allow us to experience it in quite the same way again.

More examples would emphasize further, but not change, the essential point that the body of writings we call literature is enormously varied and that it broadens our experience and deepens our understanding of issues, events, and people by helping us grasp their essential shape and meaning. Literature can be thought of as a kind of forum in which the members of a society reflect together and brood upon the many issues that arise in their lives. Inevitably, the thoughts of those who offer the most insight into the most interesting and most enduring issues—that is, those with an unusual gift for doing so, the great writers—float to the top and get the most attention. How could it be otherwise? But the collective judgment as to what is most important is the only limit on the scope of the forum, which means that the diversity of theme, content, and viewpoint found in literature is of the essence: only that diversity fulfills the function of literature.

If we look at race-gender-class criticism with such thoughts in mind, it is clear that this one-note criticism is far too restrictive to deal with the great diversity of content in literature.[6] To say only this, however, still does not get to the heart of the problem. Criticism that restricts itself to one issue might seem to have some use within this restriction, but when we look at what is typical of single-issue critics, a more fundamental problem comes to light. The examples I gave earlier of single-issue users of literature were scholars interested in the history of handwriting, printing, or hunting. Most of them would freely admit that they are not really concerned with literature, because they are involved in another kind of study. There is, after all, only one possible reason to restrict literature's content to a single issue, and that reason must lie in a purpose that has nothing specifically to do with literature. What this means is that race-gender-class criticism belongs firmly in the category of activities that may involve literature but that center around something else. To put the matter simply, when you reduce literature to a single issue, your reasons for doing so must have nothing to do with literature, and consequently neither will your results.

Race-gender-class critics try to avoid the issue of diminishing the content of literature by claiming that they are setting literature in a wider context, hoping to make it seem that they see more, not less.[7] But their wider context is merely a different context, wider, to be sure, in the sense that it encompasses more phenomena than literature, but also narrower, in that it addresses nothing but a single strand that runs intermittently through that widened body of phenomena. In the relevant sense, then, the context is narrower, not wider.[8] The question remains as to whether these critics' treatment of even that one issue is coherent and intelligent. In the next two chapters I shall show that their politics is just as dubious as their criticism.

Some race-gender-class critics may sense that they are vulnerable on the question of their misuse of literature, because many of them deny that there is any such thing. This paradoxical claim evidently does not mean that *Hamlet* is something we imagined but that the category "literature" is not a coherent one—its boundaries are not clear enough to prevent it from merging with all other uses of language. The purpose of this claim can be seen in the next step in the argument, which asserts that because "literature is an illusion" (as Eagleton puts it),[9] treating literature as if it existed results in the "dislocation of 'literature' from other cultural and social practices."[10] Literature is therefore a bogus, elitist category, and there is no real difference between literary texts and other texts. This argument is now commonly used to justify what is known as "cultural studies"—virtually another name for race-gender-class studies—as the proper framework for studying literature.

Because Eagleton's is the most influential version of this argument, it is worthwhile to see how he reaches his conclusion. As we shall see, he begins by citing and building upon someone else's analysis of how literature should be defined, citing it with evident approval, but he misunderstands that analysis and its conclusions. What he then erects upon this foundation shows that he has not grasped the nature of the issues that arise in a definition. I make this judgment with some confidence, for the analysis Eagleton makes the basis of his argument was my own.

The question What is literature? has been a perennial concern of theory. What is it that differentiates literature from other uses of language?[11] Early attempts to define literature focused on the features common to all members of the category; possession of those features then became the diagnostic basis for deciding whether a given text was or was not literature. This approach breaks down, however, because no aspect of either form or content is common to all literary texts and only to them. Political speeches can be subtly composed, newspaper articles can be stylish, and real-life stories have plots, dialogue, beginnings, endings, and turning points. Attempts to diagnose a specifically literary form of organization as the diagnostic feature have sometimes seemed plausible, but only at the cost of being too vague to permit a clear test.

In *The Theory of Literary Criticism* I suggested that this problem can be solved by recognizing that definitions do not require common properties; the basis of categorization is as often a matter of common purposes as of common properties.[12] A common pattern of use is in fact the basis of many everyday categories, for example, clothes, food, poison, weeds. One food, or poison, may have nothing structurally in common with another; what matters is that they are put to the same use or have a similar result. I suggested that literature was a similar case. It is a functional category, one whose members have a common function. The ordinary use of language is directly related to its immediate context and is governed by the purposes of that context. When it has achieved its purely local purpose, a piece of language is rarely recalled except when that context is studied in retrospect. By contrast, the pattern of use characteristic of literary texts consists in recurrent attention, without any interest in the context of their origin per se, and therefore in a more general kind of concern with their content. In this view, the category "English literature" is the group of texts that are continually looked at in this way.

My approach had been to show how a better understanding of the logic of definition could solve the problem of defining literature, because what had made this question such a puzzle was simply a logically inadequate notion of what a definition is. This was the analysis that Eagleton took as his starting point, glossing it with a remark that completely misrepresented my point: " 'Literature' in this sense is a purely formal, empty sort of definition."[13] It is nothing of the kind. All kinds of perfectly ordinary, coherent categories are based on function rather than on defining physical properties, and many more have fuzzy edges, for example, book, shirt, and tree: at what point is a book no longer a pamphlet, a shirt not a tunic, or a tree not a bush? Eagleton seizes on the idea that literature is not a category based strictly on physical similarity in order to dissolve literature as a real category, but that argument would dissolve most of the other categories that we live by. So wedded was he to the idea that a real definition required common properties that he went on to conclude that a definition without them amounted to no category at all. This elementary mistake of logic has now become the basis of race-gender-class theory on the question of literature as a category.

Eagleton's logical misunderstanding was highly congenial to all those critics who treated literature in the same way they treated any other historical document and for whom any categorical difference between them was an embarrassment. And yet a theory requiring that no distinction be made between Shakespeare and an Elizabethan cookbook should not have been persuasive. Moreover, no amount of theorizing about the concept can ever abolish the fact that people who speak English have no difficulty understanding what the word *literature* means. Those people also know that many different kinds of writing about very different issues fall within its scope and that when race-gender-class critics show themselves to be interested only in exploitation and oppression, that narrow focus is their limitation, not literature's.

Because they have decided in advance what any particular text will have to say to them, race-gender-class critics cannot receive anything from literature: what they go away with is no more than what they brought to it. No insight can be gained from writers and thinkers whose work has stood the test of time, because these critics are determined to stick to their own thoughts and measure literature against them. For generations, literature has opened minds and propelled them beyond their previous limits, but race-gender-class critics in principle exclude any such experience of literature. Instead of letting the broader perspective of different situations and conditions work to open up new thoughts about their own time, race-gender-class critics project only their own obsessions (which are already narrow enough even as they relate to their own time) onto the literature of past ages.

What, then, does it take to be a good critic? For many years, Frank Kermode has been one of the most respected critics of English literature. A fellow critic, attempting to define what made Kermode the great critic he is, recently said that it was "his acute responsiveness to a great variety of texts."[14] Receptiveness is indeed the key: in effect, a good critic has to be a good listener. To be able to deal appropriately with a great body of diverse texts, one must be, like Kermode, acutely responsive to the particular agenda and emphasis of each one. If, however, critics have a fixed agenda and a predetermined set of concerns, they will never be able to do justice to the diversity that confronts them.

Both monotony and irrelevance will be the result of looking for and finding just one issue—one kind of political content construed and judged in a predetermined way—regardless of the text. Critics who become obsessed with a single factor cannot do the job because they cannot be listening to what the text says. And that makes it doubtful whether critics should declare a specific theme for their work. The term "feminist critic," for example, is hard to square with the fact that the critic's job is to deal with the subject of a given text, not to impose her own.[15]

Race-gender-class critics often try to evade the issue of receptivity to a text, but never with any real success. Reading the classics with an interest in what they have to say to us (rather than diagnosing their race-gender-class attitudes) is described scornfully by Gerald Graff as an uncritical search for "a repository of uncomplicated truths" or "universal values that stand above controversy."[16] (Another popular catchphrase used for this purpose is "eternal verities.") Graff also complains of an attempt at "protecting [the classics] from disrespect."[17] But his argument is transparently an attempt to avoid the issue. What Graff needs to explain is why alert reading and receptivity to the emphases of the text are not preferable to a critical agenda that is set even before the text is read; he evades that problem, however, by caricaturing receptive reading as a search for "uncomplicated truths." In doing so, Graff also misrepresents literature and its appeal. Western literature can claim universality—that is, it is interesting to anyone who wishes to read and think—precisely because the diversity of attitudes contained within it is so great. Because the values of one classic writer frequently clash with those of another, the great writers present more questions than they do answers; one can contemplate *Hamlet* or *King Lear* a long time without finding any uncomplicated truths. Students of German literature will smile grimly at the notion that Goethe's *Faust* gives easy answers. And one will not find in Dickens' London "values that stand above contro-versy." Many of the classics are remarkable precisely for provoking long-lasting controversy and taking no clearcut stand between compet-ing values.

It would be more true to say that we get eternal questioning, not eternal verity, from Shakespeare, which is something we do not get from race-gender-class critics. To the contrary, they give us a set of simple and eternal verities, namely, their extraordinarily rigid ideas about race, gender, and class. They choose books for their course read-ing lists because those books contain viewpoints they see as eternal truths. They grant to the "truths" of Foucault, for example, an extraor-dinary degree of credence, even reverence. The same point holds for philosophical works in the Western tradition: few of the university teachers who urge us to read Plato believe that he found the truth about anything. Instead, they generally want us to read Plato because he asked some excellent questions that we should all think about. And so here, too, the talk of eternal verities only diverts attention from the logical problems of race-gender-class scholarship.

An older moralizing tradition that measured literature and philoso-phy against the conventional pieties of its time also required resistance rather than receptivity to what the classic authors had to say to us. That tradition was always mocked as the work of dull, pious middle-class folk who had no ear for what transcended their narrow understanding of the Bible—but now their essential spirit is with us again. As they, too, now respond to Shakespeare's subtlety and complexity with simple and rigid moral judgments, race-gender-class critics seem not to understand their kinship with the dullards and philistines of yesterday.

Gerald Graff is charmingly frank in admitting that "being alone with the texts only left me feeling bored and helpless." Just imagine: being alone with Dickens or Shakespeare made this professor of literature bored. And so, race-gender-class ideology can help to relieve the boredom: "The classics, I suggest, have less to fear from newfangled ideological hostility than from old-fashioned indifference."[18] The notion that we need to enliven bored readers of Shakespeare or Dickens by monitoring the correctness of their politics makes no sense except in the context of the particular fact that Graff was bored. But one can only wonder: Why did one so deaf to literature want to study and teach it in the first place?

The sad fact is that politically inspired criticism never speaks of the enjoyment or intellectual excitement of literature, and certainly not of the love of it. A visitor from another planet who read this kind of criticism might well wonder what sort of institution literature is: Why, he might think, do people buy those books? The question would baffle him. Race-gender-class critics think of themselves as having more serious things on their minds than enjoyment. The word *aesthetic* is not valued in their vocabulary. It conjures up an image of someone turned inward on himself and his own pleasure while others deal with a grim reality. Aesthetic enjoyment is thus for irresponsible people with no social conscience. And yet for centuries the institution of literature has been based only on people's *liking* books so much that they choose to read them repeatedly, not on their having a duty to read what is morally or politically correct.

Race-gender-class critics have profoundly misunderstood the meaning of aesthetic pleasure, which does not involve a self-absorbed withdrawal from serious matters. It is, rather, one example among many of the way human nature supports activities that are useful through the pleasure experienced in performing them. We need to eat to survive, and nature ensures that we do so by having us enjoy food; we need clothing and shelter to protect us, and so find clothes and houses attractive; we need to procreate, and here nature made special efforts to ensure that we should like to do so; our children need to be protected, and we are fascinated by them; we need to maintain our physical capacities, and so find exercise exhilarating. But we also need to exercise our imagination, our capacity to think and feel, and hence we enjoy literature.

If we did not enjoy this exercise of the imagination, we would soon deteriorate intellectually, just as we would starve if we stopped eating and our species would die out if we no longer enjoyed making love. The pleasure we take in any of these activities can be heightened without necessarily being divorced from the essential benefit the activity provides. We therefore have gourmet food, attractive architecture, well-designed clothes. In just the same way, literature makes a heightened appeal to our imagination, and works of literature that have what we call an aesthetic appeal do so in an exceptionally powerful way. That is why they survive generation after generation.

We can be sure that the kind of victim-centered literature being written today to illustrate politically correct precepts will soon die for lack of an ability to excite or inspire: group grievances will not hold people's interest for long. Take the case of Alice Walker's "Am I Blue?" a short story that the California State Board of Education recently adopted for use in public school achievement tests.[19] This short text (of about two thousand words) boils down to little more than a series of complaints. In it, whites are mean to blacks, whites are mean to Indians, white men are mean to Asian women, boys are mean to girls, and people are mean to animals. (There may be hope for the son of the narrator's "partner," who learns to piece quilts.) For all its attempt at seizing moral high ground, this series of remarkably narrow and mean-spirited racial stereotypes reads like a race-gender-class parody. Who could ever learn to love reading if this recitation of grievances were all there was to literature?

The aesthetic sense is not divorced from real issues, then, but is the same kind of force that draws us into many activities that are important in our lives. The recognition of this close connection between the functional importance of literature and its aesthetic impact has a long history in criticism. In classical and neoclassical poetics it was said that poetry delighted and instructed. This has been a durable view, and if its two key terms are formulated somewhat more broadly, it is still viable;[20] we can extend the word *delight* to include other nuances of a strong and immediate response: to involve, to intrigue, to move, to fascinate. Similarly, we can broaden the scope of *instruct* to include such ideas as "give cause to reflect" or "develop understanding." It is worth noting, however, that the classical formula avoided any restriction of content: both instruction and delight could be about anything. By contrast, the chief difficulty of race-gender-class criticism lies in its departure from this level of generality and in the lack of any justification for its extreme narrowing of focus.

Race-gender-class critics often try to justify this narrowing with the claim that it is not of their making, because (they argue) Western literature is itself monolithic and dominated by a restricted set of ideas; and since these ideas are harmful, they must be exposed. In this view, the canon of Western literature is the record and the instrument of the sexism, racism, and class oppression of Western civilization, and it both embodies and perpetuates the anti-egalitarian values of politically dominant groups, mainly upper-class white males. Writing in this vein, Eagleton states that "departments of literature in higher education are part of the ideological apparatus of the modern capitalist state."[21] But this idea is supported only by its constant repetition; to anyone willing to look at the factual record it is simply wrong.

All the unreal tidiness of conspiracy thinking is present in the suggestion that a single, tightly knit, well-disciplined, highly effective social group with a clear idea of its interests pursues those interests with a well-executed plan. Reality is quite different: the literary canon is the result of the activities of all kinds of writers, many of them loners and oddballs who irritated their ruling classes. Far from being willing propagandists for the social order, they were often viewed in their own times as dangerous subversives.

The canon is also the result of the actions of all kinds of readers; when we use this word, we are employing a kind of shorthand that sums up the present state of our collective reading and theatergoing. There is nothing oppressive about it: it simply summarizes what we do. Race-gender-class critics charge that the canon is elitist, because culturally dominant figures impose their choices on others. But far too many people are involved to make this kind of control possible in anything but the short run. Professors whose reading lists consist of books that students find uninteresting or directors who put on plays the public won't pay to see soon find their cultural influence declining sharply, if they ever had any. The real difference between the Western canon and the politically correct books chosen by race-gender-class critics is that the latter are ideological choices imposed on unwilling readers by a cultural elite and only the former are backed by a long history of appreciation and interest on the part of a genuinely diverse reading public.

Although the historical record is full of attempts to make literature monolithic and to force it to reflect the values of the ruling class, such attempts generally failed. The most prominent examples recently are the attempts of Marxist regimes like Stalin's and Mao's to control their subjects' reading, though dictators of the right are (almost) as likely to do the same. The outcome of such governmental repression is instructive, for the light it sheds on the process of canon formation. Usually, a coterie of compliant writers gathers around the dictatorial regime and enjoys success, whereas more courageous writers are either censored or executed. When the regime falls, however, those who conformed to its values are discredited, and they run for cover. (The East German writer Christa Wolf is an excellent example.) The works of courageous individuals who spoke their minds and offended the regime either survive as underground classics or are rediscovered, and many make their way into the canon—as is happening in Russia today.

What this shows is that, once again, the race-gender-class attack on the canon has things the wrong way round: canonical status goes not to the mediocrities who do as the ruling classes tell them but to individuals who write as their consciences dictate. Oddly enough, the race-gender-class critics who want to reshape the canon according to their political beliefs (instead of allowing it to be shaped by the diverse forces of the citizenry at large) share Joseph Stalin's view of the uses of literature. These critics think of themselves as liberators, but they follow in the footsteps of dictators.

The idea that literature is a means of social control is again the reverse of the truth. By broadening our horizons and giving us access to a wider range of thoughts and attitudes, literature has always been likely to shake the conventional pieties: it is liberating and subversive, not repressive. That is why dictators, fearing that literature will subvert the status quo, try to restrict access to books. The former monarchs of many European countries were generally suspicious of poets and thinkers, and their eventual fate proved that they had good reason to be.

The claims that race-gender-class critics make about the objectionable ideas spread by the canon are once more not just wrong but the exact opposite of the truth. The charge that the Western literary canon embodies and promotes sexist attitudes, for example, is repeated endlessly, but if this is so, then one must wonder why it has not been more effective than it is, for the position of women is certainly better in Western than in non-Western cultures. The truth, of course, is that the

Western canon has helped to produce that result, and one can easily see how. Take the example of Gotthold Ephraim Lessing, the quintessential rationalist writer of the German Enlightenment. Just the kind of white male that race-gender-class critics talk about, one might think. Yet in his most important play, *Minna von Barnhelm,* the voice of reason and insight is given not to a male but to the play's title character—a woman. Compared to her, the male characters are weak, irrational, and confused. Another still-popular play by Lessing—*Nathan the Wise*—is an eighteenth-century attack on racial prejudice.

The French playwright Molière is a similar case. Molière loved to satirize all kinds of human follies, from hypocrisy and pretentiousness to hypochondria, but when he wanted a voice of common sense and decency in his plays, he usually gave it not to an upper-class male character but to a servant girl who commented on events with devastating clarity and intelligence.

The examples I have pointed to are neither atypical nor minor—Lessing is the most prominent literary figure of the German Enlightenment, and Molière one of the three great dramatists of the classical age of French literature. They point to a truth that utterly confounds the race-gender-class case: Western poets and writers have generally been leading, not lagging, in humanitarian movements. To be sure, the canon has its share of works that extol male bravery and heroism, but its greatest figures are rarely wholly admirable: Hamlet, Lear, Macbeth, Achilles, Faust, all have their faults. Strong women, however, are everywhere: Portia, Lady Macbeth, Cordelia. Still, the really important point is that the Western canon is far too large and diverse to permit the simple generalizations of the race-gender-class critic.

Contrary to feminist dogma, women have often had a marked influence on the production of literature. In the French classical age, the literary salons had great authority in matters of literary taste, and those salons were controlled by women. And in the eighteenth century the cult of sensibility in the novels of the time owed much to the fact that an enlarged audience for books had been formed by the rising middle class, especially the daughters and wives, who now had both the education and the leisure time to make reading possible. In Goethe's play *Torquato Tasso* it is said that the realm of taste and the arts is that of women.

What is true for women is just as true for egalitarian developments in society generally, including the struggle for racial equality. Egalitarian sentiments are far more common in Western than in non-Western cultures, and this, too, is the achievement of the Enlightenment, in which educated people (that is, those despised elite groups) played a leading role. The free expression of ideas by the creative writers and philosophers of that period led the way and those ideas have been spreading since the eighteenth century: many inhabitants of the Third World would be delighted to see them arrive more quickly. Far from being a repository of repressive ideas, then, Western literature is a record of our progress toward the kind of society that race-gender-class critics want. Political correctness itself is a legacy of dead white males like Tacitus and Rousseau. Remember, however, that all this is part of the great diversity of Western literature and thought, which contains voices raised against Rousseau as well.

Those who want social justice in matters of race, gender, and class should be the loudest voices raised for the Western canon—the source of, and the support for, their egalitarian ideals. But radicals always demand perfection, and that perfection alienates them even from the roots of their own ideals; it is on this basis that they criticize the Enlightenment for its incompleteness (here read simply as hypocrisy), as if the work of that group of writers could have been completed overnight. They fail to see that the Enlightenment initiated a process whereby conditions within its sphere of influence began to depart radically from those that remained outside.

Even the most vocal of the insurgent groups among race-gender-class critics—homosexuals—seem not to understand their enormous prominence and influence in Western culture. The list of remarkable figures in this group includes possibly the greatest philosopher of this century (Ludwig Wittgenstein); Russia's greatest composer (Tchaikovsky); the most influential economist of this century (John Maynard Keynes); Germany's greatest twentieth-century novelist (Thomas Mann) and most important political figure (Frederick the Great); many great English writers (W. Somerset Maugham, E. M. Forster, Oscar Wilde) and actors; the greatest military figure of the ancient world (Alexander the Great); many great figures in the world of dance; and the list goes on.

The objection to the Western canon is sometimes framed as an objection to the rigidity of its defenders, who are allegedly resistant to the natural process of change and want it to be immutable and beyond revision. But although resistance to change is a notion that is valid in many human contexts, it does not fit well with the specific situation we are dealing with, for few have ever thought the canon immutable. The greatest figures stay in it year after year, to be sure, but new names are being added all the time, and all but a very few regularly rise and fall in stature. The annual bibliography of critical books and articles published by the Modern Language Association (MLA) can be used to follow these changes. The bibliography shows, for example, that in German literature E. T. A. Hoffmann's standing has improved during the past forty years, as has that of Kleist, whereas Schiller's and Hebbel's have declined during this period. The rise of twentieth-century authors such as Kafka and Grass has evidently had the effect of sharply reducing interest in other early twentieth-century authors, for example,

Remarque. All of this happens not because of a conspiracy to control us but simply because patterns of reading change over time. People make their own reading decisions, and the present canon is the result; future changes in that canon will also be the result of such decisions.

Although race-gender-class critics often say that pronouncing one book better than another is oppressive, the act of choosing to read this work rather than that is unavoidable in a modern world where no one could begin to read what is printed in a year. The basis of evaluation is the need to decide how to spend limited time. The resistance to the race-gender-class critic's agenda is not a matter of resistance to change in the canon, then, but of resistance to a *particular way of changing it;* the objection is both to changes brought about by fiat, rather than naturally through readers' decisions, and to narrow, politically correct criteria that are rigidly applied.

Because literature as a body of texts is essentially and necessarily diverse, it cannot have a specific agenda, but critics who do not understand this are always tempted to impose one of their own. But now a paradox arises: What makes this move so tempting is the promise of grand results from an all-encompassing critical system, yet the results trivialize literature. It is simply parochial to read Shakespeare or Chaucer primarily in the context of twentieth-century political obsessions (the dreamed-of egalitarian transformation of human society or the destruction of the patriarchy).

One can see just how the impulse to find an agenda for literature leads to totalitarian criticism when an advocate of politicized criticism argues against Frank Kermode's criticism. Peter Parrinder makes his case with disarming candor: "Whenever [Kermode] outlines the purpose and function of criticism he tacitly redefines criticism as interpretation."[22] This means in turn that his "attachment is not to any particular interpretative system but to the notions of the canon . . . and of the professional practice of interpretation." Because Kermode has no system, his is "permissive and pluralist" criticism, and it is complicit in the academy's "obsessive and monotonous return to a core of texts which might seem scarcely in need of further elucidation." All this removes criticism from the sphere of cultural politics, and because, for Parrinder, "what qualifies criticism as criticism is [that]. . . it assails what it takes to be false values in the name of true values," it follows that Kermode's criticism is barely criticism at all: he is guilty of "neutralizing and perhaps neutering the critical act." According to Parrinder, we need a "clear message to convey to the people outside," for "if criticism prefers to reduce itself to interpretation and to stop asking what is taught and why it is taught . . . somebody else, perhaps somebody far more sinister," does it instead.[23]

For Parrinder, there exists one set of true values, these values control everything, and critics must know and apply them—no room for diversity here. Critics must also decide what people will read and what they are to think. Who will decide all of this? We are not told, but he or she will certainly be a social engineer with grand ambitions.

The health of our social system in general, and of particular institutions within it (such as the one we call literature), can be attributed to the fact that a large number of people are constantly making decisions for themselves. Literary commissars have no place there. Many will try to shape taste to their liking, but they must compete with others who want to do the same. The public will have the last word, however, as to whom they will listen to, and for how long. Professors of literature have more influence than most, but their opinions are as varied as they are. In this situation, there can never be a single, decisive choice, nor can a single criterion ever be enthroned. That kind of centralization could happen only in the police state that Parrinder conjures up with his sinister "people outside," blissfully unaware that this phrase is more likely to alert readers to the dangers of his own politics rather than to those he offers to protect us from.

Parrinder had accused Kermode of being narrowly professional and of serving only the internal needs of the university world, but in a stinging reply Kermode said that Parrinder had everything backward: "The entire operation of high-powered academic literary criticism" ultimately depends on the preservation of a reading public, without which literature cannot exist; and "university teachers of literature . . . can read what they like and deconstruct or neo-historicize what they like, but in the classroom they should be on their honour to make people know books well enough to understand what it is to love them. If they fail in that, either because they despise the humbleness of the task or because they don't themselves love literature, they are failures and frauds."[24] When a man as noted for his tact and tolerance of other viewpoints as Frank Kermode speaks so trenchantly, we would do well to listen. Kermode rightly insists that it is the race-gender-class critics, not he, who have a narrowly professional outlook and that it is they who have lost touch with the wider world of readers. This situation exists because these critics have no real interest in what literature might have to say, only an interest in what they can use it for. They do not love books, so they cannot inspire love for them. Yet unless they do, they have no business teaching literature.

3

Gender,
Politics, and
Criticism

In the previous chapter I argued that politicized critics ignore the diversity of literature and treat all kinds of writing in the same way. They attempt to justify this reduction in the content of literature by insisting that some issues should take precedence over others. This approach enables them to say that even if a variety of issues are present in literature, we should turn our attention to those that are the most important. And the most important are those with political content— that is, *their issues*. These issues actually subsume others, for, as Fredric Jameson puts it, "everything is 'in the last analysis' political."[1]

But this argument for a single factor taking precedence over all others is more slippery than these critics think. When they tell us that everything is political, they are assuming that to argue against them one would have to *deny* that every action has a political dimension. And because this cannot be denied, they think that they have made their case. What matters here, however, is not whether it is true or false to say that everything has a political dimension: of course it's true. What matters is what this truth implies, because once properly understood, it does not support the radicals' case at all. Politically motivated critics understand it to imply that politics is always the *most important* dimension of every action, but that is certainly not so: the political significance of an action may be important in some cases but trivial in others.

Political analysis is indeed a general framework within which everything is potentially relevant. An analysis with this comprehensive reach must be uniquely powerful, these critics think. But here they are mistaken, for all frameworks of analysis are equally general in their scope—there are environmental, physical, chemical, ecological, economic, and many other dimensions to everything, too. All actions have ecological consequences, for example, and so, using the same logic, it could be said that everything is ecological. Yet the ecological impact of a given action may be enormous or negligible. If, like race-gender-class critics, we confuse generality with priority—that is, if we think that the statement "everything has a political dimension" implies "politics is the deepest and most important consideration in any situation"—then we shall reach the contradictory conclusion that a dozen or more factors can all claim to be the most important aspect of an action.[2] The inference from the first statement to the second is true only if the first is unique—and it is not.

For instance, scholars in various disciplines can look at crop failure in the former Soviet Union from different perspectives: they may examine it as a factor in the political life of the country or study its effects on global climate, world food production, the ecology of northern Europe, or the world economy. A study is defined not by the facts it considers but by the kind of concern it has with those facts. If one wants to do a political analysis, no fact or event is in principle irrelevant to that analysis, but the same is just as true of many other kinds of analysis. "Everything is political" is equivalent to "politics is the basis of everything" only for those who do not understand this. That everything has a political dimension has therefore nothing to do with the claim that political analysis is the most fundamental type of analysis.

Race-gender-class critics use all manner of fallacious arguments in their attempts to install politics as the central issue in literary criticism. A typical case is that of Gerald Graff, who asks a rhetorical question about literature and politics that is loaded for easy victory: "Is literature a realm of universal experience that transcends politics, or is it inevitably political?"[3] Here the fallacy lies in Graff's attempt to force a choice between two positions, one being patently foolish, the other being but one of many possible alternatives. For who could doubt that politics is a part of universal human experience? Graff thus uses an absurdity as a lever to compel us to adopt his view—that politics must be central to all literature—as the only possible alternative to it, which it is not. The corrective to the view that literature has nothing to do with politics is that it has *something* to do with politics, not that it has everything to do with politics. The two crucial issues Graff avoids are: Must political considerations take precedence over all others? and Is the particular politics we are offered by literary radicals a viable politics?

Consistent with the principle that a political analysis can consider any evidence it wishes to consider, there is no reason to exclude literature from its purview, as long as we understand that this is still *political* analysis and that in many cases (though this will depend on the particular text) it will have little to do with literary criticism. Some literary works are centrally concerned with politics, but most are not, and criticism must give priority to the central, not the tangential, issues of each work. Even with this substantial caveat, however, there are two good reasons to question whether race-gender-class critics' writings are useful even when politics is central to a particular work.

First, a political analysis grounded in the conviction that politics is the basis of everything will not be of much use even as politics. A meaningful politics must recognize other important values in human life. Indeed, politics makes no sense when it stands by itself. If the question who wields political power is not broadened to take account of what that power is to be used for—that is, what human values it will serve—then it reduces to a matter of who manages to subdue whom, and that question, taken by itself, has no interest for us. It acquires interest only to the extent that we care about the human values that will be advanced as a result.

The second, more practical reason for skepticism about claims for a politicized criticism is that whether or not political analysis takes precedence over other kinds, it must be done in an informed and intelligent way. Literary critics are not trained in political analysis, and as we shall see from their attempts at it, they do it badly. As a result, political scientists usually have a low opinion of the political thought of such critics. What they do to politics is in fact analogous to what they do to literature: just as they narrow the content of literature to politics, they also reduce the content of politics to oppression and victimology. Thus they not only reduce all of literature to one issue but handle even that issue reductively. Instead of a realistic approach to politics as the art of the possible, race-gender-class critics think in terms of a perfect egalitarianism and want to denounce groups that, in their view, stand in the way of our reaching it. In the real world, the formula for a perfectly just society has proved elusive. Nonetheless, race-gender-class critics speak as if we need only overcome the resistance of certain malevolent groups —for example, the ruling class, or the middle class, or males, or heterosexuals, or the imperial West—that conspire to prevent this otherwise attainable goal.

In this chapter and the two that follow I shall look at the content of political analysis offered by race-gender-class scholars, considering each part of the triad separately. Race, gender, and class are, in reality, three separate issues, and to allow the same concept (oppression) to govern them adds yet another layer of distortion.

It is becoming increasingly clear that somewhere along the line feminism has taken a wrong turn. The movement used to be identified with eminently sensible goals that enjoyed broad support but seems now lost in outlandish, wildly unrealistic ideas. Prominent feminists tell us that men pursue a "war against women" and are bent on destroying, subjugating, or mutilating them (Marilyn French) or that all heterosexual sex is coercive and hence like rape because "for women it is difficult to distinguish the two under conditions of male dominance" (Catharine MacKinnon) or that the trouble with men is that they think vertically whereas women think laterally—"vertical" denoting the (defective) mode of thought that gives us modern science (Peggy McIntosh).[4] French seems to have lost sight of the enormous stake that men have in the happiness of their mothers, wives, and daughters, MacKinnon has sunk into such a bitter view of normal heterosexual relations that she no longer has any grasp of what they mean to both men and women, and McIntosh repeats essentially the old antifemale slander that women cannot think logically but believes she is doing women a favor in giving new life to that view. These ideas seem to interest campus feminists, whereas the wider public has no difficulty in recognizing their absurdity. Similarly implausible ideas are so pervasive that they can reasonably be said to characterize the present state of the movement; this, in practice, is what feminism now is. When we are told, for example, that Arthur Sulzberger, Jr., publisher of the *New York*

Times, considers himself a feminist and is "an ardent fan of the writer Marilyn French," we are no longer surprised that an extremist is chosen to illustrate a feminist viewpoint.[5]

What was formerly a defensible feminist agenda, at least in part, has given way to destructive attacks on the allegedly exploitative character of the traditional family and of male-female relationships; as a result, feminism is losing support among men and women alike and is in danger of isolating itself in angry campus enclaves, where its slide into ever greater unreality can continue unchecked.

How did the women's movement degenerate to such an extent? Although many factors are at work, the most important, in my view, is a severely distorted view of the past, which in turn leads to an unrealistic view of the present. Any movement for social change looks to a better future but makes its case by arguing against the past: change means that some existing condition needs to be altered. The case for change becomes more compelling, therefore, if the past is made to seem ugly. For this reason movements for social change are likely to take the dimmest view of the past. But now a tension arises: concrete proposals for change will work only if they are based on a realistic appraisal of the existing state of affairs and of how it got that way. One must understand well the nature of what one is trying to change to avoid doing damage. So even though reformers are tempted to make the worst case for the past to convince society that change is needed, successful reform requires that the past be viewed in a sober and accurate way. The rhetorical temptations of the situation are at odds with the practical needs.

In the case of feminism, one of these two competing factors has overwhelmed the other; the rhetorical urge has taken control to such an extent that disparagement of the past has completely eclipsed a rational understanding of it. The result is so unrealistic a view of how the present circumstances developed that it disables the movement. The word that captures the essence of this view is *patriarchy,* shorthand for the belief that what has obstructed political and social equality between the sexes is a conspiracy by men to treat women unfairly. Some feminists believe that patriarchy is a worldwide phenomenon, as well as one that has endured throughout recorded human history; for example, Marilyn French thinks that it "probably arose in Mesopotamia in the fourth millennium BCE, and gradually spread across the world."[6] Others see it as the product of our Western society; in this vein, Sandra Gilbert and Susan Gubar speak of "patriarchal Western culture."[7] Limiting criticism to a particular group of men, however, does not indicate a more moderate attitude, because a narrow focus generally results in greater hostility being concentrated on a smaller target. Yet the idea of the West as the focal point of patriarchal oppression is so hard to square with the documented plight of women in the rest of the world (for example, the forced suicide of widows, genital mutilation, foot binding, the killing of female babies, and countless other horrors) that it can surely be disregarded.[8]

If patriarchy were the source of the problem, then we would need to get this malevolence on the part of men under control by taking appropriate steps to enforce equal outcomes for men and women. Historically, many situations seem to give plausibility to this way of thinking —for example, differential rates of pay for men and women, the routine promotion of men over women of comparable ability, the virtual absence of women in the professions, the exclusion of women from government, and the lack of suffrage for women.

These are certainly facts, but as feminists insist in all other contexts but this one, facts need to be interpreted. Feminists have claimed that the interpretation was obvious: men have systematically treated women badly. But one can show that this interpretation is superficial and misleading and that these injustices are, instead, partly a predictable consequence of the conditions of life before the modern era and partly an equally predictable result of progressive change itself. This difference in interpreting the past is critical, for here lies the wrong turn that feminism has taken, one that increasingly isolates it from the reality of what is happening to women in the modern world.

One simple question is difficult to answer: If an enduring patriarchy has indeed been the source of our troubles, why is it being challenged now rather than at some earlier time? The usual answer—that women will not put up with it any more—only moves the question back a stage: Why this recent assertiveness? Did women of earlier centuries lack the spirit of today's women? Were they, too, to blame for the patriarchy? The idea of an evil patriarchy commits feminists to a dim view of their sisters of yesteryear, yet there is no reason to suppose that the temperament of those women was any different from their own. There is a more plausible answer to the question of why now, but it does not support the bitter feminist view of the past. Change is coming for women not because they have at last woken up to the enormity of the plot against them but because the conditions of human life have been changing.

The way people live has changed significantly in recent times, and some aspects of that change—for example, modern birth control— affect women more than men. But the full impact of modern conditions on the lives of women can be appreciated only if we examine how several aspects of life before the modern era interacted to produce a synergistic effect.

Consider first of all infant mortality. Not long ago the rate of infant mortality was by modern standards appalling. The historian Fernand Braudel, writing about the period from 1400 to 1800, calls it "terrifying," for royals and paupers alike.[9] Even in the late nineteenth century, stories like one I saw recently in a newspaper clipping from 1870 were not unusual: all four children in one family died of diphtheria within a period of a few weeks. Today the decision to raise, say, two children usually involves no more than two births, but in former times a woman might have to bear perhaps six or seven children to assure that two would survive to maturity.

Seven pregnancies and infancies would be considerably more of an obstacle to a woman's having a professional career or a role in government than would two, but we cannot grasp the full force of this obstacle unless we consider it with other factors, such as life expectancy. Life expectancy for both men and women was formerly much shorter than it is today, and because of the increased risk of death from frequent childbirth before modern medicine, the life expectancy of women did not exceed that of men by a decade or more, as it does today.[10] So we are not looking at a simple difference of two births versus six or seven; instead we must compare time for two births and infancies taken out of an expected lifespan of seventy or more years to time for seven births taken out of perhaps forty years (the figure for mid-nineteenth-century Europe as well as for modern-day Tanzania). The difference between these two cases becomes even more lopsided if we compare only the adult years, in which case the time for those seven births has to be taken out of an average of perhaps twenty-five years.

But did this really have to affect all women? Might not some have chosen to downplay the importance of children in their lives in order to pursue professional careers? No, because here another factor comes into play. Having children today can be a conscious quality-of-life decision, in which a woman weighs career against family and makes the choice or compromise that suits her. Remember, however, that Social Security is a very recent phenomenon. In earlier times children were social security, and old age without them would have been a frightening prospect. From this perspective, they were a virtual necessity.

Modern birth control is the one factor commonly mentioned as a liberator of women, but it is much less important than the combined effect of the three factors I have mentioned so far. Even if modern birth control had been available in earlier times, it would not necessarily have changed career opportunities for women while those other factors were in place.

Feminists generally dismiss the idea that childbearing had much to do with creating the unequal situation we inherit from the past, referring contemptuously to it as "biology is destiny" in order to insist that human beings have freedom of choice. But here they are evidently thinking of the freedom of choice their own era gives them: they know that *they* are free not to have children if they so choose or to have just one, or perhaps two, and return to their careers after a short time at home. What they do not see is how unrealistic this attitude would have been in a time of high infant mortality, shorter lifespans, no social security, and no birth control.

Yet even these factors do not begin to give a realistic sense of how unavoidably restricted most women's lives must have been by today's standards. Imagine caring for several children when there was no refrigeration, when transportation was primitive and slow, and when communications were virtually nonexistent. Again, feminists tend to react with some impatience: Why should all this make any difference to the relative position of men and women? Why would men not have taken an equal part in caring for their children? But such arguments would miss the point: the absence of refrigeration meant that the great majority of women had to breast-feed, and for a longer time than is usual today. This responsibility tied them to their children far more closely than it does modern women: there was no bottle of formula in the refrigerator for someone else to give the baby while the mother was at the office. This fact, together with the lack of motor vehicles and telephones, would have made it difficult for a woman to work even five miles away from home: unlike her modern counterparts, *she* could not dash home in the car to feed the baby when the babysitter—or her husband—telephoned to say that it was feeding time.

To be sure, wealthy women might have employed others to nurse their children, but they would not have been exempted from the other factors we have noted. Additionally, the pattern of life of the vast majority was bound to have a spillover effect on the career expectations of all, including women who were wealthy or unmarried.

There are countless other features of modern life that affect the way women live their lives, and they go well beyond the obvious labor-saving devices that enable both men and women to spend more time doing what they like. For example, electricity has leveled much of what was formerly a decidedly unlevel playing field for women. As a result, very few jobs are left that require the greater upper-body strength of men; that difference is trivial compared to the energy made available by electricity. Men and women alike can now push buttons or pull levers to operate heavy equipment, position a fire ladder, fly a plane, fire a heavy gun, or even kill millions with nuclear weapons. And so today it makes sense to ask why there should not be more women in the armed forces and police and fire services—but it makes no sense to deplore the fact that women have begun to enter these services only recently and to blame sexism for the small number of women presently in senior ranks. When upper-body strength was still a major factor in the use of weapons and equipment, no one could have thought that women and men should be equally represented in the military and the police.

Or consider the modern highway patrol: in former times even roads that connected major settlements were dangerous, especially for an unaccompanied woman. This was yet another factor that made a career in the professions almost impossible except in the relatively few places with large population concentrations.

What most irks modern feminists is the image of the housewife, stuck at home and thereby excluded from the stimulus of the outside world and from access to power. But in the past the contrast between the home and the outside world cannot have been what it is today. The present-day world is large, diverse, and beckoning and is brought to us by rapid travel, television, books, and the telephone. Today part of the attraction of a career for both men and women is getting out of the home into this enormously stimulating larger world. But when thirty miles was a major journey, roads were dangerous, and most people stayed within the few square miles of their home area from one year to the next, the wider world must have been perceived as more dangerous and less tempting.

These are just some of the recent changes that illustrate the lack of historical perspective in blaming patriarchy for the unequal situation we have inherited from the past. The differentiation of the roles of men and women in past ages was due not to an enduring patriarchal conspiracy but rather to conditions of life that existed until quite recently. Modern women have changed expectations not because of their sudden awareness of past discrimination against them but because of profound advances in science, technology, medicine, communications, travel, and social legislation, advances that for the first time make the same opportunities available to men and women—and what a wonderful development in modern life this is.

But what about the openly unjust acts that men have sometimes routinely and systematically committed against women in the past? Don't they prove that patriarchal attitudes were a significant factor in the unequal past? Yes and no—the no being the more important part of the answer.

There are two parts to this question, but both relate to human rather than specifically male failings. In answer to the first: there is no doubt that the customs and legislation of former times could be grossly unfair to women. Remember, however, that the conditions of human life in those times all but excluded most women from a role in government. The consequences of any interest group being unrepresented in government are predictable: that group will not fare well. If we imagine a situation in which women held virtually all governmental offices, we might expect that over time legislation would slight men. In this case it would be foolish to think that such self-interest was simply due to prejudice against men rather than to other well-known limitations of human nature: legislation is enacted under competing interests, and the outcome always reflects that competition. When one group is absent from the process, the outcome will reflect that fact.

The second aspect of past injustices toward women—the once fierce discrimination against them in the workplace—is essentially a transitional phenomenon, resulting from an all-too-human resistance to change. As modern conditions began to allow women to entertain thoughts of careers that had previously been inconceivable, many men —and women—obstructed this drastic social change. Such resistance made change much slower and more unpleasant than it might have been, but we all know that human beings show signs of distress when faced with disturbance of their settled ways. A natural preference for what is familiar, a reluctance to give up privilege, and the persistence of habits and attitudes formed in earlier times will always impede change.

There is no need to postulate a conspiratorial patriarchy or ingrained male prejudice against women to explain this: it would be surprising if major changes like these did not meet initial resistance. Two points clinch the argument for the interpretation of workplace prejudice as resistance to change rather than male hostility to women. First, many, if not most, women were as hostile to this kind of change as men were—inexplicable according to the second explanation, but exactly what would be expected according to the first. Second, much of this resistance has now subsided, again exactly what we should expect according to the first explanation. Given time, people adjust. But this is not consistent with the patriarchal explanation, because these are still the same men, only now acting differently.

How we see the past will inevitably shape the approach we take to the present. If women see their present situation as one that has coalesced gradually over the past century and could never have existed earlier, they will simply move to take advantage of their new opportunities. Determination is still needed to overcome some remaining pockets of resistance, but it is also wise to approach a new situation carefully. We can only guess how women will eventually take advantage of it. Will they show the same pattern of career interests that men have shown, and if not, where will the differences occur? Will the greater bond with children that comes from carrying, bearing, and nursing them necessarily keep the percentage of women in government and the professions noticeably under fifty percent—say, thirty, or forty? We shall find out in time.

Nonetheless, for feminists committed to the patriarchal theory, only male oppression has prevented women from having professional careers, which means that past and present are essentially the same. Anything less than a fifty-fifty split in numbers, power, and prestige in the workplace is for them ipso facto evidence that oppression continues. The caution that is appropriate to any new situation is therefore unnecessary, because the situation is not new; a wrong done to women by men needs correcting now, just as it always has. We do not need to explore new possibilities carefully, learning from experience as we go; instead, we must simply set things straight.

If misrule by an oppressive patriarchy were a correct interpretation of the past, the logical remedy would indeed be immediate corrective measures such as hiring goals and timetables for reaching the parity feminists believe should have existed all along. And so instead of letting the situation take shape from the choices women make as they choose among newly available careers, anger about the patriarchy leads feminists to distort the situation by forcing it into what they consider the correct shape. This distortion could be seen in the recent search for an attorney general. Not content to remove barriers and then wait for change, the Clinton administration decided to force change by limiting the search to women. The result was a public relations disaster that demeaned women (and the office) by implying that they needed to be protected from competition with men.

This is by no means the only damage done by an obsession with patriarchy. It also creates a "victim" culture within feminism that misdirects emotional energy into resentment and hostility. It poisons relations between the sexes, and it catapults into leadership roles in the women's movement angry, alienated women who divert that movement from the necessary task of exploring feasible changes. What is most relevant to this book, however, is that this destructive attitude corrupts the work of women who should be making contributions to knowledge and scholarship. In one field after another, their work is at best damaged and often rendered valueless by the unrealistic and anachronistic victim-centered framework of their thought.

The most extensive examples of such corruption are found in the field of literary scholarship. Typically, work by feminist critics is shaped so completely by the notion of patriarchy that an intelligent contribution to the understanding of literature becomes almost impossible. The greatest problem is anachronism: when feminists use literature of the past only to find evidence of patriarchal oppression, or of resistance thereto, they are in effect taking the conditions of modern life as the universal standard. The result is that their work becomes irrelevant to literature produced by societies whose conditions they have fundamentally misunderstood.

A preoccupation with slights to women has led one feminist critic after another to miss an opportunity to make useful and distinctive contributions. Sandra Gilbert and Susan Gubar's *The Madwoman in the Attic,* for example, could have been a ground-breaking study of the great nineteenth-century women writers: Jane Austen, the Brontës, George Eliot, Mary Shelley, and others. But from the outset Gilbert and Gubar talk about how these women had to struggle against "patriarchal poetry" and "patriarchal poetics," among other manifestations of patriarchal mistreatment.[11] Inevitably, their book says a great deal about the alleged oppression of these writers by the patriarchy but little about their remarkable literary imaginations.

When the feminist critic's attention is turned to female characters in great books, the results are just as predictable. It is easy enough to use the theory of a malevolent patriarchy as the basis for commentary on how Ophelia or Desdemona[12] or Cordelia is mistreated, or how *The Taming of the Shrew* is full of misogynistic prejudice. But quite apart from the fact that this approach applies a historically unrealistic theory of relations between the sexes, it also applies indiscriminately a preconceived idea as to what will be important. We are back to the central critical sin discussed in the previous chapter—that of letting the critic's obsessions determine in advance what is going to be important for a particular work.

A logical problem faces those who believe that the condition they call patriarchy is present everywhere. If patriarchy is an evil, it must be regarded as an aberration; yet the universality of differentiated roles suggests that they are deeply rooted in the human condition, which would immediately throw doubt on the feminist analysis. Feminist archaeologists have attempted to resolve this dilemma by making the whole of *recorded* history the aberration. They discover in the era immediately preceding recorded history the reign of a "Goddess," a benign deity of prehistoric times who presided over an era of peace and harmony before she and that harmony were swept aside by misogynistic and violent Westerners with their patriarchal God. It was they who introduced the patriarchal system to the rest of the world, and they who ended the era of a nurturing, pacifist, egalitarian spirit. One consequence of this theory congenial to race-gender-class ideology is that even if the Third World is now a miserable place for women, responsibility still lies with the West. The search for Rousseau's primitive harmony finally succeeds, then, and the Noble Savage turns out to be the child of the loving earth mother.

Skepticism is of course natural when something sought so fervently (and for so long) as the original harmony is eventually located after so many disappointments at a time and place where evidence is both scarce and ambiguous—that is, before recorded history begins. The paucity of real evidence and the huge gaps in our knowledge allow more latitude here for wishful thinking and leaps of the imagination. It is scarcely surprising, therefore, that two careful recent critiques—by Philip Davis and Mary Lefkowitz—both find that the feminist cult of the Goddess rests on an overinterpretation of flimsy evidence.[13]

Davis's general conclusion is that "like other conspiracy theorists, the Goddess' proponents twist evidence blatantly, when they do not simply invent it." For example, Goddess theorists appeal to the archaeological findings of James Mellaart to argue that a certain ancient Anatolian city was a paradise whose people lived at peace with one another and in harmony with nature, though they neglect to mention that "Mellaart reports evidence of a flourishing weapons industry. . . . Many of the human skulls he found had sustained wounds."[14] Lefkowitz shows that even Marija Gimbutas, an academic archaeologist of considerable distinction, "must resort to speculation and imagination at almost every stage of her discussion."[15]

The extent to which the theory of patriarchy dominates all areas of feminist research can be seen in the recent, weighty compendium *The Knowledge Explosion: Generations of Feminist Scholarship.*[16] This volume contains forty-four essays by different hands surveying feminist work in a variety of disciplines (literature, physics, politics, sociology, and so on). Although the editors clearly intended to display the considerable achievements of recent feminist research, the impression they create is quite different. What they really show is how an unreflective acceptance of the patriarchal theory constricts feminist work everywhere, for though their title announces a concern with new knowledge, the individual chapters give far more space to complaints about the victimization of women. The chapter on political science, for example, takes as its point of departure the statement that women have been marginalized; the one on engineering deals with women's threat to male control of the field; that on physics also talks about male domination of the field and how men are trying to preserve it; that on law begins similarly and goes on to consider how the law slights women's work; that on economics soon focuses on the "outrageous abuses of women, in both theory and practice, made in the name of economics"; that on sociology begins with concern over the marginalized position of women in the discipline and goes on to "basic tenets devaluing women";[17] and so on. Again and again, these essays recite a litany of insults to women.

Even the general chapter entitled "The Principles of Feminist Research," which ought to be the intellectual showpiece of the volume, recommends research principles for feminism whose intellectual content is limited to victimization by patriarchy, for example, "doing research with people rather than on them; having women do research; doing research in ways that empower people; valuing experiential knowledge; honoring female intelligence; and seeking the causes of oppression."[18] A more superficial and contentless set of research principles would be hard to imagine. How, for example, would such principles have helped in the search for the structure of DNA? Hopes are raised by the inclusion of a chapter in which Cheris Kramarae promises to look at problems that arise in defining the term *patriarchy*. But even though she devotes much care to distinguishing "capitalist patriarchy" from "racist patriarchy," Kramarae never even considers the possibility that the analysis of human affairs implicit in the term might need further thought.

Because of the broad scope of and the numerous contributors to *The Knowledge Explosion*, the index of names cited gives a reasonable measure of a particular feminist scholar's influence.[19] The results are startling. Catharine MacKinnon is the most frequently cited, and Andrea Dworkin places fourth. Both are associated with the extraordinary view that normal heterosexual relations are tantamount to rape. Dworkin is the blunter of the two: for her all sex is rape because women are powerless, and therefore even their consent cannot be a free act.[20] She also believes that women's inequality originates in their having sexual relations with men and that men retain their power through this means.

If feminism were less patriarchally obsessed, views such as these would probably never be taken seriously. The dismal message of *The Knowledge Explosion* is not only that these views get serious attention from feminists but that they get more attention than any others. Many observers imagine that Dworkin's views consign her to the lunatic fringe of feminism, but her writings are in fact a staple of Women's Studies courses. Catharine MacKinnon, however, whose views are just as extreme even though formulated less bluntly, is widely thought of as a leader among feminist legal thinkers. She has been the subject of innumerable puff pieces in the national press for her "innovative" views, has been a visitor at the Harvard Law School, is published by Harvard University Press, and has been called upon by NBC national news to speak as an expert in feminist legal thought. She received thirty-three votes from the Harvard Law faculty in favor of a tenured position as professor of law there, a grim indicator of the intellectual decline in major universities that race-gender-class thinking has brought about.[21] Her books are routinely reviewed in the nation's most prominent and intellectually ambitious journals, a treatment usually accorded only the few most important books among the thousands published each year; even reviewers who categorically reject her views write analytically and at length about them (a case in point is Ronald Dworkin, writing in the *New York Review of Books*), all of which suggests that hers is a case to be reckoned with.[22] But Richard Posner has pointed bluntly to a consideration so obvious that it should have precluded this degree of public attention: MacKinnon's argument has very little in common with legal scholarship. She proceeds not by setting out a thesis and then carefully scrutinizing all the arguments for and against it but by engaging in careless and intemperate diatribe.[23] Looking at the MacKinnon phenomenon from the other side of the Atlantic, Anthony Daniels, who refers to her as "one of the leading current celebrities of American feminism," is just as clear: her latest book is "not so much an argument leading from evidence to conclusion as a prolonged howl of inchoate rage."[24] By contrast, the prominent philosopher Richard Rorty, in an advertisement for MacKinnon's *Only*

Words, says admiringly that "MacKinnon states her case in prose that is as distinctive and trenchant as Orwell's," a judgment certain to prove embarrassing in the long run.

In its overwhelming concern with grievance rather than knowledge, *The Knowledge Explosion* is typical. Other standard feminist anthologies such as *The New Feminist Criticism* or *Making a Difference: Feminist Literary Criticism* will disappoint in the same way; they too contain a great deal about grievance and comparatively little about new feminist knowledge of literature.[25] When a large number of people lose their way, usually more is involved than individual misjudgment. Systemic factors are likely to be the problem, one of which is a contradiction in the entire program of feminist "knowledge."

The starting point for feminists is a conviction that the lot of men and women is unequal. And this judgment must be *global,* for if the condition of men and women is unequal only in certain respects, then one might be left with a series of apples and oranges that cannot be compared. (Women have had to look after children, but men have been drafted and killed in wars; women have been paid less, but men have shorter lives; and so on.) For feminists, women have fared worse, period. But now a problem arises. To reach this point, it was necessary to assume that there are no serious differences in the capacities or interests of men and women. For if the existence of such differences were conceded, then it would also have to be conceded that they might be relevant to and even explain some differences in the conditions of men and women in the real world. And that might return us to the incommensurability of the apples and oranges, which would steer us away from grievance and complaint.

It is precisely this rejection of the possibility of serious differences between men and women—whether expressed overtly and stated as principle, as some feminists do, or covertly by adopting the framework of grievance—that makes the next step so difficult: How can feminists, without contradiction, expect to find a contribution to knowledge that is unique to women and characteristic of them? For that would require a distinctive *difference* between men and women. As Catharine Stimpson admits, candidly enough, yet without seeing how this admission must undermine feminism's ability to sustain its grievance posture, "there is no reason to study women unless women represent something else again."[26] Stimpson does not understand that if a difference does exist, then she and her sisters can no longer insist that *only* male oppression accounts for the differentiated roles of the two sexes in the world. At the very least, one other factor that leads to that differentiation would now have to be considered, and it could not be a trivial one if it is to be capable of generating a distinctive and important female contribution to knowledge.

Two contradictory impulses are at work, therefore: the insistence that there are no good reasons for the past differentiation of roles pushes feminists in one direction, whereas the claim that there is a distinctive female contribution to knowledge pushes them in the other. The result is paralysis; a concern with new knowledge is often announced, but a recitation of grievances always follows, both because it is easier and because that is the nature of the underlying drive. And the more that grievance is stressed, the more difficult it becomes to arrive at a female contribution to knowledge.

Some feminists break out of this paralysis by taking the next step— that of diagnosing a distinctive female contribution to knowledge—but only if they fail to see the underlying contradiction, and that is not a hopeful sign of what is to come. The proof that progress beyond this point is only possible for those who manage to forget how they got this far can be found in a curious fact. The notion of a female way of knowing is usually found in those hated stereotypes of female behavior, which in all other contexts feminists denounce as demeaning to women and as excuses for males to treat them as less than equals: to name a few, women are less competitive and more nurturing, less logical and more intuitive, more caring and less rational, less individualistic and more social, less quantitative and more qualitative.[27] The same qualities that in one context were denounced as patriarchy's excuses for inequality are embraced in another as valuable female traits.

Even more curious is the fact that some feminists go much further in adopting these stereotypes of female behavior than society did in the past. Peter Shaw has written that "in the past, surely, stereotypes of the sexes were understood as tendencies, not absolutes. When men and women were stigmatized, it was typically because of their occasional, not their immutable, vulnerabilities."[28] One might add that some stereotypes did not stigmatize at all: the stereotype of men rather than women as soldiers was understandable in a time of primitive weaponry, and neither sex felt it embodied hostility or prejudice.

Peggy McIntosh is among those who have revisited the old stereotypes with great enthusiasm. McIntosh is associate director of the Wellesley College Center for Research on Women, arguably the most influential of campus feminist groups. She believes that men and women think differently—men "vertically" and women "laterally." The formulation is new, but the idea is not; this is the old contrast of logical, mathematical, individual, and competitive with intuitive, qualitative, social, and nurturing. What McIntosh contributes is a thoroughgoing commitment to this line of thinking that does not balk at even its most absurd consequences. Looking for the right answer in science, for example, is competitive and hierarchic; quantitative thought is simply *bad*. (Both are part of the patriarchy.) She would prefer that we develop "a decent relationship with the invisible elements of the universe."[29]

But if generations of scientists had not looked for the right answers, McIntosh would probably not be here to argue her point.

What matters to McIntosh is that women are much nicer than men, but in no other respects are her views flattering to women.[30] For example, she gives us an implicit answer to the question of why there are so few women scientists: women don't think like scientists. One must wonder why McIntosh's radical feminist colleagues do not complain about this slander. If I am correct, the answer to this is that the inherent contradiction in looking for female ways of knowing makes finding anything that will qualify so difficult that the seekers become desperate.

The idea that women are nicer people than men is often given specificity by portraying them as antiwar, pro-environment, and so on. For Sue Rosser, "most girls are more likely to understand and be interested in solving problems and learning techniques that do not involve guns, violence, and war. . . . Many are uncomfortable with experiments that appear to hurt animals for no reason at all."[31] Or Ruth Bleier: "A feminist approach to scientific knowledge . . . would aim to eliminate research that leads to the exploitation and destruction of nature, the destruction of the human race and other species, and that justifies the oppression of people because of race, gender, class, sexuality or nationality."[32] For these feminists, women's ways of knowing seem indistinguishable from strongly left-wing political beliefs.[33] Here radical campus feminists imagine their views to be those of women generally, which they certainly are not. Helen Vendler has attempted to introduce a note of realism into these attempts to sentimentalize women: "The abuse of power by both sexes, and the deficient moral behavior of both men and women to each other and to children, is the truth concealed by feminism. . . . A de-idealizing of women is necessary for the women's movement."[34]

If women's ways of knowing are nice, men's are nasty. In fact, much of feminist science is devoted to showing that males are mean to Mother Nature, whom they try to dominate and control, even to violate. She is oppressed by men, just as women are. The parallel is worked through to its inevitable conclusion: scientists and engineers actually rape nature. This commentary on science is represented by Sandra Harding, for example, who refers to Newton's *Principia* as "Newton's Rape Manual."[35] To be sure, a doctor monitoring a fetal heart beat is trying to control the situation—by preventing an infant's death—but most women would view this as a unique blessing, not as a sinister plot. Harding's extraordinary views are as much part and parcel of campus feminism as are McIntosh's.[36] The judgment by Paul Gross and Norman Levitt of feminist work in science seems apt: "The most widely known attempts at feminist science . . . are all undone intellectually by the moral ferocity which motivates them in the first place."[37]

The most modest attempt to isolate a specific feminist contribution to knowledge speaks not of a female mode of thinking, or of female benignness in research, but of greater emphasis on research topics that are in the interests of women. The most often cited example is research on breast cancer: more women scientists, it is said, would mean more such research. More women involved in funding decisions in science would also, it is argued, mean more equitable funding for women's health issues. But even this more modest position is hard to sustain. Two questions must be asked: first, do the facts really bear out the claim of skewed research emphasis and funding? And second, should we expect women scientists to pursue women's issues?

Andrew Kadar convincingly answers the first question in his recent article "The Sex-Bias Myth in Medicine."[38] Kadar argues that the statistics quoted to show bias against women in the funding of medical research are misinterpreted. For example, in 1987 funding at the National Institutes of Health for diseases unique to women was 13.5 percent of its budget, which might seem low until one learns that 80 percent of the budget goes to diseases common to both sexes, and only 6.5 percent to diseases unique to men. He concludes: "Though it is commonly believed that American health-care delivery and research benefit men at the expense of women, the truth appears to be exactly the opposite." Statistics on longevity underscore the point: before modern medicine, women had the same life expectancy as men, but now they live many years longer.

In answer to the second question, scientists are motivated not by gender issues but by their career interests. Science is a crowded and competitive enterprise, and any aspiring scientist aware of an opening in the field would seize the opportunity, regardless of whether it benefited men, women, or both. Women scientists who chose to pursue women's issues exclusively would hamper their careers by shutting themselves off from most of the great issues in science. Serious women scientists will want to be in the main arena, taking on projects of concern to everyone; the alternative is automatic second-class status. Here the unrealistic obsession with imagined past evils leads to a proposal that would guarantee real future inequality.

The grandiose claims made for the new feminist knowledge only draw attention to a sorry reality. The editors of *The Knowledge Explosion* boast that "some areas of achievement . . . go beyond even the wildest dreams of some of the early academic activists. . . . Women's Studies explodes the traditional knowledge-making practices, and their products." Yet the unbiased reader will note the discrepancy between the great claims and the meager results.[39] When Sandra Gilbert tells us that "the intellectual excitement generated by feminist criticism" can regenerate literary studies, she seems out of touch with the reaction of the wider world beyond the charmed circle of campus feminists, where it is dismay, not excitement, that is generated.[40] Peggy McIntosh also claims much with the title of an article: "Warning: The New Scholarship on Women May Be Hazardous to Your Ego."[41] But she gives not a single example of intellectual achievement as she gloats about the insult to men's consciousness of all this new knowledge. Meanwhile, falling enrollments in the humanities carry a message that is not getting through: students are voting with their feet against the direction that the humanities have taken recently.

The sad truth is that once anger about patriarchal oppression starts, it spins out of control and productive thought ceases. It is now not only acceptable but expected that feminists will rehearse their rage publicly. *The Knowledge Explosion* is full of such expressions, and one chapter is even devoted expressly to rage: Susan Arpad's "The Personal Cost of the Feminist Knowledge Explosion." Arpad recites a kind of ritual credo: "I recognize that, as a woman, I am a marginal human being; I live in a society where at any time I can be dismissed, trivialized, ignored, or brutalized."[42]

In this climate, it is no accident that leadership among campus feminists is now in the hands of people distinguished chiefly by the degree of their alienation rather than by solid intellectual accomplishment—women like Catharine MacKinnon, Annette Kolodny, Catharine Stimpson, and Peggy McIntosh. Perhaps it is inevitable, too, that in such a climate those who are most likely to be alienated from the mainstream world of heterosexual relations—that is, lesbians—will exercise disproportionate influence. The severe intellectual deterioration that has taken place has at last been challenged by several spirited critiques from within the academy, for example, Christina Sommers' *Who Stole Feminism?*; Elizabeth Fox-Genovese's *Feminism is NOT the Story of My Life*; and the extraordinary whistle-blowing of two committed teachers in women's studies programs, *Professing Feminism*, by

Daphne Patai and Noretta Koertge, whose eloquent subtitle tells all: *Cautionary Tales from the Strange World of Women's Studies.*[43] These books, however, have met with the bitter hostility of campus feminists.

Because of modern conditions, women now have unprecedented access to all sectors of the job market. But even though their numbers in colleges and universities have increased rapidly—55 percent of college students are now women[44]—feminism, as currently constituted, is causing many of them to miss the opportunity to take their places among the genuine intellectual leaders in their fields. New and damaging female stereotypes are being created by the obsessive harping on victim status that has become so obtrusive a part of public thought and comment. The fact is that when women believe that a continuing patriarchal conspiracy is the only reason for the differentiated roles of the past, that belief becomes yet another barrier to their progress.

Sadly, this wrong turn occurred just as women had largely overcome initial resistance to change in the workplace. That there will be further significant change in the numbers of women in the professions and government is no longer controversial. A short list of the most able members of the last Republican administration, for example, would have to include Lynne Martin, Carla Hills, Linda Chavez, Condoleezza Rice, and Lynn Cheney. But the excesses of feminists are now undermining these gains, and the very word *feminism* has become so tainted that more and more women shy away from it. The feminism typical of campus women's studies departments has little credibility among the general public.

The question of how to interpret the past is the heart of the matter, because it determines the crucial question of how change should come. We shall get the best from this new situation only if we see it more positively and more realistically than the preoccupation with an imagined patriarchal evil will allow. We need to be clear about the fact that the technological and medical advances of Western society, together with the social changes they have brought about, now give women opportunities that were unavailable in the past. These developments, rightly understood, explain why feminism is a fairly recent and Western phenomenon and why these changes are slowly spreading to the rest of the world as it, too, is increasingly affected by the process of modernizing. Nonetheless, powerful emotional resistance prevents many feminists (especially radical feminists) from accepting the fact that the capitalist economies of the West have been the engine of change for women. Rather than lament the entire past of humanity as one long display of male oppression, they should focus on exploring the promising but uncharted future.

4 The Academic Politics of Race

Race is another central ingredient of new-style campus studies in the humanities. It enters into scholarship in literature and history in a number of ways, but the common thread is an insistence on the white European's mistreatment of other races. There is an intense focus on a limited number of specific historical events: the enslavement of blacks in North America; the disruption of the peaceful lives of the New World Indians by Europeans who took their land; the imperial expansion of Europe beginning in the Renaissance; and the colonial administration of Third World countries. Moral indignation over these episodes becomes not only the controlling framework for many race-gender-class critics but often the entire content of their writing on literature. They seek to uncover the racism that underlies even benign-looking texts by famous white American writers or the imperialist arrogance and chauvinism beneath the surface of classic European writers. Even Shakespeare is found to be complicit in this meanness of spirit, this white moral sickness. Historians of a similar mind-set stress the cruelty and belligerence of the European explorers and the smugness and racism of the colonial regimes.

Let us look at some representative examples of critical judgments in this vein. Here is Edward Said on the novel: "Without empire . . . there is no European novel as we know it. . . . The novel, as a cultural artefact of bourgeois society, and imperialism are unthinkable without each other. . . . Imperialism and the novel fortified each other to such a degree that it is impossible, I would argue, to read one without in some way dealing with the other."[1] More generally, Said accuses Western culture of "Orientalism," that is, of constructing a self-serving set of stereotypes about the Orient to justify "European-Atlantic power over the Orient," specifically colonialism: "To say simply that modern Orientalism has been an aspect of both imperialism and colonialism is not to say anything very disputable."[2]

Here is Stephen Greenblatt on Shakespeare: "Shakespeare became the presiding genius of a popular, urban art form with the capacity to foster psychic mobility in the service of Elizabethan power . . . [and] approaches his culture, not, like Marlowe, as rebel and blasphemer, but rather as dutiful servant." And on Spenser: "Spenser worships power . . . [and] is our originating and preeminent poet of empire." The complexities of his art "are not achieved in spite of what is for us a repellent political ideology—the passionate worship of imperialism—but are inseparably linked to that ideology." Greenblatt insists on the "impossibility of sealing off the interests of the theater from the interests of power."[3]

I introduce these writers as representative examples, but they are more than that. Even a critic of Greenblatt's—Paul Cantor—says of him that "if I were asked to name the most influential literary critic of this generation, it would be Greenblatt."[4] Said, University Professor at Columbia University, is also among the most prominent literary critics of our day. Their followers are legion.

For some, these attitudes do not seem inconsistent with the continuing study of works by white males—the European classics. (This position is what makes it possible for race-gender-class critics to claim, when on the defensive, that not much has changed—students still take courses on Shakespeare and other European classics, just as they always have.)[5] Others, however, want to study texts by authors less blighted in spirit. Yet the books that are new candidates for inclusion in literature curricula are obsessed with the same moral problems. They express the same moral judgments, usually about the same historical facts. (Alice Walker and Toni Morrison are good examples.)[6] These books in effect make politically correct criticism into literature; grievance is their content.

Evidently, a great deal is now invested in this attitude toward race and guilt, for it determines the content of much literary criticism and even contemporary literature. Yet although this attitude has a factual basis, it is seriously flawed. Everything depends on the context that is assumed for the facts, and once that context is understood, the case for this approach to literature and criticism collapses.

Before we look at specific cases, it will be helpful to formulate some general principles. Take the following theoretical sequence of events: let us say that General Motors announces a loss of half a billion dollars for the preceding year. Yet despite this bad news, the price of the stock goes up, not down. The market has apparently placed a positive, not a negative, judgment on the news. The explanation for this initially puzzling situation lies in a general context of facts and expectations.

Suppose that during the same period auto manufacturers in the United States had a terrible year because of foreign competition, that both Ford and Chrysler had already reported losses of well over a billion each, and that General Motors had been expected to report an even bigger loss. Then the half billion loss is good news. The point here is that the loss taken simply by itself meant nothing. Its meaning could be understood only in light of the even greater losses of comparable companies, so that GM performed well relative to what could have been expected at this time and in this context.

The first general principle, then, is that facts do not carry their own interpretation; they must be evaluated in relation to expectations within a given context. Now for a second principle: imagine that a man is walking toward me, and I am asked to say what I see. But what kind of thing should I say? Just describe what he looks like, you reply. But there must be more to it than that, for if I say that he has two legs, you will react with impatience: everybody has two legs. You don't want just any facts about him—you want significant facts, facts that will *differentiate* him from other individuals, facts that are notable in the context. Once more, facts are never just facts; some are commonplace and therefore not worth mentioning, whereas others are distinctive and command attention.

With the aid of these two principles, we shall see how race-gender-class critics misinterpret the facts that obsess them—how they evaluate facts without reference to a context of expectations and focus on the commonplace rather than on the distinctive.

The most crucial aspect of the context of expectations in all the historical events referred to lies in the great change ushered in by the Enlightenment. When we accuse people of "racism"—that is, of acting in a way that allows the inference that one group matters more than or is superior to another in more than superficial ways—we are assuming a sense of common humanity. But although that idea may have been expressed by individuals throughout recorded history, it is relatively modern in the sense that it did not achieve real power in human affairs until the Enlightenment—the eighteenth-century current of political, social, and philosophical thought that was largely the product of northwestern European thinkers and their North American cousins.

The idea of a common humanity was the Enlightenment's precious gift to succeeding ages. Up until that time, tribalism had been universal, as it still is in parts of the world where the Enlightenment's influence has not yet penetrated. (Calling a twentieth-century Yoruba bent on annihilating the Ibo in the Nigerian civil war of the 1960s a "racist," or accusing him of "genocide," would simply have puzzled him.) Formerly, people identified with those that they saw as their own, and when the interests of that group clashed with those of other groups, an individual's loyalty to his or her people was never in doubt. One could leave it to other groups to press their own claims.

In this context, clinging to one's own was not regarded as evil or as insensitivity to others; it was a matter of seeking security in a hostile world, because other groups were always seeking their own interests. Tribalism provided collective security in a context where the dangers faced by individuals were too great to allow concern for individuals from other tribes. Yet this attitude also entailed risks; the individuals could rely on their own group, but if it was overrun by another, annihilation could result. In the modern world, those risks have been heightened by numerous factors—for example, weapons of war that are many times as destructive as weapons of earlier times. For this reason, tribalism has become counterproductive. The case of Bosnia, for example, shows that it now results not in greater security for the individual but in less. In the twentieth century, greater security is afforded by the Enlightenment idea of belonging to a common humanity rather than to a tribe, for that idea widens the circle of those who might protect the individual.

The central Enlightenment idea that all peoples share a common humanity, and that their allegiance to that commonality transcends any allegiance to their national or racial group, brings with it a set of related ideas. Words like *racism, genocide,* and *imperialism* belong in this new context but would be out of place in an environment not imbued with Enlightenment attitudes. In fact, all these words signal various ways the Enlightenment's philosophy of a common humanity is violated. If all human beings have equal value, regardless of tribe, then it must be wrong for one tribe to exterminate another or to set itself up over another. Torture now occurs for the most part only in those areas of the globe where Enlightenment values have not yet fully penetrated, and so its decline is also part of this same process. The spread of Enlightenment values has led to the ending of many other un-Enlightened customs, such as cannibalism, human sacrifice, head-hunting—*and slavery.*

One can easily forget how much the Enlightenment has changed (and is still changing) the world and how recently those changes began. One way to grasp the magnitude of the movement is to visit the Tower of London. Tourists are still shocked at the array of ingenious instruments of torture in use just a few hundred years ago in England, the same country that gave the world habeas corpus and the mother of parliaments. Shakespeare seems very much part of us, yet the Tower assaults our senses with evidence that his world was not ours: the varieties of torture, the ugliness of methods of execution, and the monarch's ability to subject anyone to them at whim, all attest to the low value placed on life at that time. What is it that accounts for the difference between a world full of such horrors and present-day England? The Enlightenment.

This spread of the idea of a common humanity has been a significant aspect of modernization. There have been many milestones in the history of the human race: the invention of the wheel, agriculture, building, writing, democracy, and systematic knowledge itself. These great innovations are the legacy of many different peoples from different eras. Northwestern Europe's contribution of the idea of a common humanity deserves to stand with that small number of other fundamental changes in human life because of its role in ending the horrors mentioned above. European pride in this achievement is justified, but it should be tempered by the thought that leadership in human affairs regularly moves on from one group to another. It is a sobering thought that the Germanic tribes whose descendants were so prominent in the Enlightenment were largely illiterate peasants only a few centuries before, the Mediterranean cultures having advanced far ahead of them at that time.

The Enlightenment was the beginning of a worldwide cultural revolution that is ongoing, and in this sense we might talk of a spreading European cultural hegemony; but this is not a hegemony that race-gender-class critics can pounce upon and vilify. For they are among its agents: though professing cultural relativism and a solidarity with non-Western cultures, they are in fact the most ruthless and uncompromising enforcers of the Enlightenment's cultural revolution.[7]

The world is still in the process of coming to terms with Enlightenment values. Take, for example, the notions of racism and genocide, with all they imply about the need for respect for the humanity of tribes and groups other than one's own. Third World ethnic strife and tribal massacres in recent decades are clear evidence that the attitudes implicit in those words are far from having been eradicated. In Nigeria, whole populations of the Ibo have been annihilated by rival tribes. Civil war in Ethiopia has produced horrendous numbers of dead. In

Mozambique, the number who have died in the civil war that has been going on since 1975 approaches one million.[8] In Somalia, tribal warlords have been using mass starvation to improve their own tribe's position. In Rwanda, the war of extermination between the Hutu and Tutsi tribes has claimed at least half a million lives. A ferocious racial war has broken out in Sri Lanka between Tamils and Sinhalese, in which "tens of thousands of people were massacred in the most gruesome way."[9] (This occurred after government-imposed racial preferences in employment and education to achieve racial equity had worsened, not improved, race relations.)[10] In Timor, up to two hundred thousand East Timorese have been killed by Indonesians or starved to death by famine since 1975.[11] And this list is just a beginning. By post-Enlightenment standards, these are incidents of racism and genocide, but their sheer numbers show that they are not just *lapses* from those standards and that the Enlightenment revolution has yet to reach many areas of the world.

It is essential that we be clear that when we denounce racism in absolute terms, we are measuring all cultures and all times by a standard that is distinctly modern and Western. In this respect, race-gender-class critics are not cultural relativists but cultural absolutists. In his recent book *Sick Societies,* Robert Edgerton describes the variety of cultures on earth with devastating realism and in the process demonstrates how impossible it would be for race-gender-class scholars to retain their professed relativism in the face of cultural situations that must profoundly offend them. In some, life is often short and very unpleasant; in others, relations between men and women are bitterly unhappy; in still others, women are educationally and socially restricted and even physically mutilated, and debilitating tribal warfare is a way of life. Edgerton does not shrink from saying that some cultures are simply dysfunctional—they do not offer their members satisfying lives. Given a choice, nobody would be indifferent to whether they lived in a modern European society or in the wretched pre-Enlightenment situations Edgerton describes. Michael Berliner puts the matter forcefully: "Some cultures are better than others: A free society is better than slavery; reason is better than brute force as a way to deal with other people."[12]

This, then, is the context within which the moral judgments that concern race-gender-class scholars must be evaluated. It is easy to see that, in this context, they violate both principles I set out above. They make moral judgments without regard to the general morality of the context, and in specifically criticizing Europeans, they focus on actions that do not distinguish Europeans from others and ignore other things that make them truly distinctive.

Let us begin with the most emotionally charged of all moral issues: slavery. Just as General Motor's report of a substantial loss suggests a negative judgment, so does white involvement in slavery. But what are the standards of the context, and how do Europeans stand in relation to those standards? Before the Enlightenment, slavery was widespread. In general slavery was part of the universal habit of regarding the claims of one's own group as more important than those of outsiders. The Arabs were the first to run an organized slave trade in the late Middle Ages, but it had been common to use captives as slaves regardless of race.[13] Before the arrival of Europeans, Indians practiced slavery in North America. It was also common in Africa, where Africans sold other Africans to Europeans for transport to North America.

Relative to the context, then, how do Europeans (including their North American branch) appear? The distinguished historian of Islam Bernard Lewis puts the matter simply: "In having practiced sexism, racism, and imperialism, the West was merely following the common practice of mankind throughout the millennia of recorded history."[14] Europeans seem no worse in this respect than non-Europeans, then, and perhaps somewhat better: they were at least ambivalent, as evidenced by the illegality of slavery in some states in North America.

Now to the second principle. To say that Europeans practiced slavery is true, at least in North America, but this fact does not distinguish them from other groups. A statement like this has the same force as "this man has two legs," that is, very little. Is there anything with regard to slavery that is distinctive by virtue of being true of them but not of others? Clearly, there is. What sets Europeans apart from other groups is their unique role in ending slavery, and the European Enlightenment began the process. A standard account summarizes what happened: "The slave system aroused little protest until the 18th century. Rational thinkers of the Enlightenment then began to criticize it for its violation of the rights of man. . . . By the late 18th century, moral disapproval of slavery was widespread. . . . The trade to the British colonies was finally abolished in 1807. . . . In 1807 the United States also prohibited it." By 1865 slavery in North America had ceased to exist, and a worldwide movement to end slavery was well under way. In 1919, "the principal Allied Powers (Belgium, the British Empire, France, Italy, Japan, Portugal, and the United States)" signed a convention to "secure the complete suppression of slavery in all of its forms and of the slave trade by land and sea."[15]

This sequence of events is extraordinary; in not much more than a century, a practice that had existed all over the globe for thousands of years was virtually ended. The heroes of this process were Europeans who responded to the thinkers of the Enlightenment. One group from among them deserves special mention—the North Americans who tore their society apart to fight what proved to be the decisive battle in the defeat of slavery, the American Civil War. And yet in the upside-down world of race-gender-class scholars, this is precisely the group that is blamed for slavery.

One aspect of the situation, however, predisposes all of us to see it in a misleading way. The Civil War was the decisive moral struggle over slavery, so in looking back at this great symbolic drama, it is natural to admire the winners and despise the losers. For that reason, the losers in this one battle tend to have all our indignation at the institution of slavery heaped upon them and to be perceived as its representative. But this is an illusion: the losers had that position only because their society contained the vanguard of the abolitionist movement. In that respect their society deserves credit for being unique, not opprobrium for containing anti-abolitionists, for in that respect it was far from unique.

The point is reinforced if we look at the pockets of slavery that still exist. They are found only where European influence—that is, Enlightenment influence—is weak. A recent article in *Time* magazine, headlined "Alas, Slavery Lives," reported that "tens of millions of people around the globe, including children as young as six, are working in bondage—in dangerous and degrading conditions that often involve 18-hour days, beatings and sexual abuse. Many are the victims of opportunistic slave raiders."[16] Another article reported not only that child slavery exists in many countries throughout the world but that "traditional slavery persists in the Sudan."[17] Still another headline proclaimed "Female Slavery a Get-Rich-Quick Scheme in China."[18]

What is true for slavery is just as true of the clashes between different cultures that race-gender-class scholars denounce as imperialism. Once again, if we ignore the mores of the context, we can easily say that European imperialism and colonialism are morally unacceptable; they violate the Enlightenment idea of a common humanity in which all have equal value. But how should the Europeans be judged in context? Again, in pre-Enlightenment times a tribe almost invariably pressed to the limit its advantage against a neighboring tribe. As Dario Fernandez-Morera said recently, the peoples that the Europeans conquered shared the values of their conquerors and would have done as much to them had they had the power to do so.[19]

It must be remembered that what we now call genocide had earlier been a temptingly permanent solution to competing claims. This was the way of the Plains Indians, for example;[20] the Pawnees were drastically reduced in number through clashes with their neighbors. Their persecutors, the Sioux, were also legendary for their love of torture.

Modern readers of the Greek classics are probably shocked by the casual assumption in *The Odyssey* that when a town is captured, its men will be killed and its women taken captive. But in pre-Enlightenment times, wars between tribes were often fought to the finish, that is, until one side had been exterminated, because the first priority of a group was to secure its survival. In sixteenth-century Europe the best defense was a good offense: if you were not growing stronger, your neighbors were. A king's duty to his people was to secure their peace, and in that dangerous world a strong state was a large one; the more powerful the state, the fewer dangers it faced. What may sound like flagrant national chauvinism in Elizabethan England was, for Elizabethans, simply exultation in the knowledge that foreign powers could not threaten them with devastation. If England had not contested Spanish influence around the globe, it would eventually have had to face conquest by a stronger Spain.

All of us who live where the Enlightenment cultural revolution is virtually complete can now condemn expansionism, but a pre-Enlightenment state could not afford such an attitude. This point cannot be emphasized enough: to reevaluate centuries-old situations in terms of the most fastidious late twentieth-century rules is absurd.

As to the second of my two principles: if pressing their advantage over that of other groups did not distinguish Europeans from other peoples, was there anything in this area that did distinguish them? Again, the answer lies in the fact that they led the world in moving away from this pattern of behavior. The Enlightenment is the source of the still emerging consensus that aggression by one people against another is intolerable and that one people may not subjugate another. The Europeans themselves turned against colonialism; if there is a parallel in world history for the peaceful British withdrawal from India and its motivation in domestic anticolonial sentiment, I do not know of it.

Even the anticolonialism of the Third World owes much to the spread of Western values. Mohandas Gandhi was an inspirational leader in India's fight for independence, but he was a Western-trained lawyer as well. He, too, had absorbed the values of the Enlightenment. The bloodless transition to self-rule in India was in no small part due to Gandhi's ability to speak to the British in terms they understood; he used the Enlightenment language of a common humanity. Indeed the very ideas of independence and self-determination were part of the colonial legacy.

Although this distinctive European renunciation of expansionism and aggression comes to full fruition only in this century, there are signs of something new happening much earlier. J. H. Elliott aptly says of the sixteenth-century Europeans that "greed, arrogance, dogma—all these played their part. But there was a more generous spirit also alive in that European civilization."[21] If we look at the entire sweep of the colonial era, from the Renaissance[22] voyages through the nineteenth-century empires and beyond to the process of decolonizing, the Europeans typically shrink from the kind of thoroughgoing solution to the competing claims of different peoples that was common elsewhere—that is, genocidal rooting out of the rival culture. With rare local exceptions, Europeans did not set out to annihilate populations that stood in their way; they already felt the need to excuse what they were doing by assuring themselves that they were ruling other populations for their own good. They were, of course, rationalizing, but their need to do so indicates an ambivalence and the beginnings of a new set of values. For here the legitimate claims of another group were being acknowledged, even while they were being denied. The more permanent solution to competing claims (slaughter) was no longer acceptable to a people who had begun to have such thoughts. Seen in historical context, colonialism is an intermediate stage between the unrestrained pressing of one's claims without regard for those of others and the complete renunciation of that mode. A society that must convince itself that the occupation of another is for its own good is not too far away from accepting that it should not do so at all.

Let us return to the trenchant judgments of Stephen Greenblatt and Edward Said that I cited at the beginning of this chapter: Greenblatt's, that Shakespeare and Spenser put their talents into the service of the repulsive ideology of imperialism; and Said's, that the European novel is implicated in imperialism and colonialism and that Europeans see the Orient not as it is but through stereotypes designed to justify colonialism. Evidently both violate my two principles.

Greenblatt ignores the prevailing morality of the context in order to apply his own twentieth-century morality to Shakespeare and Spenser—a flagrant anachronism. He speaks as if the Elizabethans had already experienced the Enlightenment. The devastating answer to his charge that Elizabethan literature attempts to justify colonial adventures is that at that time nobody felt the need to justify them. The English did not have to be persuaded that England should extend its influence and power—they simply thought it was a self-evidently good thing to do. Other countries thought England's expansion of its empire bad because they themselves would lose power and influence, but morality (Greenblatt's "repellent political ideology") had nothing to do with it. Although the losers did not like losing, they would have been happy to have played the same game and won. Said also ignores the context of expectations: who can doubt that expansionism and conquest in the Arab world was limited by feasibility rather than by morality? Here, too, the losers were unhappy about losing, not about the rules of the game.

In criticizing Europeans for attitudes that were simply those of their time, both Greenblatt and Said miss what was distinctive about them— their ambivalence and the strong signs of their eventual renunciation of those attitudes. And so Greenblatt and Said both preach historicism yet judge ahistorically; they both preach Enlightenment values yet attack the very group that originates and spreads those values.

Race-gender-class scholars sometimes acknowledge implicitly that their critique assumes the very values of the West; in this mode, they see the West's failing as the gap between its ideals and its performance, in other words, as hypocrisy. A common example is criticism of the discrepancy between the theoretical high-mindedness of eighteenth-century talk of the rights of "man" and the sordid reality of slavery. Similar discrepancies are found in colonial contexts.

This charge of hypocrisy is worth careful consideration, because it does raise an interesting point about transitional periods. Once the Enlightenment idea of a common humanity becomes *widely* accepted, its consequences are clear: behavior that was once common comes to be regarded as unacceptable barbarity. But this change requires a period of transition. That transition is now well advanced. It has been going on since the eighteenth century and is not yet over.

A period of transition is, of necessity, one of inconsistency, in which parts of the old and the new exist side by side. Change will occur more quickly in some regions than in others, but even in regions that lead, there will be ambivalence. The form that this inconsistency takes among Europeans is interesting but hardly surprising. The Enlightenment gives them a new view of humanity and also advances their scientific and technological knowledge. They use their new knowledge to advance their power, but their developing new morality begins to undermine their confidence in what they are doing. For a while old ambitions given new scope by new power are in conflict with their new beliefs. This transition period is, however, relatively short; as it begins, European nations still have relatively little doubt about empire, but by the end they can no longer justify it to themselves.

During the transition there is much soul-searching and not a little rationalizing of pre-Enlightenment practice by appeal to Enlightenment values. The idea of the "white man's burden"—a wise colonial regime prevents tribal warfare, brings medicine and literacy to Africa, and so on—exemplifies this stage. The important question here is, Is it possible to imagine the introduction of a wholly new set of values without a transitional period full of double standards? This question answers itself. It is possible to say that particular individuals were hypocritical, but to label a whole period and a whole people hypocritical must imply that the Enlightenment revolution could have occurred overnight, without a transition. Human affairs do not work that way.

Another interesting point about transitions is raised when the same argument is made about the hypocrisy of the U.S. Constitution in the matter of slavery. Here universal rights were enunciated in ringing tones, yet they were not to apply to everyone. An instructive parallel is the development of habeas corpus. Today we celebrate its introduction in the Magna Carta of 1215 as a defining event in establishing limits to the power of governments over individuals, yet its scope was also limited at first. Habeas corpus originated in a dispute between King John and his barons, who were intent on limiting the king's power over them—though such protections were not to be extended to the entire population. Should we worry about hypocrisy here too, because only an elite was protected? History gives us the answer: what proved to be supremely important was a principle, namely, that if the government wants to deprive a person of his or her liberty, it must demonstrate the reasonableness of its action to the satisfaction of a jury of his or her peers—that is, to people who are like the accused—not to the satisfaction of government agents. The idea that governments must behave in a manner that ordinary people understand and condone was far too profound to be disparaged simply because it was not fully implemented at the time of its conception.

This principle was in fact so important that over time it gradually spread not only through all classes of English society but beyond England, to one country after another. We need to be realistic about situations such as these. *If, when a great moral principle is introduced, its full cost must be paid immediately, progress will never occur.* What matters is that the principle be implemented, however imperfectly at first, because its moral force will inevitably work to increase its scope.

Similarly, the great moral principles enunciated in the U.S. Constitution could never have been implemented immediately; once they were introduced, however, the progression to universal applicability was irresistible. Resistance to change makes inconsistencies of this kind unavoidable; to bemoan this is not to impugn Americans but to refuse to accept human nature.

What is true of individual instances of this kind is just as true of progress toward Enlightenment values in general. Europeans at first stumble toward a new system of values that (it now appears) the world will eventually adopt, but this stumbling can hardly be seen as morally reprehensible when they are the authors of the standard being used to judge them. Inconsistent situations are always open to the competing judgments that the glass is half full or half empty, but in these cases we know that the glass had been empty, and that must be the standard against which they are judged.

There is a considerable irony in the fact that race-gender-class scholars consider all systems of belief "socially constructed" except their own; yet nothing is more clearly an introduced and learned system than the Enlightenment value system they adopt as their universal basis for the denunciation of sexism and racism. It is the value system of what V. S. Naipaul recently called "our universal civilization."[23] We call its values "civilized," and appropriately so.

There is still another kind of blindness here. Given their aggressive and uncompromising insistence on value judgments (antisexism, antiracism, and the like) that are unmistakably part of the Enlightenment's legacy, it is odd that race-gender-class critics judge colonialism so harshly. For colonialism was the means by which the Enlightenment system of values they espouse was spread around the world. A small thought experiment will prove the point: imagine a world in which European expansion had never happened, one in which there had been no influence of European ideas beyond Europe. What would the world outside Europe be like today? Would the rigid caste system of India be more, or less, in evidence? Would there be more, or fewer, genocidal tribal clashes in the world? Would there be more, or less, brutalization of women by suttee, foot binding, genital mutilation, exposure of babies, forced segregation? Would there be more, or less, slavery in the world? Would there be more, or less, human sacrifice, torture, cannibalism? Would life expectancy be higher or lower?

The answers to these questions are not in doubt. Without European influence, the world would be much less to the liking of race-gender-class scholars than it is today. The positive and negative effects of that influence vary with particular areas, but in the case of Africa, for example, the noted Africanist L. H. Gann points to a host of beneficial effects brought about by the colonial legacy.[24] The other side of the coin is presented by George Ayittey, who argues that in the immediate postcolonial period "thirty years of independence have brought nothing but economic misery, famine, senseless civil wars, wanton destruction, flagrant violations of human rights and brutal repression."[25]

Although it is sometimes argued that this postcolonial misery is itself the legacy of colonial oppression, the very terms of this diagnosis—for example, the "flagrant violations of human rights"—are clearly Western in their formulation. Their use could not even be imagined outside the sphere of influence of the European Enlightenment. Would anyone even bother to accuse the nineteenth-century chief Shaka—the great, and extraordinarily brutal, founder of the Zulu Empire—of "violating human rights?" And can it be doubted that the genital mutilation of females is a traditional African custom rather than one introduced by the West through colonialism? The principle of the self-determination of peoples must take precedence over the facts that Gann and Ayittey present—it, too, is an inescapable legacy of the Enlightenment. But it is worth remembering that throughout human history modernity and progress were always spread by the influence of one culture on another, including conquest.

In spite of the aggressive modernizing implicit in the values they espouse, race-gender-class critics blame Western influence for destroying many a settled, established way of life. (Annette Kolodny's complaint about the fate of North American Indian cultures is typical.)[26] But this attitude is unrealistic in yet another way. All cultures change and adapt, rise and fall; nothing is a given for very long. One of the very same American Indian cultures discussed by Kolodny provides an interesting example of this principle. Although the horse was supremely important to the Comanche culture, it must have been a relatively recent introduction, because Comanche horses were descended from those that the Spanish brought to the New World. Comanche culture therefore illustrates the principle that a unique way of life often arises from the contact, and even the clash, between different cultures.

In the Old World, Scotland illustrates the same point. Scottish culture, with its quaint folkways—kilts, bagpipes, and so forth—also has an aura of antiquity, but it is really a relatively recent blending of many cultures, including Irish, French, Viking, and Brittonic Celt, a blending that could not have occurred without clashes between those cultures. Just as a favorite dish is a product of assimilated ingredients, cultures too are unique syntheses of prior elements mixed together by various historical accidents; they are always changing as new elements are taken in. Changes in American Indian cultures through contact with other cultures were therefore inevitable. To lament such change is to be unrealistically sentimental; the spread of the wheel was no less inevitable. Change occurs even without external stimulus; Robert Edgerton shows that even undeveloped cultures are not harmonious wholes without internal strain and that they also have dissenters who occasionally manage to bring about change.[27]

At the bottom of this static view of cultures is a Romantic aestheticism about folk traditions, a fascination with colorful and exotic costume, dances, and so on. When one considers the cost to a people of not modernizing—for example, foregoing the benefits of modern medicine and having a life expectancy of only 25 to 30 years—a preference for the aesthetic over the practical seems curious on the part of scholars who in other contexts are only too ready to argue that the aesthetic dimension of Western culture is a sugarcoating of unacceptable material conditions.

If we are to make any statement about Westerners with regard to race and racism, it is that Enlightenment values have led them to invent the term *racism* and to be severely troubled by it. Despite many accusations that American society is racist, for example, careful empirical work by Paul Sniderman and Thomas Piazza has demonstrated a remarkable openness and flexibility in the attitudes of American whites toward racial questions.[28] Evidence of their hypersensitivity to any charge of racism can also be seen in their vulnerability to racism baiting.

This hypersensitivity also makes it difficult for Americans to talk honestly about race, but recently, during deliberations of a New York State commission on the social studies curriculum in the public schools, antiwhite racism baiting became so extreme that Arthur Schlesinger, Jr., a member of the commission, was provoked to an angry but truthful reply. In *The Disuniting of America,* published shortly thereafter, Schlesinger addressed assertions of the moral superiority of the African over the Western tradition: Europe, he said, whatever its sins, was "the source—the unique source—of those liberating ideas of individual liberty, political democracy, the rule of law, human rights, and cultural freedom that constitute our most precious legacy and to which most of the world today aspires. These are European ideas, not Asian, nor African. . . . There is surely no reason for Western civilization to have guilt trips laid on it by champions of cultures based on despotism, superstition, tribalism, and fanaticism. . . . The West needs no lectures on the superior virtue of those 'sun people' who sustained slavery until Western imperialism abolished it . . . who still keep women in subjection and cut off their clitorises, who carry out racial persecutions not only against Indians and other Asians but also against fellow Africans from the wrong tribes . . . and who in their tyrannies and massacres, their Idi Amins and Boukassas, have stamped with utmost brutality on human rights. . . . Those many brave and humane Africans who are struggling these days for decent societies are animated by Western, not by African, ideals."[29]

Two important points must be made about Schlesinger's outburst: first, everything he says is so obvious that it can hardly be questioned; and second, on college campuses today few dare to say as much. But even Schlesinger suppresses a good part of the truth: he blames black activists for this unrealistic denigration of the Western tradition, avoiding the equally obvious fact that feminists and white liberals have done far more to create the climate of opinion he objects to and to further "multiculturalism" on college campuses than have those he singles out for criticism.

Schlesinger's realism contrasts strangely with the unreality of prevailing academic discussions. Johnnetta Cole, for example, is convinced that "we live in a society where tolerance, not to mention respect for differences, is particularly low" and believes that America is exceptionally racist: "Racism is dyed into the very cloth of the American way."[30] She does not understand that in making these charges she is speaking a language that embodies the system of values—a Western system—of those she is criticizing. Henry Louis Gates also complains that the high canon of Western masterpieces "represents the return of an order in which my people were the subjugated. . . . Who would return us to that medieval never-never land?"[31] But he, too, has things upside down. It was Western thinkers who rescued us from a more primitive moral order. It was they who moved us away from the subjugation of one people by another.

Said's complaint that Europeans see and judge Arabs by Western, not Arab, lights shows the same lack of realism. That Europeans see other cultures through the eyes of Europeans is hardly surprising; all of us bear the mark of the environment we grew up in. The crucial question is whether the West is more, or less, open to and curious about other cultures than are non-Western societies. That question is easily answered. Stereotyped thinking about other races and cultures is rampant outside the West. If Said could muster sufficient objectivity to look at both sides of the relationship between Europeans and Arabs and ask himself on which side one finds more expressions of hate and prejudice, he could never have reached his unrealistic conclusions.[32]

Said's unrealistic view of Western, as opposed to non-Western cultural openness is pursued in a whole new genre of scholarship that has arisen recently—one concerned with travel writing. Before modern technology made world travel a common experience, European travelers sometimes published records of their surprising experiences in unfamiliar parts of the world for a readership that was understandably curious about those experiences. Race-gender-class scholars find in them a convenient record of European chauvinism and prejudice toward other races and cultures. Typical is Mary Louise Pratt's stress on the "great significance of travel writing as one of the ideological apparatuses of empire" through which "metropolitan reading publics have been engaged with expansionist enterprises whose material benefits accrued mainly to the very few." She shows us "how travel books by Europeans about non-European parts of the world went (and go) about creating the 'domestic subject' of Euroimperialism."[33] ("Creating the domestic subject" is race-gender-class jargon for "forming public opinion.")

Again, a nearly total lack of realism prevails. Pratt does not see that empire needed no justification in these contexts; that the impressions recorded by the writers would not have differed from those the readers would have formed; that travelers *from* these foreign lands would have had equally culture-bound impressions themselves; that public opinion could not have been formed by a few travelogues alone—indeed prior public opinion probably had much to do with the tone of the travelogues.[34] Pratt prefers instead a conspiracy theory.

One can only hope that knowledgeable scholars will increasingly shed their inhibitions and frankly insist that the Western tradition has been the unique source of opposition to racism and slavery, not the reverse. The truth is the only thing that has any chance of setting us free from the unhappy past in matters of race. Great damage has resulted from our reluctance to speak plainly about the historical record.

The unrealistic attitudes toward race and racism that have been preached on campuses across the country by race-gender-class scholars have produced results that should alarm everyone. "For the first time in forty years," a 1993 poll found, "young white adults are more biased against blacks than are their older counterparts."[35] There is now more racial resentment among college-educated whites and blacks than among those without a college education. This attitude is something we might legitimately call socially constructed. In more familiar language, it is the result of the present campus climate. Formerly, college-educated people were more enlightened about race, hence less racist than those without a college education. That was natural enough: education should enlighten and broaden perspectives. The divisive, unrealistic preachings of campus ideologues have reversed this pattern, however, and have succeeded in dividing us. These ideologues have a vested interest in the discord and chaos that will make their theories self-fulfilling prophesies, but the rest of us ought to recognize that they and their theories are leading us to disaster.

Race-gender-class orthodoxy on campus urges us to "celebrate ethnicity," but our Enlightenment heritage should have taught us to fear anything that puts group membership ahead of common humanity, thereby pushing us toward tribal thinking and tribal politics. Enlightenment thinkers realized that humane values can prevail only if we identify ourselves as human beings first and foremost. The celebration of ethnicity is what Herder prescribed for the German Volk and what Hitler found it in his interest to revive. We have recently ignored such warnings from the past, with the result that race relations have deteriorated. Arch Puddington recently noted that "the diversity agenda has deepened racial, sexual, and ethnic tensions at universities all across the country," and it would be hard to challenge that judgment.[36] If we vote, choose friends, take sides in a dispute, give credence to one person over another—or do anything else—for reasons of ethnic pride or solidarity, we are choosing not to give our first loyalty to principle, integrity, truth, and honesty. That is why ethnic politics and ethnic separatism must always be a threat to humane values. The good intentions of affirmative-action programs are not in doubt, but their results should by now have taught us that the principle of a common humanity was too important—and too fragile—to be tampered with.

Anything that encourages people to see themselves primarily as members of an ethnic group must also encourage tribal thinking, with all of its destructiveness. In scholarship, the subordination of knowledge to ethnic pride has led to Afrocentrism, that is, history that grasps at flimsy or nonexistent evidence as a means of supporting claims of African cultural achievement.[37] Arthur Schlesinger is correct when he observes that tribal separatism (on campus or anywhere else) must lead to mutual suspicion and rancor, to self-ghettoizing and self-pity, and that separatism in dormitories makes for worse, not better, race relations;[38] but he cannot bring himself to mention the factor that has done most to create the situation he deplores, because it encourages and rewards tribal identification: affirmative action.

Race-gender-class scholars tell us that an emphasis on a common humanity is a cover for white hegemony, but the proof that they are wrong can be seen in the global improvement in the human condition that the Enlightenment has brought about. The way to make a multiracial society work is neither by celebrating ethnicity nor by revisiting primitive innocence but through continued progress toward a civilized post-Enlightenment modernity. Multicultural orthodoxy interprets any deviation from perfect racial harmony as a sign of underlying evil so that it can keep resentment and bad feeling alive, but the truth is that when judged by any known standard, we already do well and would do much better but for the damage that is caused by that orthodoxy itself. It will be difficult to change the tenor of campus race discussions of recent decades, but the effort must be made to introduce a more realistic historical perspective into them.

5

Class and
Perfect
Egalitarianism

Human life is a complex and diverse phenomenon. The number of factors and values at work in any human situation is always so large that no single factor or concept is likely to give one an adequate understanding of it. The conceptual framework that race-gender-class critics use for their analysis of human situations is therefore discouraging because of its narrowness. The basic analytical tool is the concept of oppression, which is used equally for race, gender, and class. There is far more to human life than oppression, and it is never clear why that is the only issue we must address in discussing literature.

The practical effect of this exclusive focus on oppression is to make a utopian egalitarianism the reference point in analyses of race, gender, and class; anything less than full equality counts as oppression and exploitation. In the two previous chapters we have seen how this framework deflects attention from what should be the focal point of thought about gender (the development of modern conditions that now allow women to make choices that were seldom available to them in the past) and race (the spread of the Enlightenment conception of a common humanity). What of the specific issues raised by the notion of class?

Here the collapse of Marxism as a viable system of political thought has left campus radicals in a state of disarray. Marxism had built its case on the notion that capitalism was morally wrong and that a successful economy could be built without competitiveness and the unequal outcomes that a free market presupposes. Bitter experience in over twenty countries has removed any doubt that those ideas were thoroughly mistaken. This historical development poses a problem for race-gender-class critics in that their entire framework of thought and vocabulary—particularly the concepts exploitation and oppression—can hardly be disentangled from this now obsolete base of Marxist economics. Previously, unequal outcomes could be considered evidence of exploitation and oppression, but that automatic equation is no longer possible

Race-gender-class scholars seem to have noticed that a catastrophe has befallen their conceptual framework, for certain changes in their behavior are unmistakable. Many are less willing to use the words *Marxist* and (to a lesser extent) *capitalism,* the former for obvious reasons, the latter because it is so closely tied to the former. Some now deny that their thinking is, or ever was, Marxist, whereas others adopt the curious tactic of transferring the obsolescence of Marxism to the criticism of Marxist thought—as though it was the questioner, not Marxism, that had suddenly become outdated.[1] There has been little evidence, however, of what the situation really demands—namely, a rethinking of the entire radical egalitarian framework of ideas, of which oppression and exploitation are a part.

Let us look at some examples of the kind of rethinking presently required. The idea of exploitation arises in Marx's thought directly from his labor theory of value. Workers increase the value of the materials they handle and are then deprived of the difference between the wages they are paid and the increased price that the capitalist receives for the resultant goods (the surplus value), which, because workers created it—so the argument goes—should belong to them. Yet according to accounts of events that led to the downfall of the Soviet system, stores were full of items nobody wanted but empty of food, while vegetables rotted in the fields. The inadequacy of Marx's labor theory of value was exposed: it had entirely failed to grasp the importance of management, distribution, and buyers in creating value. This theory is the bedrock of ideas like exploitation and oppression; take away the labor theory of value and those ideas have no basis. Race-gender-class critics have essentially continued to use ideas that are integral parts of this defunct system of thought and appear to believe that all they need do is to stop using the name Marxism.

Class remains a fundamental organizing principle for race-gender-class scholars because it offers classifications for victim and victimizer, but the fluid social structure of modern America looks very different from the rigid nineteenth-century European class system that Marx made the basis of his political theory. One economic group flows into another, and movement up and down the social scale is constant. By contrast, the true class systems of Europe differentiated people by dress, speech, food, entertainment, and much more, but they have either weakened or disappeared, England having perhaps the best preserved of them. In America, a clearly defined "us" and "them" is much harder to discern. Generations of low-status immigrants have become affluent, and access to higher education has never been greater. In these circumstances the notion of class, too, evidently needs rethinking.

Another difficulty for the Marxist proclivities of race-gender-class critics is that America is a country whose prosperity, living conditions, and individual political liberty are envied almost everywhere, the result being a flood of people wanting to live there. If people vote for their preferred form of society with their feet, then America wins that election. Race-gender-class scholars find this an uncomfortable reality. They are unwilling to abandon their denigration of bourgeois individualism and thus continue to criticize its concern with individual rights as selfish; they would put the community first. Yet even before the demise of Marxism, history had given us good reasons to be skeptical about this idea.

Most race-gender-class critics would readily assent to the following statement: "The greater the readiness to subordinate purely personal interests, the higher rises the ability to establish comprehensive communities. . . . This state of mind, which subordinates the interests of the ego to the conservation of the community, is really the first premise of every truly human culture." But they might be rather upset to learn the origin of the statement just cited. It was written some seventy years ago in Landsberg am Lech prison, in Germany. It is in fact part of chapter 11 of Adolf Hitler's *Mein Kampf.*[2] The irrational animus of race-gender-class critics against their own society, allied as it is with their innocence in matters of political theory, allows them to stumble into political stances characteristic of some of the most brutal and despotic regimes in the history of the world.[3]

The collapse of faith in a socialist economics has created an even deeper problem for race-gender-class scholars. It is now clear that achieving equality involves problems of great intellectual complexity.

But the race-gender-class case puts heavy emphasis on a *moral choice* as being the only impediment to equality: the implication is that we could achieve it if we wanted to, but white males do not want to and that is why inequality persists. The assumption that we lack the will, rather than the understanding, to bring about full equality is essential if one wishes to denounce the wickedness of those who obstruct it; if the problem is mainly one of understanding, then righteous indignation is out of place. But race-gender-class criticism without righteous indignation would be like Shakespeare's play without Hamlet: that is its center and its raison d'être.

The Marxist societies of this century all proceeded as if implementing true egalitarianism were a simple matter. Because they thought that moral choice was the only important issue, they ruined the economies of the countries concerned and brought about a considerable reduction in what was available to be shared equally. Once we acknowledge that achieving a society that is both highly productive and maximally egalitarian involves enormously difficult intellectual problems, the mind-set of race-gender-class critics seems irrelevant; they want only to denounce, not to confront, real intellectual issues. They live in a fantasy world in which good intentions and moral superiority should be enough to make any society just and to abolish the barriers to equal outcomes.

A good measure of the coherence of the political thought of race-gender-class critics is provided by the works of Fredric Jameson, arguably the most influential of all American literary critics. The considerable vogue of Jameson's writings compels us to confront an exceedingly strange fact: just at the time when in the real world Marxism was collapsing so completely that its viability as a political theory seemed almost at an end, its influence in the universities of the English-speaking world was increasing just as dramatically. Anticapitalist rhetoric was heard more than ever among campus intellectuals. Nobody has been more central to this strange development than Jameson, and his recent activity is almost a symbol of the situation: as the Wall crumbled, Jameson was building a new Marxist edifice of his own in the form of five books: *The Ideologies of Theory* (2 volumes), *Signatures of the Visible, Late Marxism,* and *Postmodernism.*

Jameson's current influence in literary studies cannot be overstated. He is probably the most quoted of all American critics, and citations of his work are commonly accompanied by almost abjectly respectful phrases: "Jameson tells us that . . ." or "Jameson has shown us that . . . ." With the publication of *The Political Unconscious* in 1981, Jameson became the patron saint of the race-gender-class criticism that was to dominate departments of literature over the next decade. Since that time, his influence has grown even stronger. His dictum that "there is nothing that is not social and historical—indeed, that everything is 'in the last analysis' political" became an article of faith for all branches of the new wave in criticism, from feminism to cultural studies.[4] But why should the popularity and influence of a scholar peak at precisely the moment it became clear that the central thrust and inspiration of his work was completely mistaken?

To begin with the obvious: Jameson views politics as inseparable from and presupposed by literary and cultural criticism. If we follow Jameson's priorities, therefore, we should look first at his political thought—even though his readers are in the main not political scientists but literary scholars. Before we consider Jameson as political thinker, however, it is best to acknowledge a potential problem. The essays in the two-volume *Ideologies of Theory* were written between 1971 and 1986, and those in *Signatures of the Visible* between 1977 and 1988. The speed of events in the transformation of the formerly communist countries was startling. Views and predictions of just a few years ago have been cruelly treated by the passage of time, and much of what was written about the likely future course of events now seems foolish. Is it fair to judge Jameson with the benefit of hindsight? To be sure, the judgment of history is uniquely relevant to political ideas, and Marxists are especially committed to that relevance. ("Always historicize!" Jameson insists.)[5] But Jameson himself abolishes this dilemma, for what is most characteristic of him is an attribute that is hard to label without immediately striking a partisan note: an observer sympathetic to Jameson might call it a remarkable consistency and constancy, whereas one less sympathetic is likely instead to see it as a dogged resistance to any change in his views or to learning from experience. When Jameson confronts events that must have surprised him, he shows a marked tendency to assimilate those events to his preexisting framework of ideas instead of allowing them to modify that framework.

In the earlier essays, for example, Jameson's great admiration of Mao Zedong and Herbert Marcuse is evident. Maoism is for him the "richest of all the great new ideologies of the 60s," and Marcuse "the greatest Utopian thinker of that period." In the years since Jameson wrote these words the reputations of both have declined sharply—Mao, in particular, is now largely discredited. One might assume, therefore, that Jameson would be somewhat embarrassed by these judgments. But that assumption would be wrong, for the same attitudes recur in 1990 in his *Late Marxism,* in which Jameson continues to tell us that Marcuse is "the thinker of the sixties."[6]

In the case of Mao, Jameson's determination to stick to his initial judgment produces extraordinary results. Take, for instance, his view of Mao's cultural revolution. By now it is almost impossible to find defenders of this disastrous upheaval; Chinese and non-Chinese, communists and democrats, are united in their condemnation. The stories of disrupted lives, of wasted talent, of death and torture, of cruelty and humiliation, are far too widespread to be ignored. From our present perspective, who could view the cultural revolution as anything but the self-indulgence of an old man grown too used to absolute power?

Yet in characteristic fashion Jameson responds by redoubling his faith in Mao's correctness. The only problem with the cultural revolution, Jameson tells us, was that Mao stopped it too soon: "Mao Zedong himself drew back from the ultimate consequences of the process he had set in motion, when, at the supreme moment of the Cultural Revolution, that of the founding of the Shanghai Commune, he called a halt to the dissolution of the party apparatus and effectively reversed the direction of this collective experiment as a whole (with consequences only too obvious at the present time)."[7] Jameson's dark parenthetical hint is tantalizing—he doesn't tell us just what consequences he has in mind—but his main point is clear enough: China would not be in the mess it is now if Mao had just given it more of the same. Jameson does not shrink from the idea of an "experiment" with human lives, though the added word "collective" may betray some awareness of the need to make that idea more palatable. But it is a word hard to justify in the context of a decision first taken and then abandoned, as Jameson acknowledges, by one man.

The same determination to concede nothing, and to resist revisionism at all costs, is visible in Jameson's defense of Stalinism: "Stalinism is disappearing not because it failed, but because it succeeded, and fulfilled its historical mission to force the rapid industrialization of an underdeveloped country (whence its adaptation as a model for many of the countries of the Third World)."[8] This defense assures us of the success of Stalinism by ignoring everything except industrialization; but Stalinism also represents extreme ruthlessness, cruelty, paranoia, senseless purges, the extermination of the kulaks, mass murder, government by terror, and more. Can the notion of success be applied to

Stalin's record in this unhedged way? Jameson seems blind to the huge scale of the human misery caused by Stalin, but even if we leave moral considerations aside, the widespread revulsion against Marxism that resulted ought to be factored into any judgment of the so-called success of Stalinism.

In all of these volumes the pattern of Jameson's moral judgments is extraordinary. He is capable of expressing outrage when discussing Mao and Stalin, yet the outrage is directed not at these two for having caused such suffering but at his intellectual opponents because they exploit that suffering in their arguments. For example, he denounces the "current propaganda campaign, everywhere in the world, to Staline-ize and discredit Maoism and the experience of the Chinese cultural revolution—now rewritten as yet another Gulag to the East—all of this, make no mistake about it, is part and parcel of the larger attempt to trash the 60s generally."[9] Here Jameson presents a startling supposition: that criticism of the cultural revolution "everywhere in the world" (including, presumably, criticism by the present Chinese government, by Eastern Europeans, and even by those who suffered it and survived) is motivated by nothing more than a desire to undermine a Western Marxist intellectual's nostalgia for the 1960s. How can it not have occurred to him that people who experienced the cultural revolution had more important things in mind—their own survival, for example— than damaging his image of the 1960s? In Jameson's mental world, larger and smaller issues seem not to be distinguished. When he goes on to exhort his readers not to concede any of this terrain too quickly to "the other side," he leaves the impression that he has lost sight of the real human issues in these events and that in dealing with actions that make or break millions of lives all that matters is how rival intellectuals may use these tragedies to score points against each other.

Given his determination not to concede any point to critics of

Marxism, Jameson's own Marxism is inevitably orthodox, conservative, and even somewhat antiquated. The thinkers to whom he returns again and again are from the first half of the twentieth century, for example, Georg Lukács and the Frankfurt school figures Theodor Adorno and Max Horkheimer, all men whose ideas were formed before Marxists had to face what Stalin had done. *Late Marxism* even offers us Adorno as the thinker for the 1990s—surely an improbable notion when so much that is critical has happened since Adorno's outlook was formed.

Not surprisingly, there is no trace in these volumes of the more recent (and more realistic) debate about Marxism among political scientists. Some Marxists have recently attempted to reformulate certain aspects of Marx's thought that have not held up well while retaining the general spirit of his work. It is not hard to see why this is necessary: experience has presented Marxism with some very tough questions. For example: When the state owns and runs everything for the public good, a huge bureaucracy and powerful state apparatus must be the result. Yet Marx also wanted the state to wither away.[10] How could one half of a Marxist's mind be reconciled with the other? Does the destruction of the environment in the former socialist countries mean that Marxism is unable to provide the kind of vibrant public opinion needed to protect the environment? Was Stalin's cruelty an aberration, or do the little Stalins of Albania, Romania, and other such countries indicate that Marxism fails to take account of the old maxim that power corrupts and absolute power corrupts absolutely? Does a one-party state, in criminalizing all dissent in advance, inevitably require fear of a repressive secret police to make it work? And to these questions must be added the one I posed earlier: Is not the labor theory of value, on which the entire notion of the exploitation of workers depends, just plain wrong, as proven conclusively by the state economies that ground to a halt because of it?

History has forced thoughtful Marxists to take such questions seriously, and as a result a number of Marxist writers (for example, G. A.
Cohen, Jon Elster, and John Roemer) have attempted to reformulate
Marxism in light of the lessons of experience.[11] But Jameson never even
tries; by contrast with this analytical approach to political theory, his
thought seems most unsophisticated. Rousseau's fantasy of a blissful
state of primitive innocence before the ravages of civilization is never
far from the surface, the one difference being that Jameson makes
Rousseau's general view that man's natural goodness is subverted by
social institutions more specific: he limits the field to one institution—
capitalism. Accordingly, he tells us that "nature and the Unconscious"
are the last bastions, the "precapitalist enclaves" that late capitalism is at
last penetrating. A variation of this theme has it that "the last vestiges of
Nature" are "the Third World and the Unconscious."[12]

Capitalism, according to Jameson, "systematically dissolves the fab-
ric of all cohesive social groups without exception"; and "authentic
cultural creation is dependant for its existence on authentic collective
life, on the vitality of the 'organic' social group. . . . Such groups can
range from the classical polis to the peasant village."[13] Dreamy words
like "authentic" and "organic" invoke a fantasized original harmony,
but one can only wonder how long it would be before a Jameson in his
morally beautiful and authentic Third World village discovered its
rampant (judged by his Western standards) sexism, authoritarianism,
homophobia, tribalism, and racism, to say nothing of its much lower
life expectancy and vulnerability to disease and warfare. History shows
that Rousseau had things backward, as Jameson still does: civilization
alone manages to tame *some* of the natural failings in human beings, and
it is always an uphill battle. Rousseau's fantasy of a condition totally
devoid of those failings is an exaggerated and misconceived response to
the fact that civilization's successes are never more than partial.

When Jameson tells us more about authenticity, it turns out that his examples are mostly products of the Western society he disdains: "The only authentic cultural production today has seemed to be that which can draw on the collective experience of marginal pockets of the social life of the world system: black literature and blues, British working-class rock, women's literature, gay literature, the *roman québecois*, the literature of the Third World; and this production is possible only to the degree to which these forms of collective life or collective solidarity have not yet been fully penetrated by the market and by the commodity system."[14] This strange grab bag must surely be among the most comic cases of a Western intellectual's fantasy of solidarity with the common people.

Jameson's world is evidently that peculiar mix of protest movements, blind Third World adulation, Utopian dreams, and hippie back-to-nature primitivism that was the 1960s. He relives the fantasies of that time when he tells us of "the widely shared feeling that in the 60s, for a time, everything was possible; that this period, in other words, was a moment of a universal liberation, a global unbinding of energies"[15]— even though he is forced to concede that this was a historical illusion. What he is unable to face, however, is that it was a peculiarly Marxist delusion, for he remains at heart a child of the 1960s who really believed that the revolution was at hand.

The quality of Jameson's contribution to the modern debate on more technical issues in Marxist theory can be judged from his comments on the notion of class. As I noted above, the fluid social structure of modern America is very different from the rigid nineteenth-century European class system that served as the basis of Marx's political theory. That raises the question of whether Marxism might be a theory tied to a particular historical situation and thereby doomed to obsolescence as that situation recedes into the past. Jameson deals with this problem by telling us that we can only speak of "a fundamental class structure inherent in a system in which one group of people produces value for another group" if we allow for "the dialectical possibility that even this fundamental 'reality' may be 'realer' at some historical junctures than at others."[16] But surely, after George Orwell's *Animal Farm* we should have been spared this kind of obfuscation and evasion: "All animals are equal but some animals are more equal than others."

Jameson's response to the difficulties of Marxism in the modern world is, as usual, to attempt to hang on to everything and to concede nothing to critics—but at a considerable price. His "solution to the so-called crisis of Marxism" is to argue that we are entering the age of global capitalism and must therefore wait for labor to become global too; that is, we must wait until "proletarianization, and the resistance to it in the form of class struggle, all slowly reassert themselves on a new and expanded world scale." Further: "That a new international proletariat (taking forms we cannot yet imagine) will reemerge from this convulsive upheaval it needs no prophet to predict: we ourselves are still in the trough, however."[17] In other words, when we have a united global proletariat, the socialist transformation will follow, after all. Jameson brushes aside all that we might have learned from the practical experience of Marxism in nearly twenty diverse nations. Once again, the same formula he employed to rescue Mao can be seen: if a concept fails, more of it will bring success. But this formula makes learning from experience impossible: no empirical test of anything will ever be allowed to count. Jameson never explains how Marxism on a global scale will differ from what it has always been locally, but the prospect of even more territory and power for the next Stalin to abuse is not a reassuring one.

Jameson has his own, characteristic methods of dealing with both anti-Marxist arguments and embarrassing historical events, but they fall well short of genuine counterargument. Frequently, he simply cites the argument or event, highlighting the key terms in scare quotes, as if this scornful gesture were sufficient to deal with the substance of the issue. How does one deal with the preference of one nation after another for free elections and free speech? Easily: just talk of "freedom" of speech and "free" elections. What about the problem of socialism's failure in the real world? No problem: just refer to this as " 'socialism does not work.' " What about the problem of Utopian thought resulting so often in mass murder—Robespierre, Pol Pot, Stalin, Mao? Simple. Just speak of "the 'massacres' of the French Revolution, etc." Are the revelations about Paul de Man difficult to handle? Not if you make them "the now notorious 'revelations,' " and the same technique will work with the "notorious 'anti-Semitic' article." Is the equation of public ownership with a huge bureaucracy hard to handle? Then just label it "the anti-Marxist thematics of 'bureaucracy.' " Terrorism? It's just " 'terrorism,' as a 'concept.' "[18] In none of these cases is an argument presented.

Jameson also makes liberal use of all those fudging devices that Dario Fernandez-Morera so wittily exposed recently—for example, the habit of qualifying "Marxism" with the word "late" to remove it from the reach of objections to "classical" Marxism that could not otherwise be answered.[19] But a more characteristically Jamesonian device is to accuse his opponents of exploiting historical facts when they fashion arguments that cite those facts. And so he hints darkly that the "massacres" were "freshly rediscovered" during the bicentennial celebration of the French Revolution; that anti-Utopian sentiment was "helpfully revived" by the Cambodian atrocities; that "the twin Heidegger and de Man 'scandals' have been carefully orchestrated to delegitimate Derridean deconstruction";[20] that the cultural revolution is being seized upon to discredit Mao. Jameson never explains why building an argument by analyzing real events becomes exploitation, and he never hesitates to refer to historical events he finds useful for his own purposes ("always historicize!").

What makes matters worse is that Jameson's epistemology is riddled with contradictions. On one hand, he wants to have it that Marxism is a science that recognizes "fundamental realities." But on the other he wants to pour scorn on epistemological naïveté on the part of people who refer to historical accounts "sometimes called 'the facts' " to " 'prove,' for example, that the French and Russian revolutions accomplished very little." The same contradiction is visible when he suddenly drops the pose of epistemological sophistication to rest his argument on the primitive and unanalyzed notion of authenticity. Another example is the discrepancy between his attempt to shock us by asserting that Nazism and the New Deal are related systems and his righteous indignation over "the networks' truly obscene coverage of Gorbachev's 1989 visit to Cuba, where Fidel was compared to Ferdinand Marcos!"[21] Yet Nazism and the New Deal have little more in common than their both being responses to the Great Depression, whereas Castro and Marcos could easily be juxtaposed as obdurate, aging dictators who were propped up by the substantial financial support of superpowers, who installed close relatives in key governmental positions and imprisoned critics of their regimes, and who avoided at all costs the elections that might have deprived them of their power.

Although Marxism makes moral as well as intellectual claims, Jameson, on the evidence of these books, appears to lack any moral sensibility. His excuses for even the most outrageous behavior of those not on "the other side" will astonish the reader. For example, he brushes aside the matter of the savagery of Stalin or Pol Pot with the following: "What can be 'postmodern' about these hoary nightmare images, except for the depoliticization to which they invite us, is less clear. The history of the revolutionary convulsions in question can also be appealed to for a very different lesson; namely, that violence springs from counter-revolution first and foremost, indeed, that the most effective form of counterrevolution lies precisely in this transmission of violence to the revolutionary process itself."[22] In essence, then, Jameson's reply to the charge that the millions dead in the killing fields of Cambodia, the mass starvation of the kulaks, and the Stalinist purges—and more—must be laid at the door of a system that has so often given absolute power to monsters is as follows: the victims asked for it, and in inviting their own murder they waged very effective propaganda warfare against Marxist regimes. But even the rapist who callously says that his victim asked for it and that she would not have been hurt had she not resisted never has the gall to blame her as well for his reputation for violence. It would, I am sure, not impress Jameson if one pointed out that in each of these cases the mass killings in question took place *after* the revolution had consolidated its power and that most of the victims were helpless people who were not offering "counter-revolutionary violence."

Of all the excuses for Paul de Man's collaborationist (make that "collaborationist") World War II journalism, Jameson's is probably the shabbiest: it was "simply a job." Even Nazis who were tried after World War II did better than this, with their excuse of "Befehl ist Befehl" (they were just following orders)—they at least insisted that they had been *coerced* by orders from above. Here, for once, Jameson is out of step with Stalin, who would never have accepted this defense; Kurt Waldheim is now his model. He does his best to persuade us that one of de Man's plainly anti-Semitic articles should be read as a rebuke to anti-Semites and follows this up by explaining away Heidegger's fascism: Heidegger was " 'politically naive,' as they like to say, but he was certainly political," and this earns him Jameson's "sneaking admiration." It is hard to avoid the conclusion that Jameson's morality works on a simple principle that is devoid of intellectual content: there are ideological friends, who can do no wrong, and foes, who can do no right. For although he never expresses indignation about "blood, torture, death, and terror" in connection with the twentieth-century examples of such that are obvious to everyone else, he does so when predicting "a whole new wave of American military and economic domination of the world"—and this just when America's global economic position is in doubt and its defense industry in recession.[23] Jameson insists, nevertheless, that here he must "simply remind the reader of the obvious."

What distorts Jameson's vision is an extraordinary animus against America. He speaks wistfully of a "diagnosis of the American misery whose prescription would be social revolution," of the "rat race of daily existence," and of the "increasing squalor that daily life in the U.S. owes to big business and to its unenviable position as the purest form of commodity and market capitalism functioning anywhere in the world today." It makes him angry that the overwhelming majority of Americans do not see their lives as the miserable existences he knows them to be, and so for him one of the virtues of Adorno and Horkheimer is their capacity to "restore the sense of something grim and impending within the polluted sunshine of the shopping mall—some older classical European-style sense of doom and crisis."[24] This is an alienated, elitist intellectual with a vengeance: Can Jameson really hope that everyone will drop their commodities, read Adorno, and become appropriately miserable so that he will really have been right about them and their lives after all? Perhaps here we have the key to Jameson's repeated lament that big business manipulates people and transforms them into identical consumers, for he, too, would evidently like to control their minds. The fantasy of the single, centralized multinational corporate agenda is only the mirror image of Marxism's desire for conformity and control: neither does justice to the diversity of human life.

If neither his political thought nor his moral stance offers us anything to admire, what of Jameson as interpreter of literature and culture? The trouble here is that Jameson is correct, at least with regard to his own work, when he takes the position that everything depends on politics, for his criticism is indeed the routine application of his politics to cultural phenomena. The very considerable problems of the former automatically become the problems of the latter. Still, they are not the only problems. On the first page of *Signatures of the Visible,* for example, Jameson tells us that the "visual is *essentially* pornographic, which is to say that it has its end in rapt mindless fascination. . . . [Films] ask us to stare at the world as though it were a naked body." Here he follows the structure of well-known invalid inference. "All pornography involves staring; all staring is visual; therefore all that is visual is pornographic" is structurally the same as "All men are mortal; all mortals must eat; therefore anything that eats is a man." Because looking is not necessarily staring, and staring is not necessarily either mindless or sexual, the equation of the visual and the pornographic is arbitrary. More arbitrary assertion follows when Jameson says that a tourist taking a snapshot is making the landscape into a commodity and thus into personal property: Don't Marxists also take photographs of people or places to remember them by?

When this loose argumentation is turned on a film, the results achieve very little. Take Jameson's reading of *Jaws.* His interpretation is built on his view of the three main characters Brody (played by Roy Scheider), Hooper (Richard Dreyfus), and Quint (Robert Shaw). This is its core: "The content of the partnership between Hooper and Brody projected by the film may be specified socially and politically, as the allegory of an alliance between the forces of law-and-order and the new technocracy of the multinational corporations: an alliance which must be cemented, not merely by its fantasized triumph over the ill-defined menace of the shark itself, but above all by the indispensable precondition of the effacement of that more traditional image of an older America which must be eliminated from historical consciousness and social memory before the new power system takes its place."[25] The death of Quint, Jameson has just explained, is the "symbolic destruction of an older America—the America of small business . . . but also the America of the New Deal and the crusade against Nazism, the older America of the depression and the war and of the heyday of classical liberalism." Quint is associated with the American past, we are told, "by way of his otherwise gratuitous reminiscences about World War II and the campaign in the Pacific."

Anyone who remembers the film can easily see how badly Jameson distorts it. Quint's reminiscences in the Pacific Ocean are of sharks circling and picking off his comrades in arms while they float in the water, waiting to be rescued. What Jameson calls gratuitous reminiscences provide the central motivation for Quint's place in the film as the obsessed shark hunter. His death is that of an Ahab, consumed with a desire for revenge and punished for it; it has nothing to do with the demise of the American past. Jameson's political interpretation of Quint is so arbitrary that it makes the bloodthirsty shark killer into a classical liberal. The two other characters are similarly misinterpreted. The Hooper of the film makes a familiar kind of contrast with Quint: he is the young, inexperienced, intellectual academic, as opposed to the shrewd, worldly-wise, practical older man. As such, he is about as far removed from the idea of multinational corporations as one could imagine. Nor will Brody fit Jameson's stereotype of law and order; he has moved to the island to escape his role as a tough, big-city cop; there he becomes an anguished, liberal public servant, not a repressive tyrant.

Jameson's allegory thus projects Marxist categories of thought indis-criminately into areas where there is nothing to support them. He concludes that *Jaws* is an "excellent example . . . of ideological manip-ulation" and of tapping "genuine social and historical content."[26] The ideological manipulation, however, is his own, not the film's.

There is more of the same throughout these volumes. Van Gogh's *A Pair of Boots* shows, according to Jameson, "the whole object world of agricultural misery, of stark rural poverty, and the whole rudimen-tary human world of backbreaking peasant toil, a world reduced to its most brutal and menaced, primitive and marginalized state." Again, this has nothing to do with the painting, which shows a strong, ex-ceptionally well-made pair of boots—the kind that the abjectly poor certainly never owned. They were, in reality, van Gogh's own boots (though Jameson evidently never knew this), a fact that makes non-sense of his commentary.[27]

The Godfather, for Jameson, is not really about the Mafia but (again predictably) about "American capitalism in its most systematized and computerized, dehumanized, 'multinational' and corporate form." Jameson's obsessions blind him once more to how the notion of a family and its degeneration, for example, is explored in the Godfather films. Kafka is also subjected to Jameson's routine interpretation: "The pleasures of Kafka, the pleasures of the nightmare in Kafka, then come from the way in which the archaic livens up routine and boredom, and an old-fashioned juridical and bureaucratic paranoia enters the empty workweek of the corporate age and makes something at least happen!" Jameson finds his idée fixe in architecture too: "This latest mutation in space—postmodern hyperspace—has finally succeeded in transcending the capacities of the individual human body to locate itself. . . . This alarming disjunction point between the body and its built environment . . . can itself stand as the symbol and analogon of . . . the incapacity of our minds, at least at present, to map the great global multinational and decentered communicational network in which we find ourselves caught as individual subjects."[28]

All these different phenomena are emptied of their individual content so that they can be made to say the same thing, again and again. Jameson thinks that he is thereby enlarging their meaning: "The stereotypical characterization of such enlargement as reductive remains a never-ending source of hilarity."[29] Let me spell out, therefore, what it means to say that this habit is reductive: it reduces a diverse world of endlessly varying objects and books to the same repetitive issue, regardless of whether the issue is there or not. To do so is to end up not with more but with much less content.

Jameson's work on the postmodern is what most attracts admirers. In *Postmodernism: Or, The Cultural Logic of Late Capitalism,* the most ambitious of his works, his analysis suffers from the same problems that I have already noted (as the subtitle suggests), but it also has a weakness all its own. To identify something past by referring to the time of its origin with words like *new* or *modern* not only avoids a more useful descriptive title but also eventually leaves us with a reference to something that is actually old. The present time for the "New Critics" is now half a century ago, which means that the word *new* has become a nuisance. The word *postmodern* compounds this problem by hanging on to a present long past and then pointing indefinitely forward from it. (Even worse, the term *post-postmodernism* is now sometimes heard.) Surely, this compounding of vagueness suggests that a descriptive term should have been used in the first place.

The primary duty of anyone who writes on postmodernism is to clear up the confusion by explaining what it is, but Jameson shirks that duty. His first chapter of *Postmodernism* begins with an exceedingly strange explanation: "The last few years have been marked by an inverted millenarianism in which premonitions of the future, cata-strophic or redemptive, have been replaced by senses of the ends of this or that (the end of ideology, art or social class; the 'crisis of Leninism,' social democracy, or the welfare state, etc., etc.); taken together, all of these perhaps constitute what is increasingly called postmodernism." This definition essentially makes doubts about socialism and Utopian-ism the key to postmodernism. In *Late Marxism,* however, we are told that postmodernism is "the fulfillment and abolition of liberalism as well, which, no longer tenable as an ideology and a value . . . can function more effectively after its own death as an ideology." Further attempts at explanation occur in *Postmodernism:* he identifies postmod-ern culture as the expression of "a whole new wave of American military and economic domination" and tells us that postmodernism must be thought of as a historical, not stylistic, phenomenon. There are still other passages: "Postmodernism is what you have when the moderniza-tion process is complete and nature is gone for good"; and "Postmod-ernism, postmodern consciousness, may then amount to not much more than theorizing its own condition of possibility, which consists primarily in the sheer enumeration of changes and modifications."[30]

The confusion and incoherence are endless. Each attempt at defini-tion could be criticized individually. To take just one of them: it is a mistake to take "stylistic" and "historical" as fundamentally different kinds of definitions, because styles are historical phenomena too, and they cannot be referred to without describing them. To say that some-thing occurs in a certain historical context presupposes that one can identify what is being spoken of. But analysis of each of these attempts would not get us to the root of the problem, which lies in Jameson's logic: he has no conception of the difference between the uses of "is" that define and those that simply inform, that is, of the difference between "the Book of Kells is a ninth-century Irish gospel book" and "the Book of Kells is the subject of a new book from Blackwell." That is why his attempts to identify and define postmodernism are jumbled together with other kinds of interpretive or historical statements.

At this point we must face a puzzle. Jameson's political thought is rigid, narrow, and derivative; his argumentation is poor, and the concepts he uses ill defined; and his literary and cultural interpretation amounts to little more than the indiscriminate imposition of Marxist ideas on texts and objects that have no real place for them. What, then, is the basis of the extraordinary vogue that he now enjoys? I see only one possible answer to this question. The timing (1981) of Jameson's *The Political Unconscious* was exquisitely suited to the developing mood of literary studies in this country. His "everything is 'in the last analysis' political" was exactly what the rising tide of race-gender-class critics needed to legitimate their exclusive focus on oppression as the basic theme of all literature.

As we have seen above, the justifiable statement that everything has a political dimension does not imply the quite different and wholly false statement that politics is the deepest and most important consideration in every situation.[31] But there is still another confusion buried in this claim that everything is in the last analysis political. One of the essays included in *The Ideologies of Theory* ("Pleasure: A Political Issue") expands upon this view of the political as a category fundamental to all others and in so doing spells out some of its consequences. Here Jameson says that "the right to a specific pleasure, to a specific enjoyment of the potentialities of the material body . . . must always in one way or another also be able to stand as a figure for the transformation of social relations as a whole." That is, pleasure (if it is not to be mere hedonism) "must always be *allegorical*"—it must be capable of being "taken as the *figure* for Utopia in general, and for the systemic revolutionary transformation of society as a whole."[32]

Again, this is tailor-made for race-gender-class criticism: our response to and enjoyment of literature can now only be associated with political liberation, and that will justify narrowing criticism to a single issue with its three variants. But this argument contains a fatal flaw. Suppose that we reached Jameson's Utopia: what then? It would be natural to assume that when his politics has done its work (assuming, for the moment, that the real Marxist transformation is indeed possible), we shall have reached a state where life's pleasures are at last justly distributed. The trouble is that if we accept Jameson's model of pleasure, what we think of as pleasures could not then be counted as such, for only those that facilitate the coming social transformation can be genuine. And what this reductio ad absurdum shows is that the political cannot be an independent category of value to which all others are subservient. As far as Jameson's concern with it goes, politics is about the way life's pleasures are regulated and distributed—and to that extent it is a means, not an end in itself. The enjoyment of power itself is the only exception to this rule, but Marxism can hardly admit that power is a pleasure at all, for in the coming Utopia no one may wield power over anyone else.

Jameson's influence evidently derives neither from the power of his argument nor from the moral force of his position but only from his having furnished what seems to those who use it a serviceable underpinning for the victim-centered criticism that has overtaken university literature departments; yet that underpinning consists in a clearly fallacious argument. Here lurks a profound irony; for in the event that we were to agree that a political analysis was the most fundamental and important analysis of all, we should be committed immediately to seeking out the most sophisticated, learned, and intelligent political analysis. The field of political science itself would beckon, and one wonders if Jameson and the crude political thought dear to contemporary academic literary critics would survive in the process.

In 1991 the Modern Language Association of America awarded the James Russell Lowell Prize, which honors "an outstanding literary or linguistic study," to Jameson for his *Postmodernism*. This action tells us a great deal both about Jameson's enormous authority in college literature programs across the nation and about the kind of work that is now held in esteem by the MLA. Its message could not have been more depressing for those who still expect humanistic scholarship to be judged by the intelligence and humane values it reflects, not by its conformity to a confused, contradictory and, ultimately, inhumane radical politics.[33]

6

Activism
and
Knowledge

Most of us who teach and do research in universities and colleges still think of ourselves as part of an institution that serves the society around us in a nonpartisan way; if political considerations were to drive either teaching or research, results that proved politically useful in the short term would crowd out more fundamental thought. This assumption is now challenged by race-gender-class scholars who argue that all scholarship is implicated in social philosophies of one kind or another and that honesty demands an open admission of this. Political engagement should be neither resisted, they say, nor apologized for. Because there is no such thing as objective scholarship, we must expect it to serve political ends. Bias is inevitable and must therefore be unobjectionable.

It is easy to show that these arguments are mistaken, but before we

examine their logic, we should first look at their practical consequences, because the consequences constitute the most powerful arguments against them. They suggest that the arguments for this view *must*
be wrong; all that remains is to find the logical errors that lead to such
dangerous results.

First, what would happen if research were judged by the political
desirability of the results rather than by the soundness of the procedures and thought processes? When a researcher announces a startling new scientific finding or an original view of an important issue in
human history, the first thing that colleagues examine is the steps by
which the conclusion was reached. If those steps withstand scrutiny, the
new finding stands. If, however, everyone were to respond first and
foremost to the desirability of the result and if researchers knew that a
powerful political force would always applaud certain results and attack
others, the reasoning and evidence that led to the result would receive
less attention. Over time, research would gradually become more prone
to leaps of faith and misinterpretation of evidence.

Second, the one indispensable factor in first-rate research is intellectual curiosity—a willingness to follow wherever the facts and the argument lead. Research that is guided by political and social activism lacks
this crucial element of intellectual freedom. The mind is not free to
explore because it must go in certain preset directions. Under these
conditions, research degenerates into a search for more reasons to believe what was already believed. A passionate commitment to a political
standpoint forces the researcher to see only what he or she wants to see.

Third, strong political commitments tend to keep research to a low
level of intellectual complexity. Political goals involve specific, finite
courses of action. The need to act in the real world—to choose this
course rather than that—requires that we simplify a complex of many
different factors in order to make a specific choice among the few

realistic possibilities. Research, on the other hand, requires that simplification be resisted; it requires a mind-set that is alive to the full complexity of situations and that avoids the simplification inevitably required by action. Action is a blunt instrument compared to analysis, and if action rules over analysis, the quality of the analysis will suffer. A corollary of this point is that research depends on careful formulation of issues, whereas practical politics tends instead toward tendentious oversimplification. Politics tends to slogans, whereas research cannot tolerate them. That is why bona fide research is often not useful for political purposes: it is too full of hedged conclusions.

Fourth, when a researcher has arrived at what seems to be a viable explanation of the phenomenon being studied, he or she must next look at other conceivable explanations and weigh as dispassionately as possible the case for those alternatives. Here the activist researcher will be unreliable. When strong moral concerns become central in research, powerful emotional factors interfere with the dispassionate search for answers. If a politically desirable explanation looks promising, the researcher will be unable to perform the crucial task of scrutinizing the case for alternatives. A researcher must try to believe for a moment that his or her preferred explanation is wrong so as to look hard at the arguments for others. That is a psychological impossibility for the social activist.

Fifth, researchers need the clash of opposing viewpoints to help them advance. They may be encouraged by intellectual friends, but what they most need are hostile critics—researchers who are motivated to find the weak points in their work. Such critiques allow them to adjust and refine their work; their intellectual enemies keep them intellectually honest and sharp. Only a hostile critic can push them the last inch of the way to a solution that works even better than the one they were prematurely satisfied with. Researchers don't like criticism any more than anyone else does, but they know that without it they will die intellectually.

Here the activist researcher has a crushing weakness: he regards those who oppose him as immoral people whose lack of moral worth is the reason for their disagreement. Because nothing is to be learned from such people, he allows himself the dangerous luxury of believing that counterarguments need not be heeded because of their tainted source. There is nothing left to check a slide into slackness, self-indulgence, and wishful thinking and no pressure to refine and rethink.

Adverse criticism, however unwelcome, is indispensable to the health of any intellectual enterprise; without it, weaknesses endure instead of being exposed and discarded. It is a necessary discipline. Hostile critics are like predators. They harass their prey, but they also pick off the weaker elements in a species and keep it strong; without them, the species degenerates. Intellectual enemies also pick off weak and unconvincing elements in research and so make it stronger. Politics is quite unlike research in this respect; in politics, people who oppose you stand in the way of what you want to do, but in research contexts opponents ultimately help.

Sixth and last, in political contexts argument is commonly opportunistic. By opportunistic, I mean that arguments are deployed according to the needs of the moment: politicians can often be heard making an argument today that is the reverse of what they were saying yesterday. Democratic politicians are for congressional hearings and special prosecutors when Republicans sins are involved, but not when a Democratic administration will be placed at risk, and vice versa. In research, on the other hand, consistency is indispensable. Arguments must always be principled, never opportunistic, because research needs results that will stand the test of time, not short term fixes that serve the need of a present situation. In politically driven research, even the most obvious contradictions may be ignored if both sides of an opposing set of views are used to support a politically desirable conclusion.

In theory, then, politics is inherently likely to corrupt research in many different ways. Has this actually happened in research inspired by race, gender, and class? Let us look at some typical results that show each of these six factors at work.

First, the emphasis on results instead of process. Here there is no better example than Peggy McIntosh's theory that men think "vertically" and women "laterally."[1] How was the research from which this idea is derived conducted? The answer is that there was none; McIntosh's having thought up the idea was the full extent of the process. She never sat down to devise a program of observation that would either verify that she was right or modify the idea if she were proved wrong.

Another standard procedural question would be: How carefully are these contrasted behavior patterns defined? More problems are then revealed, for several mutually inconsistent definitions are offered. Vertical thinking is true/false thinking, it is male thinking, it is aggressive, competitive, hierarchic, and so on. Lateral thinking is similarly loose in definition: it is based on empathy, cooperation, collaboration, respect for others, it is female, it is peaceful, it places one in "a decent relationship with the invisible elements of the universe."

The use of the distinction right/wrong is said to characterize vertical thinking, but because lateral/vertical is also an example of right as opposed to wrong thinking—lateral is right, vertical is wrong—the theory suffers from a fatal contradiction at its very center. The only way to determine that lateral thinking is right is to use vertical thinking, which is wrong. Therefore, the act of choosing to think laterally is vertical thinking. The theory thus requires us to abandon hierarchic thinking and at the same time to use it in pronouncing the superiority of the theory. And so the only real basis for this pair of terms is that everything McIntosh likes is assigned to the one term, and everything she does not like is assigned to the other. This has nothing whatever to do with research; it is a confused and contradictory bundle of prejudices.

What we have here is not an aberration but a typical example of what happens when the validity of research is judged by results rather than by process. Ideas that lack both empirical support and internal consistency were nevertheless so politically welcomed by feminists—evidently because they exalt women at the expense of men—that they were virtually adopted by the American Association of University Women (AAUW) at its fall 1992 conference.[2] (Whether it is really in the political interests of women to maintain that they can neither prioritize nor judge what is right and wrong is another matter.)

Race-gender-class work shows over and over again what will happen in a results-oriented research climate. For example, Judith Herman's *Trauma and Recovery* equates the terrors of war for men with the "domestic captivity" of women, a situation in which their subordinate position is enforced by male violence; Anne Campbell's *Men, Women, and Aggression* argues that the key to the difference between men and women with regard to violence and aggressiveness is not testosterone but socially constructed attitudes, men having been socialized to use violence to control women; Susan Bordo's *Unbearable Weight* claims that "the widespread fear of women's fat is a symptom of the fear of women's power"; and Robbie Davis-Floyd's *Birth as an American Rite of Passage,* asserts that doctors and hospitals represent a sinister conspiracy against women that aims, as a reviewer puts it, "to integrate birth—a female, sexual, intimate, unpredictable and natural process—into a misogynistic and technocratic society whose central tenets include 'the necessity for cultural control of natural processes, the untrustworthiness of nature and the associated weakness and inferiority of the female body, the validity of patriarchy, the superiority of science and technology, and the importance of institutions and machines.' "³

These ideas cannot stand up to even a moment's reflection. Equating the horrible violence of war with the life of the average housewife is absurd, as is equating an aversion to obesity with a fear of power. The notion that men are encouraged to use violence against women in our society ignores the fact that men who are known to hit women are despised. As for the conspiracy of modern medicine to control women and nature in childbirth: that control is responsible for the fact that on average women now live seven years longer than men, a differential that did not exist some seventy years ago because of frequent deaths from childbirth.⁴ (Nature can indeed be a bit "untrustworthy.") Yet in spite of their patently indefensible claims, all these books were warmly welcomed by feminist reviewers in the *New York Times Book Review*,⁵ obviously because each one finds another way in which women can be alleged to be victimized by men. The desirability of the result is the driving force in the research, and corrupted research is the consequence.

These examples also illustrate the second and third features of politicized research—the stifling of intellectual curiosity because of a predetermined conclusion and the reduction of intellectual complexity.⁶ In the wider world, there is a considerable variety in relations between men and women and an endless fascination with them on both sides. There is thus much here to be thought about. But if we narrow the focus of our attention to encompass only what is skewed in favor of men, intellectual curiosity is stunted. And if the notion of women as victims is a required conclusion, any complex and interesting conclusions are excluded. A researcher who knows in advance she must always reach the conclusion that women are victimized is not engaged in genuine research.

An inability to consider alternative explanations is likely to be found whenever a strong emotional commitment to one kind of solution exists. A good example can be seen in the debate over gender bias in schools. David and Myra Sadker claim that girls, but not boys, experience a sharp drop in self-esteem around the time that they start junior high school.[7] Their interpretation of this alleged drop is that at this age girls are getting the message that they are less valuable than boys. But another possible explanation comes to mind: girls reach puberty before boys, and they do so in a way that is arguably more obvious and more traumatic. This change in self-esteem occurs exactly at the onset of puberty for most girls. The alternative explanation, which must at least be considered, is that the drop in self-esteem, if it exists,[8] may be related to the disorientation, uncertainty, anxiety, or self-consciousness accompanying this important physical and psychological change in girls' lives. But the Sadkers never mention this interpretation. Evidently, their vested interest in evidence of girls' victimhood ruled out any scrutiny of alternative possibilities.

Perhaps the most prominent of all the shortcomings of politicized research is the refusal to accept the clash of different views as a discipline that keeps research healthy. Race-gender-class scholars see any attempt to challenge their work as the result not of intellectual differences, from which something can be learned, but of moral failure or political opposition.[9] Their critics, they believe, are simply serving their interests as well as those of their race, gender, or class. Critics of affirmative action or Afrocentrism are dismissed as racists,[10] and more generally, opponents of the race-gender-class agenda are dismissed as conservatives.[11]

From the beginning, feminist research implicitly asked for, and was de facto granted, a special status in that to attack the research would be to attack women. Neither those who demanded this special status nor those who let them have it seemed to realize that this privileged position would effectively deprive feminist research of what it needed to stay intellectually viable: the kind of criticism that purges intellectual weaknesses. A more genuine sympathy (as opposed to a wish simply to avoid conflict) with feminist research would have dictated a different course of action. To be sure, bitter feminist hostility to any questioning of their work played its part in inhibiting criticism, but that cannot excuse the acquiescence of faculty and administrators who should have known better than to allow this special status to arise.

Inevitably, this determination not to take criticism by outsiders seriously has led to a crisis of confidence in feminist research, now widely considered to be more aberration than solid work. Research carried out in protected enclaves is bound to be unfit for the challenges of the real world when questions eventually begin to arise. This results in a high level of anxiety that has led to some extraordinary actions. Among these was a startling announcement in the *Modern Language Association of America Newsletter* of a "New Project on Antifeminist Harassment." It was explained that intellectual harassment of feminists was "connected to, but different from, sexual harassment." Examples of that harassment were "easy dismissal of feminist writers, journals, and presses"; "automatic deprecation of feminist work as 'narrow,' 'partisan,' and 'lacking in rigor' "; and "malicious humor directed against feminists." If the MLA had its way, any serious criticism of feminism was now to be considered harassment—a presumably punishable offense. A letter writer in the next issue of the *Newsletter* pointed to the irony in the situation: feminists whose stock in trade had been the easy dismissal and mockery of white males and indeed of entire intellectual traditions (the examples he cited included Gloria Hull's easy dismissal of the modes of white male Western thought as "bankrupt") now primly objecting to behavior far milder than their own when it was turned on them.[12] The writer might well have said: let she who has never uttered a sweeping, dismissive judgment cast the first stone.

The feminist classroom soon produced something similar for feminist teaching. Bright undergraduates, seeing how threadbare much feminist thought had become, began to speak up in class. Feminists were unprepared for challenges in classrooms that had hitherto been rather docile and began to denounce this questioning as disruptive behavior on the part of reactionary students. In reality, the students were just doing what they were supposed to do: ask probing questions.

Once again, the focus of this response to challenge was not how to use it to educational advantage by bringing out different facets of a question but how to muzzle it. The director of the Center for Research on Women at Memphis State University, Lynn Weber Canon, produced a set of "Ground Rules" for her class and required all students entering the class to sign them.[13] Students had to acknowledge that "oppression (i.e., racism, sexism, classism) exists." The rules in effect forced students to accept in advance the teacher's values, to share her beliefs about matters both of fact and of opinion, and to refrain from asking any fundamental questions. Students had to promise specifically not to ask questions about whether women were victims (or in what sense they were victims) and whether the class should presuppose political commitment to the instructor's notion of the "cause." Education and free inquiry were being replaced by indoctrination. The rules were a clear attempt to violate the students' academic freedom, which should immediately have been condemned by the instructor's institution and her colleagues. But that did not happen; the rules actually spread to Women's Studies departments on many other campuses.

Just how far this circling of the wagons can go is shown in the recent national "feminist assessment" of Women's Studies programs, which resulted in two volumes published jointly by the Association of American Colleges and the national Women's Studies Association.[14] The project director, Caryn McTighe Musil, candidly explains that it was inspired by the widespread criticism of those programs. Reluctant at first to allow any such evaluation to take place because "assessment" was a term associated with "external agencies with highly suspect motives," Ms. Musil describes her gradual acceptance of the idea. She proudly gives the first volume the title: *The Courage to Question,* in effect asking her reader to admire the bravery of feminists who did not shrink from a searching probe of their programs. But what was actually done to justify this self-congratulation?

What kind of independent agency did Musil ask to evaluate Women's Studies? Would it be composed of a random sample of academic people? Would it ensure diversity of viewpoint—say, some men and some women, some of each being sympathetic to feminism and some not? Or would the task be given to an outside agency that would make those decisions itself? And how was the comparison of the intellectual quality of Women's Studies programs with that of other academic programs to be undertaken—what parameters of comparison would be chosen?

Even someone who already harbored a suspicion that there might be some attempt to load the dice in favor of Women's Studies would have been astonished by what the assessment actually involved. This exercise that was to display the "courage to question" of these brave women did not concern itself with such questions at all. The procedure was simple: there was to be no evaluation by an outside agency and no involvement of anyone who was not strongly committed to Women's Studies! In this context, *chutzpah* would perhaps have been a more appropriate word than *courage.*

How could such a decision be justified? Joan Shapiro, an assessment team member, tells us that "feminist assessment is decentered." That is, "it begins to deconstruct the usual 'outside-in' or stringent vertical hierarchy to create a more open, varied, and web-like structure. It avoids an 'outsider' or more dominant, powerful, and seemingly objective force determining what questions should be asked and how they should be framed. It also avoids an attempt to meet some abstract notion of excellence."[15] If this had really been an intellectually serious attempt to avoid a tired, traditional procedure, then presumably the avoidance of the notion of "outsider" would have been matched by an equal avoidance and deconstruction of the notion of "insider." It was not, the proof being that it is possible to describe what took place with perfect simplicity in traditional terms. The insiders did the job themselves.

In spite of the attempt to invoke the sophisticated aura of deconstruction, the reality was that the usefulness and intellectual integrity of Women's Studies as a field was to be assessed by the leaders and instigators of the programs themselves. As a result, *The Courage to Question* turned into a volume that completely excluded serious questioning; it consisted only of individual chapters describing seven campus Women's Studies programs, written by the leaders of those very programs.

Shapiro formulated the "Guiding Principles of Feminist Assessment" that were to inform the individual chapters.[16] These include Principle 6, "Feminist assessment approaches should be compatible with feminist activist beliefs"; Principle 7, "Feminist assessment is heavily shaped by the power of feminist pedagogy"; and Principle 8, "Feminist assessment is based on a body of feminist scholarship and feminist research methodology." In other words, the only perspective that will be allowed is ours; we will make the rules, and they will be written so that we cannot lose.

These principles are rather like the Ground Rules for the classroom: the price of admission is advance acceptance of everything feminists do and say and the promise not to ask serious questions. This may seem to clash with Principle 1, "Feminist assessment questions almost everything related to evaluation," but lest you think that means what it says, the following will set you straight: "Feminist assessment is open to questioning how assessment has previously been carried out." It is certainly ingenious to borrow in this way the language of open-mindedness to justify its absence, but what this really amounts to is a declaration that the process will bear no resemblance to anything that could conceivably be thought of as assessment. For what is to be questioned—or rather, rejected outright—are the notions that no individual should be the sole judge of her own cause and that assessment must be performed by disinterested people who have not already decided all the important issues in their favor. Evaluation is not questioned here, it is abandoned.

Adding to the never-never-land quality of this situation was the fact that Musil then boasted in *traditional* terms of what she had done. In an interview with the *Chronicle of Higher Education,* she said: "I want critics of Women's Studies to have to verify their claims in the same way we've sought to give some hard evidence on our side for what is really happening."[17] The deconstruction of traditional evaluation has now been dropped, and Musil speaks of hard evidence as if she had indeed mounted a traditional evaluation and as if the mere opinions of devoted enthusiasts could count as such. Yet the *Chronicle's* Carolyn Mooney allowed this double-talk to pass without adverse comment, and the venerable American Association of Colleges, which should have known better, supported this meaningless exercise with a research grant, publication costs and, more important, its imprimatur.

The intellectually weakening effects of the exclusion of contrary opinion are bound to be felt most when new fields are created in which virtually everyone has the same political outlook—for example, Women's Studies and Black Studies. A number of recent incidents show that these new departments have become enclaves that shield their members from different points of view. A white professor who had taught black history for many years was suddenly a target of protests and sit-ins by black students demanding that "black experience" be required for the position. Absent here was the appropriately academic notion that a different perspective, one afforded by distance from that experience, might also be useful. A recent article in the *Chronicle of Higher Education* noted many recent incidents of a similar kind.[18] And at an AAUW conference, a self-styled male feminist was attacked and bitterly denounced as a womb envier but barely put up a fight in response.[19]

As an English-speaking student of German culture, I have been involved in essentially this kind of argument throughout my academic life. Credible departments of German language and literature combine the intimate knowledge of native Germans with the outside perspective of non-Germans; each contributes something that the other cannot, and both are needed. On occasion, we have heard the claim that those with native experience should be given preference in hiring, but such an attitude has generally been recognized as a parochial view that would degrade the quality of thought and scholarship. Sadly, this hitherto largely despised argument threatens to prevail completely in the context of race and gender. The notion that one might see the experience of a victim group in a broader perspective is evidently anathema to many race-gender-class scholars, who perhaps do not wish to have their focus shifted from moral outrage to intellectual understanding.

The sixth and last of the damaging features of politicized research is the opportunistic use of argument to support whatever the moment seems to need, regardless of overall consistency. Race-gender-class critics routinely use arguments in one place that they cheerfully contradict in another. Sweeping normative judgments about the oppression of women and the absolute evil of patriarchy coexist with the view that all ideologies are socially constructed. Cultural relativism is embraced to advance the case for non-Western cultures but abandoned when it might require respect for Western society. Because consistency will not produce the desired results, it is abandoned. A consistent cultural relativism would not allow the expression of anger directed at the United States, so it can only be used sporadically; and a consistent normative judgment on sexism and racism would make the West actually look good, so that, too, can only be applied as needed.

The same holds for the race-gender-class combination of Marxism and deconstruction. Whether one considers what I have called the randomness-of-meaning strain in deconstruction (meaning is infinite) or the reversal-of-meaning strain (assertions contain their own opposite), neither is compatible with Marxism.[20] When Marx attacked capitalism, he said something definite (thereby excluding the randomness strain) and what he said can certainly not be construed as covert praise of capitalism (which excludes the reversal strain).

Similar leaps between pairs of contradictory positions abound. Gender stereotypes are reprehensible—but women are more nurturing. Cultural stereotypes are objectionable—but Westerners are sexist and racist. Hate speech must be stopped—but white males must be denounced. Segregation is evil—but blacks need separate dormitories and clubs. These contradictions and many more like them are seen every day on college campuses, and they illustrate a sad absence of principled discussion.

Imagine, for example, a principled discussion of racism and racial discrimination. The first step in an academic discussion would be to confront the question of whether racial discrimination consists in *any* act motivated by racial preference (say, a black man marrying a black woman) or whether it refers instead to a specific subset of those acts, and if so, what subset. If, as most people would agree, only a subset should be stigmatized as racial discrimination, the crucial question is how that subset is to be defined. But even though the modern campus is obsessed with the notion of race, I have never heard of any such discussion, anywhere. When a great deal of energy goes into denouncing racism and very little into defining and analyzing it, we see the triumph of politics over academic inquiry.

The most dramatic sign of the political corruption of intellectual inquiry is the bullying and the thuggery often visible in intellectual exchanges. On many occasions recently an exchange of letters to the editor of a scholarly journal has degenerated into organized warfare. Having lost an argument on its merits, an individual will often attempt to beat into submission the scholar who has gotten the better of the argument by calling upon supporters to overwhelm the opponent by the sheer weight of numbers. Logic and evidence are met not in kind but with brute force and intimidation. Here are three recent cases.

In 1988 Richard Levin wrote an article about the systematic problems of feminist criticism of Shakespeare, in which he showed that a zeal to see gender issues in the plays had led a number of critics to distort them. He argued, for example, that Harry Berger's diagnosis of *Macbeth*'s "machismo" conception of manhood in Malcolm's urging the grief-stricken Macduff to "dispute it [i.e., the death of his family] like a man" conveniently ignores Macduff's reply, in which quite a different concept of manhood is expressed: "I shall do so; But I must also feel it as a man."[21]

The response to this article was an angry letter signed by no fewer than twenty-four feminist critics who attacked Levin for failing "to understand the serious concerns about inequality and injustice that have engendered feminist analyses of literature."[22] The letter insisted, in general terms, on the achievements of feminist criticism but avoided the specific issues and examples that Levin had raised. It concluded with a nasty ad hominem attack: "Levin has made a successful academic career by using the reductive techniques of this essay to bring the same predictable charges indiscriminately against all varieties of contemporary criticism"; further, it scolded the journal (*PMLA*) for having chosen to publish the essay. In this case, personal abuse and the sheer weight of numbers substituted for argument, evidence, and analysis. A later letter writer accurately described the multi-signature letter as one in which "some of the critics skewered in his essay ganged up to attack him."[23] Levin's reply demonstrated the poverty of his assailants' logic with embarrassing ease.[24]

The second case is that of Thomas Sheehan, who in reviewing a book on Heidegger in the *New York Review of Books* criticized Jacques Derrida's attempt to suppress the book, an attempt apparently motivated by the fact that material in the book relating to Heidegger's Nazism was embarrassing to Derrida.[25] This was a sensitive matter so soon after the revelation of Paul de Man's pro-Nazi writings in Belgium during World War II, which Derrida had foolishly and unconvincingly sought to defend.[26] In a letter Derrida denied that he had tried to suppress the book, but Sheehan cited convincing documentary evidence that he had done so. Another exchange ensued in the next issue, but it was by now quite obvious that Derrida had indeed tried to suppress the book. As Sheehan later wrote, summing up the point of the whole episode: Derrida was clearly embarrassed "at having the whole business exposed, both his suppression of the book (which he had hoped to keep secret) and his foolish blunder in lying about it in the *New York Review of Books*."[27] But having lost the argument, Derrida now summoned his troops. The next issue of the magazine carried an unpleasant personal attack on Sheehan signed by twenty-five prominent scholars. As before, the letter avoided the real issue (Derrida's attempt to suppress a book and his having lied about it) to mount a broad attack on Sheehan, charging that his "vindictiveness contributes to a climate in which provocation and slander increasingly take the place of serious, public discussion." The signers included a number of individuals who had already embarrassed themselves by trying to defend Paul de Man (Hillis Miller, Jonathan Culler, Fredric Jameson) and who therefore evidently shared Derrida's anxiety, though there were others from whom one might have expected better judgment. Once again, logic and evidence having failed, an unscrupulous use was made of the weight of numbers to punish and intimidate.

The third case involves Christina Sommers, who, having written several articles critical of the arguments of feminist philosophers, found that a covert attempt was being made to discredit her and to persuade the *Atlantic Monthly* not to publish an article it had commissioned her to write. Sommers published a letter in the *Proceedings* of the American Philosophical Association exposing what seemed to her unprofessional behavior.[28] The next issue contained replies by all the primary actors in the situation and a convincing response by Sommers. Once again, however, those who could not carry the day with logic and evidence summoned their legions. This time there was not just one multisignature letter but three. In all other respects, however, the pattern was the same. The letters made no real contribution to the substance of the previous argument, instead defending feminism in general terms and denouncing its enemies.

The prevalence of these episodes in which scholars organize themselves into gangs shows how academic life is degraded when political commitments become central to it: minds become too closed to inquire.

What I have tried to show in this chapter is a strong causal link between the politicization of universities and the decline in the quality of their scholarly endeavors. The well-known horror stories of political correctness are not aberrations but an integral part of the race-gender-class phenomenon on college campuses. They are warning signs of an unhealthy condition that has arisen because a great principle—that of knowledge for its own sake—has been compromised.

Race-gender-class scholars argue that political interests are everywhere and that it is naive to think that they are not present in the universities. But Peter Washington has answered this point by turning it upon itself: it is precisely because political interests are everywhere that we need a place that cultivates—not to perfection but to the maximum possible extent—detached, rational inquiry.[29] That place is the academy. The freedom of scholars to follow where the argument leads, without political guidance or interference, is essential both to its internal functioning and to its hopes of support by society; taxpayers—whatever their political persuasion—will not be willing to support universities on any other basis for long. A professor who uses his campus office, secretary, telephone, or supplies to campaign for political office or to support a ballot initiative is guilty of misuse of university resources for personal business, and there is no reason to view systematic use of the classroom for open advocacy of favorite political causes differently.

An analysis that has political implications is one thing; but open advocacy breaks the implicit compact with taxpayers, degrades the classroom, abolishes the possibility of free inquiry, and denies students their academic freedom. It is, moreover, simply foolish for professors—especially political radicals—to endanger their protected haven in this way. For although they deride the ivory-tower concept of the university, the truth is that they are uniquely the protected inhabitants of that ivory tower. Political correctness is a very academic phenomenon, and it is wildly unpopular with the general public.

An odd incident during the 1993 national conference of the National

Association of Scholars allowed this reality to emerge. One of the speakers—John Leo, a columnist for *U.S. News and World Report*—mentioned that political correctness is unpopular with the general public and suggested that publicity was a simple and effective means of combating it. Leo is correct: if the parents of college students only knew some of the things that were happening on campuses, they would be appalled. But then Todd Gitlin, former president of the Students for a Democratic Society, chimed in to warn the audience that they should beware of allowing the general public to influence what happened in the universities. Suddenly the populism of the radical left was dropped, as the radical political movement revealed itself as an elitist phenomenon. All the usual talk of the need to democratize the overly elitist universities is abandoned in a panic when the threat of genuine democratic feedback from the electorate looms.

The heart of the matter is that the mind-set of a social activist is worlds apart from that of an academic teacher and scholar. Academic analysis follows where the argument leads, but activism wants only support for a predetermined direction. Academic researchers are intrigued by the structure of arguments, whereas activists only want to win them. Activists underestimate the power of ideas to move the world and try to impose them through political power; but the pursuit of power corrupts ideas just as it corrupts people.

7

Power,
Objectivity, and
PC Logic

It is time to look at the typical habits of mind and patterns of inference that are at work in the arguments we have examined. We might call them, collectively, PC logic. Race-gender-class scholars evidently believe that their thought is highly sophisticated and that this sophistication leads them to subtle and complex conclusions. Where others have a naive faith in objectivity and truth, for example, they are able to demystify such notions and demonstrate the covert dominance of power in human affairs. Yet nothing could be further from the truth than this belief; PC logic is not an ascent to a higher level of thought but a regression to cruder and more primitive thinking that appears sophisticated only to those with limited knowledge of the history of the topics they address.

Let us look first at their showpiece argument to see how it works. This is the argument (for which Michel Foucault is the inspiration) that covert relations of power are the driving force in human situations.[1] J. G. Merquior's formulation of Foucault's notion of power is adequate both for Foucault and for the race-gender-class critics who use it: it consists in the "systematic reduction of all social processes" to patterns of domination.[2] This notion is thought to provide the corrective to a naive belief in truth and objectivity and to get beneath the surface of situations to uncover the real forces that are operating at a deeper level. The site of this uncovering can be almost anything: a novel, an essay on that novel, a political or legal theory, a law or a legal ruling, even a conversation—in fact any piece of language about anything whatever. In each case the apparent subject of the language concerned is pushed aside in order to show that the real, underlying subject is power and dominance. And this operation, so the argument goes, takes us to deeper levels of meaning and reality.

Unfortunately, this purportedly novel, sophisticated idea is not at all novel but all too familiar in everyday life. Parents of rebellious teenagers see it constantly as a predictable and thoroughly tedious stratagem. When teenagers begin to want to do things they have never done before, they are impatient with anything that stands in their way. They go through a stage in which they are apt to reduce any topic of discussion to a question of parental control, that is, power. Parents anxious for the safety of their children want to set limits—for example, on the use of a car when their children begin to drive. Teenagers see this as nothing more than parents wanting to control their lives and assert their power. Parents may try, in vain, to insist that they really are concerned about other issues, for example, responsibility and safety, but for teenagers in this mood, there is only one issue—parents having their way.

I imagine that even race-gender-class critics find it tedious to have

their children tell them, after they have explained their very real concerns about having their fifteen-year-olds on the streets at 2:00 A.M.,
that all they are interested in is asserting parental power. Anyone who
has had to face such situations quickly sees what is wrong with the
showpiece race-gender-class argument, because he knows that it represents a primitive, not a sophisticated, train of thought. It amounts to a
refusal to think about the substance of what is being said and a determination to take the argument down to the lowest, least sophisticated
level, the level at which intelligent thought is excluded. This is, after all,
an immature response, the response of a child who simply wants what
he or she wants, and now. And a primitive argument is what it remains,
whether used by Foucault and his followers or by a fifteen-year-old.

From a logical point of view, this argument works by isolating a
single factor among many in a given situation and then ignoring all the
others in order to reduce—and so distort—a complex state of affairs to
that single factor. To make matters worse, the factor chosen as really
important is the one that remains after reason and intelligence have
been abandoned—after we have in effect returned to a stage of human
development that predates civilization. In that state, presumably, the
only factor that limits human action is the extent to which the individual is able physically to get away with doing what he or she wants. All
ethical discussion of human behavior is essentially about the ways that
the exercise of power should be limited; and if power were indeed
everything, then ethical discussion would in principle be meaningless—
and all discussion of oppression would be meaningless as well.

Power is certainly a factor in many situations, but it is never the only
factor, and rarely is it the most important. Moreover, the claim that it is
the *only* important factor is not simply an exaggeration—it is also an
incoherent claim. Suppose that power were indeed the only real factor
operating in a situation. It would then follow that the only salient

feature of that situation would be who was exercising it, and over whom. But that question could have no possible interest for us until we have found a *value* in the situation on behalf of which that power is being exercised.

If we care about who is exercising power, it is because we are interested in the *uses* to which it is being put. If we care about Nazis seizing power, it is not because power is involved, but because they are Nazis. Power is a means, not an end, and it should have no independent content as an idea. Power is the power to do *something,* and if we attempt to justify whether a particular use of power is a good thing, we shall be considering arguments for or against the value on behalf of which it is used, not power itself.

If everything were reduced to power relations, we could discern neither content nor value in human life, but race-gender-class scholars are rigidly committed to a particular set of social values. This contradiction shows us that they do not understand what their favorite argument about power implies. If we look beyond their slogans to their behavior, there too it is clear that they do not believe what they say: in their own lives, they would not accept the fact that power is the basis of everything. They, too, want a relationship with their children based not on power over them but on love and respect and they, too, would protest the uninhibited use of power by the police, for example, as an abuse of power. The notion that power is fundamental is one of those academic theories that has become fashionable without its horrendous implications ever being understood.

Everything that is valuable in a society is the consequence of its having progressed beyond "might is right." Knowledge and morality begin with the recognition that might makes neither right nor truth, and so it is hard to think of any use for a university if power is the basis of everything. Whenever our will to determine right by appeal to principle rather than to force wavers, civilization is in danger. In the former Yugoslavia, might has for some time been right; the stronger force has taken what it could, the result being mass rape and genocide. If power is all there is, and the Serbs have it, why should they not use it? Race-gender-class orthodoxy has it that such cases are merely the honest and open use of power, as opposed to the covert hypocritical uses of power on the part of coercive bourgeois democracy.[3] That makes the Serbs morally no worse than, say, the government of England, which—so the rote-learned argument goes—hides its use of power behind the window dressing of laws.

Ideas have consequences, and the consequences of foolish ideas can be appalling. We cannot doubt that race-gender-class intellectuals, once ripped from the safety of their cozy campus niche and transported to Bosnia, would soon rediscover the values of the Enlightenment and begin to protest the *uncivilized* behavior of the Serbs, a word that in such a context would refer precisely to power unrestrained by moral considerations.

In spite of the crudity of this argument and indeed of the very concept of power employed in this way, a whole scholarly industry devoted to it is arising. Volumes such as the recent *Rethinking Power* promise "cutting edge" research into the concept.[4] This development is not uncommon in situations where an overly simple concept has been given too much work to do. The concept is treated as a mysterious and complex one that needs elaboration and elucidation, and plain-spoken arguments against it are then dismissed as insufficiently subtle. But the reality is that there is no mystery, only a primitive idea.

The argument for the overwhelming importance of power relations in human life illustrates two central features of PC logic that recur in many other contexts. They are, first, the fallacy of the single factor and, second, the reduction of distinctions in kind to unimportant differences in degree, black and white becoming gray, and *equally* gray.

The fallacy of the single factor is common in everyday life. We have seen it at work in the argument that politics is the basis of everything and again in the argument concerning power relations.[5] Let us now examine how it is supplemented by the reduction of differences in kind to differences in degree.

This aspect of PC logic is a variant of the "all or nothing" logic that tries to force us to choose between two extremes, excluding all intervening stages. The ultimate origin of this fallacy lies in the fact that we all have a tendency to categorize people, for example, as either good or bad: if they are not one, then they are the other. Sometimes a single transgression results in the reversal. It is language itself that tempts us to do this. There are many pairs of opposed terms that predispose us to choose between them: black/white, long/short, and so on. In reality, however, these pairs are not mutually exclusive categories but, instead, the two endpoints of a continuum. Because we have only two terms, we tend to use the two poles and forget the range between them.

Race-gender-class scholars extend this habit of thought in a characteristic way. They take a pair of opposed concepts—say, knowledge for its own sake and politicized research. They examine the first of the two poles to show that it is not absolutely and completely free of the other. So far, they are on solid ground: there is at least some political implication in every piece of research, whether in the uses to which its results can be put, the motivation of the researcher, or any number of other factors. But having apparently broken down what had seemed a clear contrast between the two kinds of research, they believe they have shown that there is no real difference between them and that all research is equally political. Notice, however, that we could have started with the other pole and reached the opposite conclusion: since there is no such thing as politicized research that does not have at least a tiny component that is knowledge independent of political inspiration, there is really no such thing as politicized knowledge, and therefore all knowledge is knowledge for its own sake. The same logic can just as easily justify the opposite conclusion. Then what is really going on here?

We can clarify what is happening by using the example of black and white. To repeat the steps of the argument, we first focus on the pole of whiteness. We can easily prove that there is no such thing as a pure white in nature and that white always has a little black in it. Therefore, the argument continues, there is no such thing as white, and everything must really be black; and so there is no real difference between things that only seem white and black. As before, the sequence can be reversed, with the conclusion that there is no such thing as black, because there is no visually pure black in nature, so that everything is really white and there is no such thing as black. This example demonstrates clearly the fallacy of such logic: what is ignored here is that *shades matter.*

This same structure is present in the attack on other distinctions that attempt to preserve the integrity of knowledge, for example, the distinction between true and false statements or that between objectivity and subjectivity. Follow the structure of the argument again. We take a pair of concepts: say, objective and subjective. We focus on the pole of objectivity and can easily show that nothing is absolutely and completely objective. As before, this first step in the argument is perfectly valid, but from this valid beginning the false conclusion is drawn that there is therefore no real difference between the two (shades do not matter), and so everything is really subjective.

This is a desirable conclusion for race-gender-class critics, because they think it protects them from being faulted for research that is frankly subjective or frankly politicized, since both truth and knowledge for its own sake are delusions. But note once more that the same logic starting at the other pole will prove the opposite conclusion: there is no such thing as subjectivity. All or nothing logic can be made to work backward, too.

Returning to the example of black and white, the crux of the matter is this: the fact that we cannot find a pure white or a pure black in nature, and the consequent fact that everything is therefore a shade of gray, does not mean that the various shades do not matter, and it certainly does not mean that everything is the same. There is still a very large observable difference—*the very same difference as before*—between what we call white and what we call black; only the analysis of those differences has changed.

In theory, we could adjust our language to make it express the fact that pure whites and blacks do not exist and speak instead of darkest gray as opposed to lightest gray, but that would not lessen the real difference between the two, any more than the race-gender-class argument lessens the *real* difference between Isaac Newton and Trofim Lysenko or between subjective impressions and documented research. Similarly, we could be hypercorrect and say that there is no such thing as research that is 100 percent free of politics; instead of talking about the contrast between knowledge for its own sake and politically inspired results, we would therefore speak of strongly politicized (hence *almost* totally unreliable) research and minimally politicized (hence quite reliable) research.

This new way of speaking would soon seem pedantic, however, and so we should probably revert to talking of black versus white and of knowledge for its own sake versus politicized research, even though aware that no pure example of either exists. The point here is that whatever the linguistic system we use, the fact remains that great differences of degree do exist and that they matter. That all research has at least some political overtones may be true enough, but a huge gulf separates that fact from the very different idea that all research is equally political. Moreover, once we have established the fact that politics is present in varying degrees, we shall have no trouble in seeing that it is better that it be present to a lesser degree, which is why Lysenko is greatly inferior to Newton.

I now want to take another formulation of this argument and juxtapose it to a different parallel example. This version begins with a perfectly true statement: we all have a political standpoint. It continues: therefore everything we do is colored by our political views; therefore we are all equally politically motivated; therefore there is no point in trying to separate political considerations from academic analysis; and so research cannot be distinguished from politics. By now what should catch the reader's eye is the word *equally*: it does not follow logically from anything that precedes it, yet everything that follows requires it.

Here is a parallel sequence: none of us is without fault. (Again, perfectly true.) Therefore we are all guilty; and because we are all equally guilty, we should not try to distinguish what is morally good and bad in our behavior. Therefore, there is no real difference between vice and virtue. Once again, nothing in this argument follows after the first (true) statement: the fact that we all have faults does not mean they are all the same in scale or kind, and it certainly has nothing to do with attempts to make all sins and sinners equal and to abolish moral distinctions. That parking illegally and committing murder are both assigned to the category "illegal acts" does not mean that they are not different in important ways. And similarly, the fact that running for election and doing a piece of academic research can both be assigned to the category "political acts" does not mean that they are not significantly different within that category or that political considerations are equally important in the two cases.

We can now generalize about the essential shape of PC logic. It begins with a pair of categories (here knowledge/politics), breaks down the distinction, assigns everything to the same category, and finally claims that, as a result, everything is the same. The fallacy at the root of this mode of argument is this: *putting things into the same category does not make them identical.* Shades matter: there is a very real difference between rallying support for a political cause and finding a cure for cancer, *however you categorize them.*

The same argument holds for objectivity and subjectivity. We can make a practical distinction between claims that are not based on conventional standards for scientific verification and accuracy—we generally call such claims subjective—and other claims based on evidence that can be evaluated by scientists, which we term objective. These real differences are in no way diminished by the fact that no case of pure objectivity can be found, because that would not imply that everything is equally subjective.

It is worth noting one practical consequence of this kind of fallacious inference. If shades don't matter, and if anything that is not pure white can simply be labeled black, then the evidence needed to make such a reversal can be vanishingly small. Anyone who is the slightest bit guilty is simply guilty, and as guilty as anyone else; anything that is just a tiny bit tainted by politics is simply political, and as political as anything else; and anyone who displays just the faintest hint of racism or sexism is simply a racist and a sexist, and as much so as anyone else. Once this habit of thought is in place, the power to make qualitative distinctions in the real world is lost. The power to see *what is there* is severely diminished.

Examples of this loss of the power to see what is there occur throughout the entire range of topics that engage race-gender-class scholars. Consider relations between men and women. The arguments of Catharine MacKinnon and Andrea Dworkin begin by focussing on the apparent difference between consensual sexual activity and rape.[6] The moves that follow are classic PC logic. Is there any sexual activity that is absolutely and completely free of the slightest hint of coercion or persuasion? Possibly not, but for MacKinnon and Dworkin certainly not, given their view of the social context of inequality for women. Then the distinction between rape and consensual activity breaks down; hence, all sexual activity is coerced and so there is no difference between rape and any other sexual activity. Here is that same plausible first step to convert everything that is black and white to gray, followed by the refusal to recognize drastic differences in the shades of gray. MacKinnon has been widely praised for her originality because of reasoning such as this, yet the truth is that her argument is merely a mechanical application of PC logic.

The evidence needed to convict even a relatively just society of oppression can be vanishingly small once PC logic is applied. Starting with the conventional distinction between oppressive societies like the Soviet Union, Nazi Germany, Idi Amin's Uganda, or Nicolae Ceauşescu's Romania, on one hand, and twentieth-century liberal democracies, on the other, we go through the familiar steps. Are liberal democracies free of all oppression? No. Then they too are simply coercive and oppressive. Yet once we look at the different shades of oppressiveness, the differences are enormous.

This failure of any sense of scale or of shading is basic to Foucault's entire system of thought, and there is no greater influence on race-gender-class scholars than he. Merquior puts the point succinctly: "Foucault had no room for the traditional recognition of basic differences between liberal regimes and despotic polities."[7] The extraordinary fact is that although Foucault led the privileged life of a professor at the Sorbonne, he nonetheless believed that his oppression as a citizen of a Western democracy was comparable to that of the victims of totalitarian societies.

PC logic is not only fallacious, it is also derivative, and its derivation does it no credit. We see it emerge in everyday life whenever someone becomes angry enough to lose perspective on what is happening. When we are exasperated by a fairly trivial event—for example, sitting through a boring lecture—we may speak carelessly and inflate the scale of the event: we may describe the experience as purgatory or hellish or torture. PC logic represents the congealing of this loss of perspective and the consequent inability to see differences of scale into a studied inability to perceive those differences; it is as if the fit of exasperation had become a permanent feature of thought. We can be sure, however, that a sense of scale would return if race-gender-class scholars ever saw the gestapo at their door. They would then rediscover the difference between real violence—torture, mass reprisals, genocide, executions of women and children, retaliation against families, sending children to die in hopeless battles—and the constraints that a modern democracy places on its citizens.

It is easy to apply PC logic to race relations, because there is no society and no institution that does not harbor at least one racist. If a collection of human beings is not completely free of racism, then away we go again: it is just racist. The resulting reduction of all situations to the single category "racist" and the refusal to recognize differences of scale will make it easier to ignore any evidence that a given society may be relatively enlightened in its racial attitudes.

If we were to focus not on whether modern America, for example, shows any sign of racism (that is, whether it deviates in any way from complete racial harmony) but instead on the degree to which it is racist, a very different result would be obtained. Then we might see that few other societies have ever made such efforts to be fair to their minorities or to see the point of view of other cultures. Similarly, when the degree of racism present among whites is compared not to an *absolute* absence of racism but to the degree of racism present in other racial groups, it can be seen that these children of the Enlightenment are indeed a relatively enlightened group.[8] It is hard to imagine that a white racist could now get an enthusiastic local audience of fifteen hundred people to cheer an unabashed display of racial hatred, as happened recently at Howard University when Khalid Mohammed preached a virulent anti-Semitism.[9] And harder still to imagine that following the outcry caused by such a speech, he would continue to be invited to one campus after another to repeat his message.[10] Yet even events like these do not prevent Andrew Hacker and many like him from continuing to castigate their fellow whites as incurably racist.[11]

Perhaps, however, there is some awareness that scale is an issue, for race-gender-class scholars use a number of stratagems to suppress it. If different shades are to count as the same, then light gray must be made to look darker. A moral factor may be added: the darker shade is more honest, the lighter more dishonest, even hypocritical. Or the emphasis may be intellectual: the lighter shade is a disguised darker one that can be seen only by the discerning. Take, for example, the case of sexual harassment. Feminists try to expand its definition so that they can expand the scope of grievance, but although PC logic is usually helpful in this regard, here it runs into a problem.

A published definition at the University of Minnesota tells us that "sexual harassment can be as blatant as a rape or as subtle as a look."[12] This is the standard elimination of shades, so that a vanishingly light gray can be counted with the darkest, compounded by the notion that discerning the lighter shade requires subtlety. It is as if the crimes were the same, but seeing one of them required more skill. But the mechanical application of PC logic has now produced an absurdity that the unsubtle minds who composed this statement managed not to see. The trouble is that sexual harassment has to be, well, *harassing*. Harassment so subtle that it is easily missed will hardly do.

Perhaps the framers of this statement sensed its absurdity after all, however, for in adding that sexual harassment can also be as blatant as rape, they must have thought that this gesture would create a balance through the even-handed extension of the definition to both greater and lesser instances. But that only makes the absurdity greater: rape is rape, not harassment.

The daily lives of race-gender-class ideologues are a constant reproach to their theoretical arguments. If a bridge collapses on them because an engineer's recommendation was ignored by corrupt politicians, then they, just like everyone else, will complain about political interference with an objective professional judgment. If they are wrongly diagnosed with Alzheimer's disease and spend agonizing months until they find that the diagnosis was false, they will not accept the excuse that the doctor concerned had let his senile mother's condition cloud his judgment. Like everyone else, they will complain that he should not have let his subjective feelings interfere with his work: he should have been more objective (more objective—not absolutely and metaphysically objective). This everyday behavior shows that they can tell the difference between politics and knowledge when they need to and that they rely on their ability to do so.

What is most disconcerting about finding this logic so commonly deployed by academic teachers and researchers is that many of its elements have traditionally seemed characteristic of an untrained mind. In my own teaching experience, all-or-nothing logic and single-factor analysis are present in most freshman papers, and part of my task has been to make students understand the inadequacies of such thought processes before the semester ends. Teachers of literature know that their beginning students will insist that poems mean whatever the reader feels, and they realize that teaching means moving them beyond this subjective absolutism to get them to talk about (and think about) what a poem actually says.

Similarly, a refusal to respond to shades has always seemed symptomatic of a mental laziness unworthy of academic thought. When a bribed judge or a corrupt manufacturer of consumer goods elicits the response "they are all crooks" or when Watergate provokes the response "all politicians are liars," we see crude thinking that blurs issues and refuses to make distinctions. Sometimes this is simply mental laziness, and sometimes it is deliberate obfuscation, but whatever the motivation the logic is the same: assigning things to one category does not make them identical. Some lies are much more important than others; some kinds of corruption are relatively minor and others are a danger to the social order; some politicians shade the truth a little and some are pathological liars.

What is so disconcerting is that this kind of thinking is no longer restricted to untrained minds; it is now common among university faculty. Worse, it has gained great prestige and power on college campuses. Stanley Fish has become a leading academic eminence precisely by having applied PC logic (in his recent *Doing What Comes Naturally*) to a whole range of issues: literary criticism, of course, but also linguistic theory, law, and social and political issues.[13] In each case, Fish rigorously follows the routine pattern: find a pair of opposed concepts; show that one pole is not completely distinct from the other; pronounce the opposition an illusion; then conclude that they are really both the same and that there are no important differences between things that originally seemed distinct.

In legal theory, for example, Fish starts with the opposed concepts of the rule of law and brute force. He then argues that the interpretation of the law by a judge (who "beats the text into a shape which will serve his own purpose") is also an exercise of force, and *no less so* than the violent criminal's use of force. His conclusion is that legal rulings and criminal violence are the same in that the bottom line in both cases remains someone coercing someone else, thereby making the force of law "indistinguishable from the forces it would oppose."[14]

In science, the initial pair of concepts is fact and rhetoric, and the predictable conclusion is that all knowledge is rhetorical. Theory of language suffers the same fate: all discourse is rhetorical; therefore, words do not constrain meaning. Literary interpretation follows the linguistic model, with the result that critics make texts mean what they do. In social theory, Fish starts with the opposition of abstract principles and individual preferences and concludes that "all preferences are principled" and "all principles are preferences."[15] Even in the minor, rather parochial issue of academic politics—should articles submitted to academic journals be judged by readers who don't know the identity of the author, to protect against editorial bias?—Fish goes through the same performance. He starts with the opposition impartial/biased, continues that no reading is completely free of bias, and concludes therefore that every reading is biased and that all readings are equally biased.

Fish is candid about the fact that conclusions of this sort are not his invention but the enlightened views of those he calls anti-foundationalists, though he also refers to them as the intellectual left.[16] Included in this term are deconstructionists, Marxists, the Critical

Legal Studies movement, Foucault, Kuhnian philosophy of science, and reader-oriented critics of literature.[17] Surprisingly, feminists are not mentioned.

Fish's argument about the status of legal rulings is worth a closer look. To break down the distinction between the rule of law and brute force, Fish argues that the policeman no less than the gunman uses force, just as the judge forces a legal text into the shape he wants. The inevitable conclusion follows: "The force of the law is always and already indistinguishable from the forces it would oppose. Or to put the matter another way: *'there is always a gun at your head.'*" The "bottom line remains the ascendancy of one person—or of one set of interests aggressively pursued—over another, and the dream of general rules 'judicially applied' remains just that, a dream."[18]

Just as Foucault's most celebrated argument (about power) was already familiar to parents in the form of teenage sophistry and prevarication, Fish's argument here reminds me of the well-known schoolboy-cynic argument, which goes like this: I choose to loaf at the beach; Mother Theresa chooses to care for the poor in India; we both do what makes us feel good and both do what we want to do; what's the difference? The schoolboy cynic, too, is trying to get rid of the distinction between selfish and responsible behavior, but once again parents have always been able to recognize a reductive and self-serving argument when they saw it. The adolescent sophistry of the schoolboy cynic is in fact perfect PC logic: he, too, argues that if a particular conceptual distinction can be broken down so that one concept can be made to apply to both of its poles, then no real difference remains. But again, shades within the new, single super-category still matter: if what makes Mother Theresa feel good is helping others, whereas what makes the schoolboy feel good is not having to mow the lawn, that difference is still important enough to allow us to begin to rebuild the notion of responsibility within a different conceptual framework. We shall then be talking about the degree to which a person's likes are devoted to his own physical comfort rather than to the physical comfort of others. That will be quite enough to distinguish Mother Theresa from the schoolboy cynic.

Like the schoolboy cynic, Fish shows no understanding of what he has really done and not done in breaking down the distinction between force and law. He appears to think that he has abolished real differences, not just a particular way of talking about them. What he does not see is that even if we decide to use a mode of analysis that makes force the basis of everything, there would still be many differences to be noted in the kind of force used, in the circumstances of its use, in the legitimacy that can be claimed for it, and in the derivation of that claimed legitimacy, all of which would effectively put back in place what Fish thinks he has gotten rid of in breaking down the distinction between law and brute force. And so even if we grant the thesis that the rapist, the bank robber, the judge, the legislator, and the soldier on Tienanmen Square are all exercising force or power, the next step does not follow: the force of the law is not *indistinguishable* from the force it opposes, as Fish maintains. Nor does it follows that all force is "principled force" ("there is no other kind," Fish tells us) or that "force is just another name for what follows naturally from conviction."[19]

Fish thinks that if he can give all these different actions the same label—"force"—he has made them all the same, but within his much expanded category of force the same distinctions will have to be made that he imagined he had abolished. What is ironic here is that in treating everything that can be fitted into a category as the same thing, Fish has adopted the view of words and categories that race-gender-class scholars reject as essentialism.[20]

Just as we can talk of different shades of gray instead of black and white, so we can talk also of different kinds of force and of differently legitimated force instead of law and force. These new differentiations will now handle the readily observable distinctions between rapists, judges, bank robbers, and legislators. Fish tries to prevent this differentiation within the category of force by claiming that every kind of force is principled force, thereby collapsing distinctions on a second level; in effect, he adds a second layer of PC logic. Now we shall have to distinguish different kinds of principles and stray even further from ordinary language, but those observed differences will still not go away.

Much the same thing happens when Fish says that everyone acts out of conviction; if we are to redefine "conviction" in this broad way, then we shall simply have to distinguish more kinds of convictions. The fundamental point remains: if we abolish one conceptual distinction that has allowed us to observe real differences in the world, we shall have to reinvent it somewhere else.

Fish's other arguments work in much the same way. The attempt to reduce principles to preferences is more schoolboy-cynic argumentation and results in our having to make distinctions among preferences according to their scope and legitimacy to replace the content of a useful distinction we have lost. The same distinctions will be made in a less familiar way. And even if all evaluations of articles for publication in professional journals are biased (true, as the first stage in PC logic always is), that does not mean that they are equally biased or biased in the same way. Biases are of different kinds, and one of them is certainly in favor of merit. The real question that needs to be examined is, Will blind submission go some way toward reducing (not removing) the effects of at least some kinds of bias? Whether it will or not is an empirical question that is not changed by the conceptual juggling of PC logic.

Fish's relentless sophistry eventually exposes some important inconsistencies within race-gender-class orthodoxy. For example, race-gender-class critics are very much in favor of "theory," because they see it as the source of useful ideas—such as objectivity does not exist or everything is political. But Fish argues that theory has no consequences, because seeking the support of an "overarching theory" is foundationalism, which is not consistent with social constructionism. (For social constructionists, there are no first principles, because everything derives from social conditioning.) Fish also argues that the intellectual left cannot complain about corrupt professional hierarchies, because that would assume the existence of noncorrupt hierarchies. Indeed, if there are only interests everywhere, and no foundational truth can transcend them, how could anyone complain about the operation of a particular set of those interests?

These insights into the contradictory nature of race-gender-class beliefs are, however, a decidedly mixed blessing. It is as if Fish had performed a reductio ad absurdum but then accepted, not rejected, the absurdity. For example, having assumed one aspect of race-gender-class dogma—that foundationalism, that is, a commitment to *any* principle—is a characteristic of the intellectual right, Fish ruthlessly asserts the corollary: left-wing intellectuals become right-wingers when they assert or imply foundational beliefs. This means that if the Marxist Terry Eagleton actually believes in the superiority of the socialist system, he violates the cardinal rule of left-wing intellectuals and becomes a right-winger. The only puzzle here is why Fish does not then brand the whole of race-gender-class a right-wing phenomenon, since it is surely based upon a rigid set of social beliefs. He ignores the fact that if race-gender-class scholars were forced to choose between their hard-edged views of capitalism, sexism, and racism (on one hand) and their pretensions to epistemological sophistication (on the other), there can be little doubt that they would abandon the latter rather than the former.

Fish complains that his intellectual opponents are beguiled by a belief in "absolutes," but it seems to me far truer to say that his own argument is beguiled by them. Again and again he argues, in effect, that if we cannot have an absolute, we must go to the other extreme.

Race-gender-class scholars pride themselves on being theorists, but theory stands or falls on the adequacy of its analysis and logic, and in those areas, as we have seen, they are conspicuously weak. In the next chapter we shall look more directly at their contributions to the field of theory.

8

Is Theory
to Blame?

Many people blame theory for the present malaise in literary studies, and there is some empirical support for this view: the now predominant race-gender-class criticism is generally laden with theoretical jargon, and the critics seem less interested in considering what literary works have to say to us than in applying a particular theory to them. But it would be wrong to deduce from this that theory is the source of the problem. What is wrong here is not theory but *bad* theory.

Theory is unavoidable, and for reasons that are more compelling than the currently popular notion that some dark ideology lurks at the bottom of even the most innocent pronouncements. Two aphorisms by Goethe put the point succinctly: "With every attentive look at the world we are theorizing" and "Everything that is factual is already theory."[1] To understand a particular case is already to have placed it among others. Kant makes the same point, but with movement going in both directions: "Thought without content is empty; perceptions without concepts are blind."[2] If the general is in the particular, the particular is in the general, too.

By contrast, current theory is largely a one-way street, going only from the general to the particular: the theory prescribes political and social attitudes as the basis of what criticism should do and literature should be, but it cannot allow for feedback from literature itself because that would show that there is more to literature than this particular theory can allow.

This idea of what theory is and what it does is too narrow in yet another way. Theory has two modes, one assertive, the other analytical. In the assertive mode, new general views of some aspect of criticism or literature are proposed: a particular theory is advocated. But in the analytical mode, ideas are examined and analyzed. The two modes are never entirely separate: new suggestions for the practice of criticism may originate from analysis, whereas a better analysis may also be a consequence of critical practice. At times when many have felt that criticism needed to change, work in theory has tended to become more assertive and prescriptive, but after the initial impetus for change has been spent, it generally returns to a more analytical mode. For example, around the time of World War II, theory was identified with the New Critics' proposals for criticism;[3] more recently, it has become identified with advocacy of social change. But this recurring tendency to identify theory with the agenda of a particular group is unfortunate, because analysis, not assertion, is the more fundamental of the two modes of theory. What makes theory valuable to us is the quality and depth of its analysis; the commitments to which that analysis may lead are a secondary concern. In the hands of race-gender-class theorists, however, the assertive mode predominates: for them, theory is knowing the right answers and applying them, not looking for a deeper analysis of the questions.

One result of this limitation is that when theorists from other fields look at the present state of literary theory, they are not impressed. The philosopher Guy Sircello suggests (to be sure, mainly on the basis of a single, indifferently argued, yet by no means completely atypical example) that literary theory contains more poetry than theory, because it generates ideas without the analysis and argument needed to support and explicate them.[4] He is right enough about the analytical incompetence of current literary theory, though his judgment of poetry sounds rather less reliable.[5] The point remains, however, that current deficiencies should not be taken to define the nature or scope of theory.

A focus on results that are politically desirable at present has also produced a discontinuity with the past and a neglect of much valuable work that is still relevant. Theory of literature is a body of knowledge and analysis that has accumulated over many years.[6] It is the result of a great deal of thought on all kinds of issues that arise in the study of literature, for example, the nature and function of literature and its relation to other aspects of a culture, the purposes and procedures of criticism, the relation of author and historical context to the meaning of a literary work, the validity of critical evaluation of literature, the nature of literary genres, and many others. There have been roughly three stages in its development. In the first, general reflections on the nature of literature and criticism were mainly sporadic by-products of the literary scene, often arising from manifesto-like writings of particular authors and literary groups or from contemporary commentary upon them. Herder's theory of cultural relativism, for example, originated in the launching of the German Sturm und Drang movement.

A new stage was reached when, in the early twentieth century, theory of criticism began to be more self-conscious and more independent of the creative writing of the time. The first organized groups of theorists for whom developing a conceptual framework for the understanding of literature became an issue in its own right were the Russian Formalists and the Prague Linguistic Circle. This more systematic attitude to theory spread to Germany, where a spate of theoretical works appeared in the 1920s as a result of the example of Oskar Walzel; to England, where I. A. Richards was a pioneer; and then to America, where former members of the pioneer groups of eastern Europe such as Roman Jakobson and René Wellek were influential. With the publication in 1949 of *Theory of Literature* by Wellek and Austin Warren, it was clear that the analysis of theoretical issues had become well developed and complex. Even so, theory of criticism remained a minority interest, and most critics were still indifferent or even mildly hostile to what they saw as abstract theorizing.

A third phase was reached in the 1970s, when a stagnant situation was energized by the influence of French thinkers such as Derrida and Foucault. There were gains and losses in this transition from the second to the third phase. For the first time, theory became accepted as an indispensable part of the knowledge and outlook of any critic—something the theorists of the previous phase had not been able to achieve—but this gain has to be weighed against the loss of analytical depth as theory became fashionable. And because France had been the most conservative of the major European nations in literary study, at first scarcely taking part in twentieth-century theoretical developments, French influence was not an unmixed blessing. The eventual catch-up was certainly energetic, but it did not build on analysis already done elsewhere. This fact, and the adoption of a new vocabulary, helped to sever links with the past. For example, the imported idea of the "death of the author" was crude compared to the results of the debate that had already taken place in America on the intentional fallacy.[7] As we shall see, when the recent treatment of most theoretical issues is compared with that of the earlier period, a consistent deterioration in analytical quality can be seen.

It has always been easy for theory of criticism to become involved in broad issues that arise in other disciplines. For example, questions about the objectivity of critical knowledge or the validity of evaluation take theory of criticism into areas explored more typically by philosophers; questions of style and meaning, into linguistic theory; questions of human behavior (both of authors and fictional characters), into psychology; and questions of the social situations portrayed in literature, into political science and sociology. Theorists in some of these other fields (most notably Freud and Marx) have become the basis of particular schools of criticism. This presents both opportunities and dangers. Literary theorists find many useful ideas in adjacent fields, but to use them well they must master their meaning in the context of their origin. Because this mastery is rarely achieved, literary critics have always been prone to amateurish misuse of borrowed concepts.

Recent theory has relied increasingly on ideas imported from other fields, and that has led to a drastic increase in the incoherence that results when those ideas are not fully understood. For example, Ferdinand de Saussure's ideas about language achieved a considerable vogue among critics because of their use by Jacques Derrida, but (as I have shown elsewhere)[8] Derrida and his deconstructionist followers garbled those ideas disastrously, in no small part because they knew very little about their context in the history of linguistic thought.

Let us now measure the contributions of race-gender-class theorists to four major issues in theory of criticism against the full context of the debate and analysis already available from the second phase of literary theory. First, consider historical context and its relevance to the literary work, perhaps the most important issue that divides literary critics and theorists. Forty years ago a great theoretical debate had already taken place between those who argued that literary works are the product of a concrete historical situation, speak first and foremost to the concerns of that situation, and must be interpreted as such and their opponents who argued that the transitory concerns of the place and time of composition would give too restrictive an account of a work's meaning, one that could not account for the vivid interest of readers who are no longer part of that context. According to this second view, the test of time resulted in the survival of only certain writings of a particular era, after the passions of that time had been forgotten. Writers who survive this test have produced work compelling enough to be of relevance not just to their own age but to a society conceived, more broadly, as continuing through time.

Historicist literary criticism originates in Herder's cultural relativism, according to which literature should be measured not by normative ideas such as those in Aristotle's *Poetics* but by the standards of its own time and culture. This idea soon developed into the literary historical orthodoxy of the nineteenth and early twentieth centuries. Eventually a major problem emerged: How was one to determine what was relevant within the cultural and historical background? In the absence of a standard of relevance, historicist literary criticism easily slipped into triviality, because without it all facts of the writer's life and times were equally relevant. It was this lack of focus that helped to produce the reaction against historicist criticism known as the New Criticism.

What contribution have race-gender-class theorists made to this discussion? They have essentially adopted the first of these two positions—the historicist position—and then added to it three additional elements: first, a belief in a zeitgeist that closely determines what can be thought or imagined in a given epoch; second, an assumption that politics is the most important content of all literature; and third, an assumption that the most basic concern of politics is oppression through imperialism, economic inequality, and unequal power relations. This complex of positions and assumptions is called the New Historicism.

The one positive thing we can say here is that the New Historicism does not suffer a lack of focus. The second and third assumptions provide the clear standard of relevance conspicuously missing in the old historicism. Unfortunately, this solution raises more problems than it solves; as we have seen in previous chapters, these assumptions sharply reduce the content both of literature and of politics. This remedy for what had been a continuing problem is therefore worse than the original malady.

The contribution of race-gender-class scholars to the more general question of historicism as a theoretical position is no more encouraging. In the case of a much analyzed issue such as this, a distinctive new contribution might consist either in new arguments for historicism or in new rebuttals to old objections. We get neither. The acknowledged leader among New Historicists, Stephen Greenblatt, brushes aside the problems of historicism by insisting that the only alternative is a belief in "a conception of art as addressed to a timeless, cultureless, universal human essence" or in "the self-referentiality of literature."[9] These are not only crude caricatures of the issues that historicism raises but unoriginal ones at that; they are a reprise of the lowest level the old debate reached. A valid contribution to the debate would have to deal with the strongest versions of the arguments against historicism, not the weakest.

The most difficult problem in historicism concerns the quality of a writer: if all writing simply reflects and responds to the problems of its age, on what basis can one say that only some writing is important and valuable? But instead of dealing with the essential logic of this tough issue, race-gender-class theorists usually avoid the question with the suggestion that it arises only from the psychological need of some critics to indulge in hero worship. For example, when Paul Cantor raised this issue in a critique of Stephen Greenblatt's work, Greenblatt replied that admiration for Shakespeare's art is "better served by historical understanding than a hierophantic *o altitudo.*"[10] From the standpoint of theoretical analysis this response is no response at all. Greenblatt seems unable to grasp the problem and so cannot contribute to its analysis. Judgments about the quality of Shakespeare's writing and thought represent an altogether different mode of response to his work, not simply a failure to seek historical understanding. Historical understanding can extend equally to Shakespeare and political pamphlets, but only qualitative judgments can separate the two.

The assumption that a zeitgeist pervades all the phenomena of a particular age is important for the New Historicism, because it is the presumed vehicle through which the climate of race-gender-class assumptions exercises its all-powerful effects. And that, in turn, provides support for the notion that these themes must be central to all literature.[11] The trouble is that this pervasive zeitgeist is part of a theory discredited several decades ago; once more, New Historicists seem unaware of the devastating arguments that put an end to it.

The German philosopher Wilhelm Dilthey was the founder of the theory in question. It was well known in Germany during the first half of this century as *Geistesgeschichte,* a reasonable translation of which would be "history of the spirit of the age."[12] Dilthey's theory was at the height of its popularity in Germany between the two World Wars until even the resolutely historicist Germans realized that it reduced all the diverse phenomena that make up an era to an artificial and unrealistic uniformity. Moreover, the need to make one idea fit an entire period led to ideas so general that they could be made to apply to anything.

Consequently, the Germans largely abandoned it. This chapter in the history of theory was not hard to find; the story is told, for example, in the classic *Theory of Literature,* by Wellek and Warren. Yet the New Historicists picked up this old and long-since discarded theory, evidently unaware that it was a blind alley we had been down before.[13]

On the question of historicism, then, the New Historicism contributes not new theoretical analysis but only dogmatic assumptions to support the unlikely proposition that, as Edward Pechter puts it, literary works are "generated from and directed toward the politics of a historically remote period."[14] And the anachronism of judging sixteenth-century Europe by modern post-Enlightenment standards means that even as history the New Historicism suffers from an elementary incompetence.

One of the best-explored theoretical topics is that of biography and the author's intention; what is the contribution of race-gender-class theorists here? "The Intentional Fallacy," the seminal article by W. K. Wimsatt and Monroe Beardsley, is among the most celebrated essays in the field.[15] Wimsatt and Beardsley argued that the intention of the author was neither available nor desirable as a standard by which to interpret and judge the literary text. Two major themes supported this conclusion. First, authors are not necessarily the best judge of what they have done; an author's closeness to the text may be outweighed by the wider perspective of a critic. Second, the text communicates its meaning through the conventions of language, and those conventions are public, not personal, in nature. A text means what it actually says, not what its author later thinks he meant to say but perhaps did not.

What had precipitated the debate was a habit that biographically oriented critics had increasingly adopted, that of using brief statements by authors as the key to a literary text, forgetting that the fullest, most explicit, and most relevant evidence of authorial intent was the language of the text itself. The discussion that followed the publication of this article constituted the most extensive theoretical exploration ever undertaken in the field.

The core of the theoretical issue here is the special status of literary texts. Ordinary uses of language have no fixed boundaries, so that it is possible to seek amplification or clarification of any sequence of words by looking more broadly at what came before and after it. But if literary texts have firm boundaries (say, the first and last pages of a novel), then the question arises, Can a critic in effect add more text taken from the author's other pronouncements? The logic of the intentionalist case requires one answer, the anti-intentionalist another.

Once again, race-gender-class theorists are a disappointing letdown after such a productive debate, and the reason for the disappointment is easy to see. Instead of immersing themselves in the logic of the question and trying to carry it further, they are content to find some snippet that can be made to support their agenda and carry it off. The superficiality of this approach to the problem of intention can be illustrated by two feminists who use different snippets from the debate to attack male hegemony, with the result that they end up on opposite sides of the theoretical question. One argues that to take a text in the context of its author's intent is to be committed to a patriarchal notion of authority and that feminists should resist this "arbitrariness of patriarchal hege-mony" by putting in question "the authority of authors, that is to say the propriety of paternity." But the other argued that to ignore author is to ignore gender and that to oppose "male critics' trivialization, contempt or neglect of the author . . . is one of the first steps in an emerging feminist critic's rebellion against the critical establishment."[16] In both cases the use of theory is opportunistic and superficial, and neither makes any real contact with the issues that are present in the well-developed argument and analysis that already existed.

The most common theme of race-gender-class theory with respect to authorial intention is an attack on the idea that an author's intention is a means to an objective account of a text, the truth about it. Such is the import of the dramatic phrase "the death of the author." But looked at more closely, this has nothing to do with the classic debate on intention, because its thrust is not a shift from one kind of valid evidence about the meaning of a text to another. On the contrary, it is part of an argument against the validity of any evidence for an account of a text's meaning.[17] In effect, race-gender-class scholars are not making a contribution to the debate between intentionalists and anti-intentionalists at all but, rather, are taking a radical and uncompromising stance on a different theoretical question: that of truth or objectivity in knowledge. Let us therefore turn to their contribution to the exploration of that question.

Here the position of race-gender-class scholars can be stated simply: they argue that objectivity and truth are naive illusions of traditional scholars and, more generally, of the Western tradition and that they have demystified these ideas. There are no value-free facts, they argue, because all knowledge is socially constructed.[18]

The odd thing about this position is that it is diametrically opposed to the reality of what both newer and older groups have actually done: first, as I have argued before, the race-gender-class scholar's commitment to his and her truths about the reality of sexism, racism, and oppression is as rigid as anything could be; and second, traditional scholars—both philosophers and critics—have often been skeptical about truth and objectivity. In point of fact, one of the most persistent questions in theory of criticism has been whether criticism gives us knowledge of the kind we get from other fields of inquiry. Philosophers, too, have a long history of concern with the question What is truth? The results in both cases long ago reached a level of sophistication that goes well beyond the simple dogma of the race-gender-class rejection of objectivity.

The most persistent opinion about objectivity in criticism has been Harry Levin's assertion that literary criticism is not an exact science.[19] From time to time, however, groups of critics and theorists have tried to establish criticism as a more systematic endeavor. These two basic positions have generally alternated as action and reaction. Race-gender-class critics constitute the most recent phase of this cycle, but far from being pioneers in their denunciation of objectivity, they represent only a reprise of the majority view of the past.

The orthodoxy of the nineteenth century represented a synthesis of both positions: literary history and biography afford genuine knowledge, but criticism in the sense of a critic's writing about the meaning and impact of a literary text is an impressionistic, subjective matter. It was precisely this fundamental skepticism about objectivity in criticism that made the literary historian cling to the objectivity of biographical and historical fact. At the turn of the century this orthodox synthesis began to break up, though two different tendencies emerged in its place. In Germany, critics began to question one half of the synthesis, namely, the assumed quasi-scientific objectivity of literary history. Reacting against what had become a rigidly positivist climate, Wilhelm Dilthey argued that literary history was unlike science in that it demanded empathy and imagination if one was to grasp the spirit of an age. But elsewhere the challenge was mostly to the other half of the older synthesis—the notion that criticism was irredeemably subjective.

A major thrust of the New Criticism was a rejection of the older defeatism about knowledge of the text and a consequent intense attention to texts through "close reading." The New Critics' refusal to rely on biography was in large part due to their rejection of the concomitant view that text-oriented criticism could only be impressionistic. That is why Wimsatt and Beardsley, in another notable article, entitled "The Affective Fallacy," argued that the qualities of the text, not the response of the reader, were the central concern of criticism.[20] The culmination of the search by Anglo-American New Criticism for a more systematic study of literature is Northrop Frye's *Anatomy of Criticism,* an ambitious attempt to develop a taxonomy of literary forms, now more admired for its ambition than its accomplishment.[21]

Even before the New Critics, the Russian Formalists had also attempted to make literary study more systematic, and when, many decades later, a belated reaction against nineteenth-century literary historicism finally appeared in France, it took a similar form, beginning with Claude Lévi-Strauss' attempt to analyze the basic patterns of narratives.[22] In conscious imitation of the mode of empirical science, Lévi-Strauss looked for the basic building blocks of narrative. Doubts about his system soon appeared, however, as his choice of underlying patterns came to seem arbitrary; some details of the plot of a narrative were declared essential, whereas others were discarded to make those that remained fit a common pattern. It was hard to justify radically different treatment of plot elements that were not inherently different at all.

As before, the overambitious systematizing tendencies of Frye and of French structuralism provoked a reaction, and by the 1960s the newest version of anti-objectivism had appeared. It is this latest swing of the pendulum that race-gender-class scholars are part of. Another manifestation of the same reactive development is reader-response criticism, which stresses the creative role of the reader in supplying meaning to an inherently indeterminate text. Still another is the strain of deconstructionism that stresses the infinite deferral of meaning in language.[23]

It is perhaps fair to say that this area of literary theory has not been analyzed with the same penetration that has been evident in others, and that the mood swings of the field—from attraction to controlled scientific methods to distaste for them and back again—have been more noticeable than serious analysis of the issue. It has also been hampered both by unrealistic notions of the mechanical quality of scientific procedure that do not allow for imagination and creative ideas in the development of scientific hypotheses and by equally unrealistic notions of criticism as a uniquely imaginative activity that has no place for controlled thought.

Even so, the best work does give the sense of a struggle to solve real problems. Leo Spitzer gave due weight to both imagination and systematic thought when he suggested that the procedure of criticism was circular: it went from general impressions of the text to scrutiny of particular passages and back again.[24] Modification and refinement could take place in each part of the cycle: thought about particular passages could suggest modifications of general interpretive ideas, and those modifications would in turn suggest a closer look at other passages that now became crucial.

This is very interesting theory, and if we compare it to, say, reader-response theory, its superiority is clear. In reader-response criticism, the reader's response is single and final and does not develop, whereas Spitzer shows us how thought about a text progresses. Interestingly, although Spitzer thought he had demonstrated that criticism was unlike scientific work, he had really shown that they are closer than we often think. His critical circle was much like that of hypothesis and experiment. By making contact with broader principles of inquiry that go beyond literary criticism, Spitzer had in fact broken through the barrier that had kept the literary critic's ideas about critical knowledge at a fairly primitive level.

By contrast, the race-gender-class view of this issue gives no sense of a productive struggle with real problems. It is excessively simple, consisting only in a denunciation of objectivity; it is uninformed, because unaware of more complex prior analysis and of the commonplace nature of its own contribution; and it is inconsistent, in that social activism requires a suspension of skepticism if a social goal is to be pursued with the necessary conviction that that goal is desirable.

The race-gender-class denunciation of objectivity and truth goes beyond literary criticism to encompass philosophical and scientific truth, but in this broader sphere, too, a strong Western philosophical tradition of questioning the nature of truth is ignored. Indeed, this persistent strain in philosophy could well be called an obsession, and the scope of the resulting conceptual explorations make the race-gender-class contribution seem small indeed.

The legacy of Charles Sanders Peirce is especially relevant to recent claims by race-gender-class scholars. Peirce looked at Descartes' deductive view of scientific knowledge, with its assumption that we proceed from the known to the unknown, and saw that it contained a major error: new knowledge is not simply added to old knowledge but can profoundly change our understanding of what we thought we knew.[25] For this reason, Peirce saw the impossibility of producing a final test of the truth of any proposition and concluded that all knowledge is in the nature of a hypothesis and that the only test of the validity of a scientific proposition is the always provisional assent of the scientific community. This view of science was in fact older than Peirce; Goethe first set it out nearly two hundred years ago, and Peirce acknowledged that his first philosophical reading was from the German classical age.[26]

Attitudes such as these have been part of the basic framework of the philosophy of science for some time, but when Thomas Kuhn popularized them in his *The Structure of Scientific Revolutions* (1962), they finally reached scholars in the humanities, with bizarre results.[27] The trouble was that the humanists who now took up these ideas knew nothing of their context and development and therefore did not realize that they had long since become familiar to philosophers of science. Instead, they thought that something cataclysmic had happened: for humanists, the nature of scientific truth itself seemed to have been undermined. Stanley Fish, for example, includes Thomas Kuhn in his list of "anti-foundationalists," along with Derrida, Heidegger, Foucault and, of course, himself, and suggests that making the criterion for good science the assent of the scientific community is "Kuhn's rhetoricization of scientific procedure."[28] Yet all that had really happened was that some scholars in humanistic fields had finally made contact with what modern philosophy of science had to say about scientific objectivity.

A parallel development in historiography is the vogue of Hayden White's *Metahistory*,[29] a work that race-gender-class scholars found appealing because it suggested that in history, too, "all interpretation is fundamentally rhetorical."[30] Once again, the objectivity of historical scholarship was undermined with the help of the false opposition of final truth, on one hand, and the imagination of the historian, on the other. White is candid about the anti-Western impulse in his position: "In short, it is possible to view historical consciousness as a specifically Western prejudice by which the presumed superiority of modern, industrial society can be retroactively substantiated."[31] The link to race-gender-class orthodoxy is clear.

In fact, earlier writers on historiography had often stressed the historian's shaping hand[32] and even claimed that the best history is an aesthetically satisfying whole, though one still answerable to the relevant facts. Literary historians, too, had often claimed to have synthesized knowledge to make it an aesthetically satisfying whole. The literary historian, said Robert Spiller, "uses many of the methods of the literary artist."[33] No one ever thought that this was inconsistent with a sense that getting the facts wrong, generalizing from the wrong facts, not knowing enough of them, or not understanding them would produce bad and inaccurate history. But White took this familiar partial truth and pressed it to its limit: historical interpretation was now fundamentally rhetorical, and its determinants were tropes, literary figures, and styles of narrative. Hans Kellner summarizes White's position: "White can find no reason to prefer one account over another *on historical grounds alone.* The version of the past we choose depends rather on *moral and aesthetic values,* which ground both the historian and the audience and are beyond the call of historical evidence."[34] (Kellner is a highly sympathetic interpreter of White.) Someone with moral or aesthetic values differing from our own (Charles Manson? Adolf Hitler?) might, therefore, also legitimately interpret the past differently. In White's theory, the distinction between history and a novel disappears: we are no longer able to learn from history as *history.* A necessary distinction vanishes.

The fourth and last of these illustrative topics is evaluation. Here again we see the contrast between a long history of struggling with difficult logical issues and the assertion by race-gender-class critics of a logically unsophisticated position that is immediately contradicted by their own actions. Although theoretically against judgments of literary value, they are, in practice, perfectly content with their own; having argued that hierarchies are elitist, they nonetheless create one by adding Alice Walker or Rigoberta Menchu to their course reading lists. They vacillate between the rejection of all value judgments and the rejection of one specific set of them—that which created the Western canon.

Race-gender-class orthodoxy on the matter of evaluation is so inconsistent and so driven by what a particular prejudice demands that it can hardly be called theory at all; and it does not begin to confront the body of thought on this topic that already existed. The three phases of theory I distinguished above have markedly different emphases with regard to evaluation. In the first, evaluation of works of art was simply assumed to be central to criticism. There was a strong interest in normative theories of poetry (for example, how should a tragedy be constructed?) and in concepts used to evaluate works of art (such as beauty). In the second stage, however, skepticism arose about the justification for both normative poetics and value judgments,[35] and criticism itself became correspondingly more descriptive in character. The normative writings of the previous period now tend to be regarded as descriptions of the practice of a particular school, each new manifesto showing the arbitrariness of its predecessor. In the third and most recent phase, value is seen largely as a question of the political interests of socially dominant groups, no other kind of value being recognized.

It was the second stage that began the serious business of examining the logic of evaluation and distinguishing it from the logic of descriptive statements: the latter, but, it was thought, not the former, could be verified by observation. For this reason, the logical positivists thought that evaluations were mere expressions of emotive response without cognitive content. Northrop Frye, a key figure of the second phase of critical theory, evidently followed this ranking when he said that descriptive criticism was a form of knowledge, unlike evaluative criticism, which was the province of journalists.[36] For Frye, as for the logical positivist A. J. Ayer, evaluative language was something of an indulgence.[37]

But this view seemed unable to account for some real facts of experience—for example, the fact (for so it must always seem to be) that Shakespeare is a writer of enormous stature. And so later analytic work tried to rescue evaluative statements from this low status. One attempt to do this distinguished different valid uses of language, one descriptive, the other appraisive.[38] This rehabilitation was not completely convincing, however, because it still allowed evaluative statements to fall short of full cognitive status.

My view is that evaluative statements are factual and do have cognitive content but that they are rather like brief summaries of a great deal of more specific information.[39] For this reason it must always seem unsatisfying to regard them as lacking in cognitive content. A brief summary can only hint at the full cognitive content of what is summarized, but it has a practical use: it allows one to make decisions such as whether to take one novel rather than another on a vacation and whether to include one book rather than another in a syllabus. The key to much of the theoretical problem posed by evaluations is this: they are not grandiose conclusions that everything leads up to but a quick orientation and starting point that must be left behind if we are to think more precisely. Only the general feeling that their greater weight should indicate a cognitive superiority misleads us.

Even in an area of theory that has been somewhat inconclusive, the contrast between the simplicity of race-gender-class thought and the relative complexity of what preceded it is striking. Instead of a genuine struggle with a difficult logical problem, we are offered only opportunistic uses of diametrically opposed attitudes to evaluation; instead of original analysis, we find only a reprise of the crass measure of literature according to its current political value that has always been used to censor and silence writers.[40]

If we add to these four illustrative topics in theory others where the race-gender-class contribution has been seen—for example, the definition and function of literature (both discussed in chapter 2)—then the inescapable conclusion is that race-gender-class theory when seen against the context of the field as a whole is poor theory. Yet this impoverished theory has managed to become so identified with theory in general that even many of its detractors accept that identification. How did this illusion arise? How did this antitheory become identified with theory? To answer these questions, we must look at the history of the field.

As we have seen, theory of criticism began to emerge as a distinct field only in this century, for prior to this time it had been largely a sporadic by-product of events in the contemporary literary scene. Theory then began to drift away from the practice of criticism, until, by the 1960s, most literary critics were mildly hostile to what they saw as abstract theorizing. The sudden popularity of French thought in the early 1970s was less a theoretical revolution than an antitheoretical coup; critics who had not been involved in the more self-consciously analytical phase of theory now returned it to a much closer relationship with the ideological currents of the contemporary critical scene. The result of this shift was that the word *theory* became identified with one of those ideological currents rather than with the activity of analysis. This development really turned the word *theory* upside down, as could be seen when Paul de Man claimed that opposition to deconstructionism was a "resistance to theory."[41] Given that theory must imply analysis, it was de Man himself who was really resisting theory, by treating his own position as sacrosanct and refusing to accept the possibility that it might be further analyzed.

As theory became fashionable, there arose a theory cult in literary studies, and its leadership became a kind of theory jet set, a professional elite with a carefully cultivated aura of au courant sophistication. In this atmosphere, only recent theory counted; anything from earlier times was wooden and outmoded. The persistent ignorance of prior theory was therefore no accident but an essential feature of this new development.

The new elite shared a set of assumptions but not a penchant for analysis. One recognized members not by their analytical skill but by the standardized quality of their attitudes. All went through similar motions to come to similar conclusions. Theory was no longer about exploration but about conformity. Stanley Fish's *Doing What Comes*

Naturally was typical both in its predictable positions and its ignoring the past: in this book, philosophy of science begins with Thomas Kuhn, serious questions about the idea of truth and the positivist theory of language begin with Derrida, jurisprudence begins with the radical Critical Legal Studies movement, and cultural relativism is a bright new idea without any previous history.

The theory culture also has its own language, which all aspirants to membership must learn to speak and which functions to preserve an otherwise unstable situation in many ways. It cuts off new theory from older thought—which is useful, since if the same terms were used, the limitations of the new would be much easier to see. It identifies those who speak it as insiders and those who do not as old-fashioned outsiders who lack the required level of sophistication. Those who have learned the language demonstrate their mastery of theoryese in titles of conference papers that are full of verbal tricks and gyrations. (Unfortunately, this also draws the attention and the well-deserved derision of the general public.) In addition, the new language serves as a protective device in that its remoteness from ordinary speech camouflages triviality or absurdity.

The drawback is that standardized language means standardized thought. Oddly enough, race-gender-class critics insist on the limitations imposed on thought by the use of a particular system of terms in all other contexts. An important part of their mental apparatus is Foucault's notion of a discourse, by which he means a standard set of terms that are both the expression of a particular mind-set and the mechanism that perpetuates that mind-set. Foucault's own examples are rarely convincing, because the normal vocabularies of both English and French are too large and varied to channel thought so rigidly. A convincing illustration of Foucault's point would require a specialized terminology that was able to shut out the rest of the vocabulary of a language. We need not look far to find such a case: the perfect example of Foucault's discourse and its stultification of thought is the highly restricted and arcane terminology of theoryese: re-presentations, marginalize, decenter, re-vision, difference, discursive practices, hegemony, phallocentrism, the "other," and so on. Genuine thought requires more than the rote learning and ingenious manipulation of a special vocabulary.

A deeper problem is that theorists do not run in packs; they are individuals who set out to crack particular theoretical problems by thinking hard about them. Their work is solitary; it is never fashionable and must always be estranged from orthodoxies. It follows that a theory elite can arise only when theory has ceased to function effectively and when the individuals who are a part of it no longer act like theorists. Real theorists thrive on the concept of argument and counterargument that is central to theoretical analysis, but race-gender-class scholars show a marked tendency to avoid facing the substance of the arguments of their critics. Sometimes, they just seem to hide: as support for deconstruction has eroded under the pressure of recent analyses and disclosures, many of its leading figures have fallen silent.[42] Yet scholars like J. Hillis Miller, Geoffrey Hartman, and Jonathan Culler, who have enthusiastically urged deconstruction upon students and colleagues for some time, surely had an obligation to defend it publicly or to recant; edging quietly toward the door when things begin to look bad is not what theorists do.

Dissent from the current orthodoxy is routinely met with ad hominem attacks on allegedly ignoble motives that avoid the substance of arguments. Critics are said to be hostile to progress for women and minorities or simply conservative, as if no further analysis were necessary. In this vein, Fish insisted that the furor about political correctness on campus was being stirred up from outside the academy by right-wingers, implying that there is no legitimate debate going on within the academy, nor any need for one.[43] (He now seems to have changed his mind, as we shall see in the next chapter.) The same implication is made when we are told that the controversy constitutes an anti-intellectual attack on the academy[44] (again presumably from the outside) or that it has been created in large part by the national press.[45] These arguments were the stock in trade of J. Edgar Hoover and Richard Nixon. Hoover routinely met criticism by claiming that it was due to outside agitators, and Nixon reduced every issue of substance to distortion by the press. Gerald Graff even resurrects a McCarthyite argument when he says that "right-wing ideologues are doing a good job of exploiting their [NAS members'] resentment and frustration."[46] Those who remember the 1950s will recall that if one were not accused of being a communist sympathizer, one could still be branded a communist dupe.

Although it is ironic that left-wing scholars have so thoroughly appropriated the tactics of figures they have always despised, the more important point is that race-gender-class theorists have moved so far away from genuine theoretical analysis that their arguments have come to resemble some of the most disreputable political behavior in our recent history. Real theorists would want to meet and engage arguments put forth against their positions by academic colleagues and to take part in the internal debate that is now under way.

The only conclusion to be drawn from this survey is that what now passes for theory is a degraded and corrupt shadow of what theory should be.

9

How Did It
All Happen—
and What
Comes Next?

The change that has taken place during the past twenty years in the study of the humanities on college campuses has been bewildering. Even with hindsight, it still seems utterly improbable, and anyone predicting this future course of events in the early 1970s would not have been taken seriously. One can imagine the seemingly ironclad case that would have been made against so absurd a prognosis, for the direction that humanist professors have taken seems to negate everything that makes their life attractive and every reason that society might have to support their work.

The life led by professors of literature before this change must have seemed enviable. They could spend much of their working lives reading and discussing great writers such as Shakespeare, Goethe, and Dostoevsky, whereas others had to make time for such enjoyable pursuits. Excellence was their watchword, and they kept company with an elite group of the greatest minds our civilization has produced. Instead of earning their living by repetitive tasks, they had at their disposal the infinite variety of literature; if they became bored with one writer, there were hundreds more to choose from. And because their work drew on thought from many times and places, it gave them—or so it would seem—a broad perspective on life.

Small wonder that professors in humanistic fields enjoyed what they did and that they argued for the educational benefits of the study of great literature. If taxpayers could be convinced that Shakespeare added to the practical wisdom of those who read him, they would continue to support the splendid life of literature professors.

We would have been amused by predictions of what was to happen, because it would have been impossible to imagine that professors of literature would throw away their advantages. Who could have foreseen so complete a reversal that philistines who had never seen any value in studying Milton and Keats would eventually derive their most convincing arguments and draw their strongest support from professors of literature themselves? Or that *they* would be the ones to tell the world that great literature, far from broadening the mind (as they used to say), actually narrows it by implanting constricting, socially harmful attitudes.

Every aspect of the earlier state of affairs seems to have been turned upside down. A concern with exceptional minds and excellence is now dismissed as elitism, and many prefer to concern themselves with Madonna videos or gay pornography. Fine writing is no longer valued; English professors now write in a style that they would formerly have denounced as clumsy and full of jargon. Many, it would seem, no longer even like the field that once so delighted them, and they write on anything but literature. Thus, professors with prestigious chairs in literature at major universities routinely write and claim authority on political and historical topics like imperialism, psychological and socio-logical topics like sexual behavior—especially nonstandard varieties thereof—or any number of topics in other fields. This practice has become so pronounced that a secondary set of scholarly fields has arisen: there is history as practiced by historians and as practiced by professors of English literature; theory of language as practiced by philosophers and linguists and as practiced by professors of English literature; and even a philosophy of science according to professors of English. But as for literature simply as literature—even to speak of it that way sounds old-fashioned.

Another drastic change is the sudden partiality to abstract theoriz-ing—in a field once so concerned with particular, concrete situations that it resisted generalization. We would never have expected individ-uals exposed to the infinite variety of human experience to reduce all books to any one issue, let alone that of oppression and victimization.

Any broad perspective on the issues of the day that might have resulted from wide reading seems also to have vanished. Professors in the humanities might have been expected to be the first to point out that people who denounce Western culture for its racism and sexism have missed the fact that politically correct values are exaggerated West-ern, not anti-Western, values; they, better than anyone, should have known that the European Enlightenment was the unique stimulus for the development of enlightened attitudes toward race, sex, and inequal-ity. We might have expected them to be the first to spot yet another reprise of Rousseauism and to warn of its historical consequences; we might also have expected them to provide a corrective to present-day handwringing about American racism by pointing to what was unique to North America—not the existence of slavery but the war to end it.

Instead, they have actually led the way in their enthusiasm for politically correct but historically ignorant and foolish opinions.

Insofar as the literature of earlier periods has played a part in their thinking, they have used it not to provide a broader context for the present but to afford more opportunities to express the judgments they already make about it, thereby adding anachronism to their other mistakes. Instead of learning from the past, they denounce it for not being the present.

How could this bizarre reversal have taken place? How could a group that would have been expected to behave in one way do exactly the opposite? Politics seems so central to this development that it is tempting to seek answers there. One such answer has become well known: the radicals of the 1960s have come of age; they have tenure, chair departments, and have moved the campuses sharply to the left. Yet this one factor, though significant, leaves much unexplained.

The political radicals of the 1960s were distributed across the full range of university departments, the most active area probably being the social sciences; yet political correctness is heavily concentrated in the humanities, which suggests more specific factors. Moreover, although the children of the 1960s have come of age everywhere, it is the campuses that have moved sharply left. In fact, the direction of political influence is not from the larger society to the campuses but the reverse: in many areas, politically correct graduates are moving the culture in their direction. The sudden leftward tilt of museums, for example, can be traced directly to pressures originating from campus race-gender-class scholars.[1] Politically correct egalitarianism has its stronghold in the university, not among the general public, and its movement within the academy confirms this: it is trickling down from the most elite to the least elite institutions.

That the most extreme distortions have occurred in literary studies makes the influence of political factors unlikely, because traditionally professors of literature have not been the most politically active group on campuses. They have been more at home reading and writing in their offices than in the world of political action.[2] Few members of my own department, for example, were seriously involved in the anti-war movement during the 1960s and early 1970s; current faculty in departments like philosophy, sociology, and mathematics were much more visible in that era. Yet despite their apolitical position at that time, literature departments are now heavily committed to race-gender-class perspectives.

Most of those who now enthusiastically embrace race-gender-class perspectives and the proposition that everything is political are recent converts to that point of view. By temperament, the great majority of them were not, and are still not, serious political radicals. The critical fact that is central both to an explanation of what has happened and to a prognosis for what the future may hold is that for the most part they are primarily members of a literary-critical movement, not a political one. For that reason the most important determinants of what has happened are to be found in the structural features of the academy, and here a familiar question arises: Whose interests are being served?

The circumstances mentioned earlier, which should have made literature professors happy and productive members of the academy, are real, but, unfortunately, other conditions work powerfully against them. Twenty years ago, W. K. Wimsatt, the most influential analytical theorist of his day, noted that literary criticism was decidedly moving in a new direction, one he evidently felt was unsound. In considering the reasons for this shift, he made a remark that would be incomprehensible in most other fields of inquiry, though it is all too relevant in the case of literary criticism and other fields in the humanities. "New persons," he said, "need new platforms."[3] New careers needed to be launched.

A remark such as this would seem odd if made by, say, a biologist; why would anyone think that a commitment to some ill-considered ideas might advance one's career simply because the ideas were new? In the natural sciences, such a misjudgment would wreck a career. The difference here cannot be explained by the usual notion that the sciences demand more precise thought; even if intelligence manifests itself in different ways in different fields, it is hard to understand why unintelligent thought should help, rather than hinder, a career.

The relevant difference between the sciences and at least some of the humanities is this: in the former, but generally not in the latter, new discoveries constantly open up new areas for research. When the structure of DNA was discovered, one area of career possibilities was taken out of circulation, while, at the same time, dozens of new opportunities were created. This breakthrough in research opened up entirely new questions, thereby helping the careers of the next generation of scientists. But in the study of literature (and to a greater or lesser degree in other fields in the humanities) we return again and again to the same basic stock of great texts; each new book or article on *King Lear*, far from opening up new fields of inquiry, generally makes it harder for those following to say something new and intelligent about the play. Yet in all fields, academics are rewarded more for their originality than for any other aspect of their performance. The few outstanding critics always find ways of demonstrating their originality, but the rest are put under increasing pressure as time goes by and the bibliographies get thicker. To be sure, new additions to the canon occur from time to time, and occasionally a piece of literary criticism suggests further intellectual pursuits for others, but such innovations in thought are too infrequent to relieve the pressure on humanists.

This pressure produces a crucial feature of literary studies, namely, its proneness to fads and fashions. Some of these grow large enough to predominate at a particular time, as deconstructionism did, but others —for example, literary Freudianism—are never more than a minority cult within the larger profession. Whatever the extent of their influence, however, their function is similar: once a new intellectual fashion arrives on the literary scene, the way is open for a new reading of every classic text. The process is quite simple: one learns the terms and categories of the new fad and applies those terms to any text, and new thought seems to have been created. New fads are thus a tremendous boon to the great majority of practitioners in the field of literary studies, which is why they are embraced with such enthusiasm. They provide professional opportunities for many who otherwise might languish.

Much becomes clearer once we understand the reason for the rule of fads and fashions in literary studies. Fads have to come from somewhere, and most often other fields are the source. This interdisciplinary borrowing explains why people whose field might seem attractive nevertheless so often stray from it, either to grab ideas from somewhere else and bring them back or, as in the more extreme recent case, to settle in an entirely new field. Thus arises the impression that some literature professors have no interest in literature.

When ideas are adopted not primarily because of their own power but because of the unrelated needs of the field that borrows them, the life of those ideas in their new setting can be strange. Everyone wonders why Marxist thought has permeated literature departments while Marxist regimes are collapsing everywhere, and the puzzle is only increased by the fact that these literature professors do not behave like Marxists in their daily lives. The answer is that these are literary Marxists and, therefore, members of a literary-critical movement that must not be confused with the real thing.

Only thus can we begin to understand why large numbers of people who have always been conspicuously apolitical now take politics to be the foundation of their literary work. This is also the way to understand the otherwise baffling contrast between the self-absorption visible in the wave of memoir writing now sweeping the Duke University English department, for example, and that department's status as the national flagship of politicized criticism; the self-dramatizing and self-absorption are real, the politics of social conscience is literary-critical.[4]

We can also find here an explanation of why people whose field is remarkable for its infinite variety of theme frequently get stuck on one repetitive and inflexible note. The cost of following the literary-critical fashion of the moment in order to achieve a semblance of creative originality and be published in professional journals is that the meaning of texts must be overridden so that the ideas constituting the new fashion can be imposed on them.

So far, this diagnosis might seem to contain both bad and good news. The bad news is genuinely bad: it is that literature professors will probably always be caught jumping from one fad to another, that is, committing mass acts of foolishness from time to time because of a built-in factor that will not go away. (This is rather like the Irish elk syndrome: competition for dominance within the species led to the evolution of ever larger antlers, but the larger antlers caused the species as a whole to become dysfunctional and dragged it down.) The good news, however, might seem to be that the race-gender-class fad, though it has been far worse than its predecessors, will be gone once it is exhausted as a source of new readings of the classic texts.

Unhappily, there are reasons to think that things are different this time. To be sure, race-gender-class was at first just one more literary-critical fashion that took hold for the same reason that others before it had. But there are new factors at play this time, one of which makes the situation entirely different from anything we have seen before. First, this latest case is on a scale that dwarfs its predecessors. In the past, literary-critical fads and fashions were embraced by particular groups within the profession, but this one now dominates the entire field. Second, it reaches beyond the field of literature and dominates or has a strong presence in other departments (for example, Women's Studies).

But what makes the current situation completely unlike its predecessors is that for the first time the fad has managed to determine the character of faculty appointments. For some time, race-gender-class concerns have been a touchstone for the great majority of junior appointments in literature, with the result that a completely new class of faculty has appeared. To understand the situation we are now in, one must appreciate that these new appointees are for the most part not literary-critical race-gender-class faddists who would normally jump to the next fad when it arrives but true believers in the race-gender-class issue who are not interested in literature and will not suddenly become literary scholars when the fashions change.

Moreover, this new class of faculty has been much strengthened by the creation of departments of Women's Studies, Black Studies, Chicano Studies, and so on, whose sole rationale is bound up with race-gender-class orthodoxy. This time, therefore, the literati will not be so free to move on to something else when they have exhausted the current fad, because large obstacles will be in their way in the form of real—as opposed to literary—race-gender-class enthusiasts who make up a large segment of their departments and virtually all of some adjacent ones. Even if the faddists were to move on to something new, the results of the appointments made during these years would remain, and the presence of the race-gender-class contingent, though reduced, would still be formidable.

How would the true believers respond to a change of direction by their colleagues? Surely, the prospect is for bitter conflict should they try to do so. This possible conflict between the literary radicals and the real ones is no longer simply conjecture. There are many signs that it has already begun. On the one side, some prominent literary race-gender-class exponents seem restive. Elaine Marks, the 1993 president of the Modern Language Association of America, having celebrated in the President's Column of an *MLA Newsletter* "the dominance of the social and political over the ontological and the poetical, the dominance of cultural studies over literary studies," suddenly in the next issue of the same Newsletter questioned whether criticism and literature always had to be about social change.[5] And at about the same time, no less a politically correct mogul than Stanley Fish wrote in the *London Review of Books* that "there is a great difference between trying to figure out what a poem means and trying to figure out which interpretation of a poem will contribute to the toppling of patriarchy or to the war effort."[6]

Coming from the other direction, Steven Watts, in an article entitled "Academe's Leftists Are Something of a Fraud," referred disparagingly to the literary race-gender-class set as "discourse radicals."[7] Watts is "increasingly annoyed by the revolutionary posturing of prosperous academics who like to pretend that they are something else," and he misses a genuine "sensitivity to real people" in all of their "otherworldly" poststructuralist politics. The conflict that we see here is also beginning to appear in the literature departments of major universities.[8]

This time the faddists evidently committed themselves to something that grew to be bigger than they were. But what made this fad so much stronger than its predecessors that it was able to transcend its origins, dominating literary studies and even re-creating itself in new departments? How did it grow so powerful that the literati lost control of it and of their own fate? Once again, there are many important factors, but one that is overwhelming.

To begin with, traditional literary scholars were all too receptive to one important aspect of race-gender-class: its bourgeois baiting. In theory, immersion in literature should afford wider perspective on everyday life, but in practice the effect has been mostly the reverse. The genteel, bookish world easily becomes a refuge that allows literary scholars to isolate themselves; they often become suspicious of, and even hostile to, life outside the academy, especially where the world of business is concerned. A casual remark by Barbara Herrnstein Smith, a recent MLA president, implied a good deal about the culture of literary academics.[9] Discussing E. D. Hirsch's ideas on a national culture, Smith referred contemptuously, though without any explanation of that contempt, to "Fourth of July speeches." She must have assumed her readers would understand what she meant and share her contempt. (They probably did.)

Oddly enough, it is the intellectual snobbery and elitism of many of the literati that politically correct egalitarianism appeals to; their partiality to literary Marxism is based not on its economic theory but on its hostility to business and the middle class. The character of this anti-bourgeois sentiment therefore has more in common with its origin in aristocratic disdain for the lower orders than with egalitarianism.[10]

Second, although one might think that the mind-set of a literary scholar would preclude any general denigration of literature, it is not necessarily so. Many are attracted to the field because they have literary ambitions of their own, and because very few achieve those ambitions, the failed poets among them are impatient with their secondary role as interpreters of the great. They would have preferred to be subjects of critical attention rather than critics. This explains, at least in part, the otherwise baffling fact that literature professors now denigrate literature and replace it with theory, for that new emphasis shifts the professor from secondary to primary status. The gyrations of Stanley Fish, for example, are the mark of someone anxious to be recognized for his own performance rather than as an explicator of someone else's.[11]

A third factor that helped race-gender-class become so powerful is found in the conditions created by the critical fashion that immediately preceded it: deconstructionism. Deconstruction's initial focus on linguistic indeterminacy and the independence of language from reality had an aura of ivory-tower amusement for scholars, which invited a sharp swing of the pendulum to the opposite end of the spectrum. Linguistic games were followed by the (apparent) down-to-earth social reality of race, gender, and class. Because deconstruction had been cultish and more than a little irrational, it was unstable and therefore particularly vulnerable to a swing to the other extreme. Moreover, its ascendancy had also cleared the ground of anything that might have stood in the way of race-gender-class; by the end of the deconstructionist era of literary studies, a generation of younger scholars knew very little about the history of theoretical debate in their field.

The most important contribution of deconstruction to the success of race-gender-class, however, was its making respectable a mode of argument that had always been despised in the academy, namely, ad hominem argument. The deconstructionist rationale for ad hominem made it now seem, at least to those who used it, avant-garde and highly sophisticated.[12] That rationale runs as follows: instead of dealing with the mere surface of an argument, we should look deeper to discern hidden ideology, at which point we have its real basis. (When race-gender-class critics say that they have absorbed the lessons of deconstruction, this is in practice what they mean.) But ad hominem by any other name is still ad hominem; it still ignores the logic of an argument and counters it only by denouncing the ignoble motives of the opponent. Under the influence of deconstruction, this crudity was not only permitted but encouraged as the deepest form of argument, and this is why feminists, for example, now think that they can brush aside objections simply by identifying a critic as sexist or conservative. In this way and others, deconstruction made matters easier for race-gender-class supporters by degrading the intellectual climate of the academy.

Although all these factors are important, they are all overshadowed by another, without which race-gender-class criticism could never have achieved the commanding position that it now has: affirmative action, which provides both the content of this new intellectual fashion and the means to implement it. Most of the key ideas of race-gender-class scholarship (oppression, discrimination, and so on) are carried over from affirmative action. (The difference is that whereas affirmative action ostensibly asks for some admissions and appointments, the race-gender-class transformation wants the entire curriculum.)[13] The intellectual catastrophe that has overtaken the humanities is not just a by-product of affirmative action. It *is* affirmative action transformed into a curricular and intellectual climate. In literary studies, what began as a program for social justice in hiring has long since developed into hiring to service a teaching program that is *about* the themes of affirmative action. A vicious circle ensues, as changed hiring patterns drive changes in the curriculum and those curriculum changes then intensify the need for more skewed hiring. Even if affirmative action on behalf of faculty diversity were to be abandoned tomorrow, much of the same kind of hiring would have to take place to service the new curriculum.

The impact of race-gender-class on college campuses has been incalculable. The academy has degenerated so much that it in some respects has become a social liability rather than an asset. For example, in the past the knowledge and analysis provided by academics often exerted something of a calming influence where a divisive issue had aroused strong emotions in the general public; the debate became better informed and more objective. Yet the reverse now seems frequently to be the case. In matters of race relations, the campus generates and exports hysteria, and it is the common sense of the ordinary man and woman in the street that must provide a corrective. The college campus is the last place one would now expect to have a rational discussion of affirmative action. And a genuinely academic discussion of multiculturalism—one that was analytical and informed by a knowledge of the experience of other multicultural societies, past and present—would also be close to impossible. Failure to conform to race-gender-class orthodoxy results in the outright moral condemnation of any train of thought, however well worked out, that does not reach the right conclusion. Thomas Sowell's account of how peaceful coexistence in Sri Lanka was transformed by preferential policies into implacable hostility and civil war, for example, is simply incorrect thinking on campus.[14] Analytical thought on multiculturalism is best aired elsewhere—say, in the *Wall Street Journal.*

The campus now also seems to be the last place where one could hope to have a serious academic discussion of women's issues. In a transitional period, one would normally expect women in the general workforce to be more unreflectively irritated by the remaining inequalities of pay and status, with women in academe exerting a calming influence because of their greater awareness of historical context. But at the moment things are the other way around: far from being a moderating influence, academic feminism drives up the level of hysteria with all kinds of unrealistic fantasies about patriarchal conspiracies against women past and present. Again, campus frenzy has to be countered by common sense from beyond the campus.

Many attitudes now popular on campus amount in principle to a complete rejection of knowledge. Take, for example, the fascination with Foucault's notion that power relations are the real basis of any situation. It never seems to occur to those who find this notion so appealing that they are adopting a twin of the despised proposition "might is right"—namely, "might is truth." Both are startling positions for educated people to adopt, especially people with much-flaunted social consciences, for these are positions more commonly associated with fascist regimes. Knowledge and morality begin with the recognition that might makes neither right nor truth.

The extraordinary degree of reliance on ad hominem rather than logical argument is also in effect a rejection of academic knowledge. Typical was an exchange of letters following Helen Vendler's review of several feminist books in the *New York Review of Books*.[15] Vendler had analyzed some typical feminist arguments, but the response from Sandra Gilbert and Susan Gubar avoided the logic of what Vendler had said and instead attacked her personally as a woman fearful of change, unsupportive of other women, and so on. The character of this attack was so familiar and so similar to hundreds of others like it that had it stopped in mid-paragraph, anyone could have finished it. Its intent was not to clarify issues and so to contribute to knowledge but, instead (to quote John Le Carré's George Smiley on the assassination of General Vladimir), "to obliterate, to punish, and to discourage others."[16] The same intent to obliterate rather than to answer, but on a much larger scale, could be seen in the desperate (but ineffective) attempts of campus feminists to suppress Christina Sommers' *Who Stole Feminism?*[17]

An even more striking sign of the extent of the degeneration of academic debate is the spate of letters I discussed in Chapter 7, in which whole groups of scholars ganged up to denounce the views of others. This is a consistent extension of ad hominem. Logic and argument go under their own steam, winning or losing by their coherence and having the same force whether signed by one or many. Personal attack, however, gains force through the number of people making the attack; multisignature letters are more punishing, more discouraging.

If there is a malignancy left over in the academy from the 1960s, it consists less in the middle-aged political radicals it has bequeathed us than in the denigration of knowledge that began at that time. The demand for a narrowly construed "relevance" amounted to rejecting any relevance to the present of our knowledge of the past. This willed ignorance has made it possible to repeat with Foucault the folly of Rousseau's primitivist attack on civilization. (A little knowledge about the consequences of Rousseau would in fact have been extraordinarily relevant.) Fits of unhappiness over the fact that civilization's advances have left us far from perfect occur with regularity throughout the history of Western civilization, and as I have already argued, many have imagined that civilization to be the cause of the evil in us, not a restraint on it.[18] But the peculiarity of our time is that the institution best equipped to correct this delusion is the one that, because of its obsession with race-gender-class, is spreading and intensifying it.

The outlook seems gloomy to me, for three major reasons: first, this latest intellectual fashion, unlike all its predecessors, has managed to create new departments and new bodies of faculty in existing departments, all of which are dedicated to the movement and will not let it fade away; second, the mechanism that has fed this development—affirmative action—is still in place and is still, day by day, generating more obstacles to its fading; and third, respect for the essential underpinnings of academic life—knowledge, argument, evidence, logic—is at an astonishingly low level. Yet one cannot help noticing that the whole edifice often seems remarkably unstable.

Although race-gender-class scholars have won control of large expanses of the academy, they seem anxious, as if aware that their position is indefensible and could fall at any minute. They run scared even as they win. When their audience is friendly, they boast about the revolutionary nature of what they are doing, but when the wider public is looking on, they are anxious to make it seem like business as usual. The leadership of the Modern Language Association, for example, has been devoted to race-gender-class for some time, yet recently it tried to reassure the public that a survey of college courses had found that the classics are being taught much as they always have been.[19] (The titles of two articles that appeared soon after suggested that this attempt was not entirely successful: "The Modern Language Association Is Misleading the Public" and "The MLA's Deceptive Survey.")[20]

Similarly, critical legal theorists when on campus make the claim that their program amounts to a revolution in legal thought, but when one of them—Lani Guinier—had to face the general public, she quickly backed off, telling television interviewers that her academic essays were just "musings" that should not be taken too seriously. She then mounted a public relations campaign to persuade everyone that she was comfortably in the mainstream after all, expurgating the most incriminating passages when she published a collection of her essays.[21]

An especially intriguing example of this awareness of two different audiences is that of Johnnetta Cole, who after many years of extravagant enthusiasm on campus for Marxist-Leninist regimes, especially Cuba, began to have national political ambitions following her appointment as president of Spelman College. Her audience having become the general public rather than the campus, she too abruptly changed her tune and tried to sanitize her record, omitting her most substantial publication—a book published in Cuba—from her vita.[22]

What we see here is not simply traditional academic disdain for the philistinism of that sector of the public that is not college educated. It is, rather, the realization that what has fueled brilliant careers on campus cannot be defended against even the most elementary criticism when the literate, college-educated public is the audience. On campus, one can answer criticism of using the classroom to promote a radical politics by saying that everything is political, but off campus that tactic will not eliminate the commonsense distinction between teaching a body of knowledge and trying to make political converts. On campus one can be applauded for the intellectual daring of the proposition that Madonna can be studied instead of Shakespeare, but off campus literate, educated people ridicule such opinions, and there is no real defense against that well-deserved ridicule.

The more naively committed among race-gender-class scholars are evidently baffled and frustrated by this recurrent strategic retreat. Gregory Jay (cofounder of the Teachers for a Democratic Culture, an organization formed to defend race-gender-class academics against their critics) laments the fact that academic leftists are losing the battle of public opinion "because they have not heralded their achievements" and "communicated the value of [their] work to a larger public audience."[23] Unable to understand this reticence, Jay, with evident impatience (another sign of the strain between the two groups), tells his colleagues: "We ought to be proud of the new knowledge and new truths we are producing and ready to defend them." But in the depth of his frustration, Jay punches a hole right through the deceptive MLA survey of books taught in college literature courses. The MLA claim misrepresents the curricular reform that has taken place, Jay says, because it "does not reveal *how* canonical authors are being taught. When you pursue *that* question, it appears that the new scholarship may be making some real headway." Here Jay sides with his intellectual opponents who charge that the MLA study is dishonest, but he does so because, unlike many of his race-gender-class colleagues, he has not grasped the fact that the public would be horrified if it knew what is happening in college literature programs.

To judge from their behavior, many devotees understand only too well that race-gender-class is a game that brings power and prestige on campus but lacks any validity in the wider world. Perhaps they even understand the contradictions involved in their using cultural relativism in support of their rigidly held views on sexual and racial matters or employing skepticism in support of dogmatic claims to political and moral truth. Still, these are the faddists, not the committed younger members of the movement. The opportunists have ridden faddish currents before, and their knowledge that those currents have a finite existence is what fuels their insecurity.

Sometimes this insecurity manifests itself in a direct, dramatic way; for example, in the attempt (in the MLA "New Project on Antifeminist Harassment") to stifle criticism by indicting it as "intellectual harassment."[24] By far the most common reflex, however, is to edge toward the center when danger threatens.[25] If this were simply the refuge of a few of the fainthearted among the rank and file of the movement, it would not be remarkable. What is truly strange about the race-gender-class movement is that its *leading* figures act in this way—its major spokespersons are the ones who seem uneasy about defending it. Catharine Stimpson, for example, though a leading partisan, likes to pose as a centrist and seems more comfortable denying that PC exists than in extolling its virtues.[26] But the oddest example of this contorted effort at safe self-positioning is, once again, Gerald Graff.

By cofounding Teachers for a Democratic Culture with Gregory Jay, Graff offered himself as a leader of the race-gender-class cause, yet his discomfort in that role is evident throughout his recent *Beyond the Culture Wars.* The thrust of Graff's argument is that we should teach the conflicts and let both sides be heard and argued in the classroom. It is strange to watch Graff rehearse the familiar arguments for listening to both sides of an issue, as if unaware of recurrent complaints about the dogmatism and zealotry of those he speaks for. He recommends the marketplace of ideas as if he had just discovered it and proclaims it to be a progressive new idea that will "revitalize American education," as Graff's subtitle put it. But that is absurd: the cornerstone of a liberal education has always been teaching students how to examine different sides of a question. What could be new about that? There is something unreal about Graff's urging the marketplace of ideas upon us as an apologist for the very people who have tried to shut it down and are under fire largely for that reason. Examples are well known: when Camille Paglia was invited to speak at Brown, campus feminists were outraged, though their voices greatly outnumbered hers; when Ward Parks criticized radical feminism at Louisiana State University he faced a harassment charge; when Alan Gribben dissented from multicultural orthodoxy at the University of Texas at Austin, he was ostracized.[27] And so on, and so on. These are not accidents; they are the predictable consequence of making the classroom a place where social and political change is initiated. Intellectual curiosity is flexible, moral fervor is not. One seeks answers, the other already knows them. Departments of Ethnic Studies and Women's Studies are in practice places where the conflicts are highly unlikely to be taught, because their members are virtually limited to a particular interest group. The subject of tough questions from undergraduates has emerged recently as a topic of discussion among feminists, yet the emphasis has been not on the value of diversity of opinion but on how to contain and neutralize questioners.[28]

Graff makes a halfhearted attempt to argue that it is anti-PC traditionalists who need to be lectured about "teaching the conflicts," because they want the academy to be a conflict-free ivory tower.[29] But professors are typically contentious individuals who will argue over just about anything, and critics of political correctness are the last to shrink from conflict—they know how roughly their opponents treat critics. Graff also complains of their use of invective (odd for people who supposedly shrink from conflict) rather than argument, but his own text is full of personal abuse of his opponents. According to Graff, his opponents use "patent falsehoods" and do not tell the truth (his pages 3 and 25), are ignorant (31, 46, 160) because they don't do their homework, criticize deconstruction because they haven't read it (158), "revel in self-pity" (49), are "frightened and defensive" (148), motivated by fear of change (3) and anger at their failure to dominate the academy (157), suffer from hysteria (3, 32), sneer instead of arguing (111), are frustrated at no longer getting their own way (8), dislike theory and don't even bother to read it (31), make excuses for social inequality and injustice (46), and are angry at the challenge to their rule by gentleman's agreement (56). Graff's penchant for ad hominem attack is so strong that it makes him unable to understand his opponents' case,[30] and his insistence that criticism of political correctness reduces to various character flaws precludes any but the most primitive understanding of the issues.

The trouble with a position that lacks conviction is that one can easily lose one's way, because nothing in it is natural. Graff eventually forgets what he is supposed to be arguing for long enough to blurt out the truth: "If the left hopes to advance it must risk entering a debate that it would not necessarily be guaranteed to win."[31] And so Graff shows that he knows perfectly well that the campus left does not want a debate and stands in the way of teaching both sides of the conflicts. He even doubts that the left's position is defensible. No wonder the real radicals doubt the integrity of the literary radicals.

Graff's fear of his newly adopted position shows even more clearly when he tries to make multiculturalists and feminists sound moderate and sensible. As he tells it, feminists do not really harp on the sexism of males; multiculturalists only want the marginal change in the canon that always happens with time; nobody really chooses texts on the basis of the author's gender, race, or sexual orientation; nor do they use their classrooms to further their social and political agendas—they just want political factors to get their due alongside others that are important. Being a moderate and a radical at the same time is evidently not easy. Something has to be sacrificed—in this case, reality.

Graff's contribution to the question of whether to study Shakespeare or pop culture betrays the same lack of conviction: "A neo-Marxist analysis of Vanna White's autobiography, *Vanna Speaks,* one that emphasized, say, the commodification of the self under postmodern capitalism, might be more challenging than any number of analyses of weightier tomes than Vanna's." Graff can only bring himself to say that when compared to run-of-the-mill traditional work the newer stuff might not come out too badly—hardly a ringing endorsement.[32]

I have dwelt on Gerald Graff because he epitomizes the evasiveness, the anxiety, and the underlying lack of commitment of the group within the race-gender-class camp that might well be ready to move on to the next fashion if only the flood of new appointees who are real believers had not created a new situation. It is this group of faddists, caught between the need to maintain their leadership position on campus and the desire to stay respectable in the eyes of outsiders, that makes the whole so unstable and the future course of events so uncertain. Even if the faddists do change course, the continuing presence of a large group that will probably never have a real interest in literature, together with the severe tension between the two groups, will cripple literature departments for many decades to come.

What can be done to reverse or at least halt the deterioration? The ambiguous behavior of the literary radicals, and the strain that is visible in their having to maintain a campus stance inconsistent with their public posture, suggests one obvious measure. The more the literate public hears of what is happening on campus, the greater that strain becomes; and the greater the strain, the sooner the literary radicals will look for something new to do that does not embarrass them. But the most obvious step that could be taken is to stop the mechanism that continues to make the situation worse day by day: affirmative action.

Fortunately, there is no conflict between what is best for college study of the humanities and what is good for society generally and minorities and women in particular. A more serious study of history and literature would enable minorities and women to gain a broader perspective on recent events in their country and to see them as part of a historical pattern in which the effects of the Enlightenment are still being played out. By contrast, race-gender-class perspectives rob them of historical context and instead channel their energies into resentment. Many of the most able move into the bureaucracy of affirmative-action enforcement, where their further intellectual development is permanently arrested.

Artificial intervention in the progress of young people through the educational system ignores the fact that the momentum gained by achievement on one level is an essential part not only of their scholastic preparation but also of their psychological capacity to perform well at the next level. Achieving mastery on one level gives a student the confidence needed to face difficult material on the next. Even the best students sometimes doubt whether they can meet the challenges. When those doubts hit, two things keep them going: first, the memory that they have done it before, and second, the certainty that they must do it again if they are to progress to the next level in the system. Students who know they owe their education to the artificial intervention of affirmative action lack both resources, and that is why affirmative action is damaging even to able students. Much as we would like to, we cannot make young people achieve, and trying to thrust it upon them only harms them. The educational system itself is damaged as pressure mounts to do more, and still more, to remedy inevitable failure; first, standards of performance are abandoned, then the integrity of the curriculum.[33] We should remember that there has long been a splendid quasi-affirmative-action program for the underprivileged in this country, one with a long record of excellent results: it consisted in high-quality public education. But that resource is precisely what has been damaged by misguided radical activism on behalf of the underprivileged groups who so urgently need it.

Conclusion

Disputes between different ways of approaching literary criticism have been common enough throughout the history of the field, just as arguments about the theory and practice of other academic disciplines have been. Seen in this light, the arguments I have made might seem no more than a normal part of academic life, business as usual. Yet something is lost if we put this recent controversy on a par with, say, the often sharp disputes between the New Critics and the Literary Historians, substantial positions both. The analysis developed in this book, if correct, points to something more serious: a startling decline in the intellectual quality of work in the humanities and a descent to intellectual triviality and irrelevance that amounts to a betrayal of the university as an institution.

The idea of knowledge for its own sake, of letting an argument go wherever its logic leads, without fear or favor, is an extraordinarily precious part of our Western heritage. Who can doubt that it is responsible for the brilliant success of Western universities? But it is also a fragile idea, and institutions based on it are, we now know, fragile, too. For we have recently had a real-world test of that fragility—a test of what would happen if we decided that it was not necessary to insist that knowledge and understanding be the unique focus and purpose of the academy and that it could also promote desirable social causes and experiments. We have seen the results, and we now know (what we should have known all along) that universities cannot serve two masters—knowledge and political and social causes. The former is a delicate creature, too easily crushed by the rougher, cruder nature of the latter. Like a cuckoo, a social cause can only make room for itself in the campus nest by ousting the rightful inhabitant— it *must* attack knowledge for its own sake and has done so with disastrous results.

The present campus left complains that any attack on what it has wrought is inspired by and serves the interests of political conservatism. The left is wrong. Abuse of the academy for political ends has been an equal opportunity pastime for despotic regimes of both left and right. Everyone who is committed to a liberal democratic way of life—again, left and right—has the same vital interest in an academy that makes knowledge and understanding its undiluted focus. In their pursuit of knowledge for its own sake, Western universities have been an important force for social change; in America, high-quality public education has provided upward mobility for generations of poor immigrants. But the lesson of recent years is that the academy can remain a force for that kind of social change only if it keeps knowledge and understanding firmly at the center and resists the call for direct involvement in social causes. On the campus, the first and last concern must be to follow where the logic of the argument leads.

In the past, a quality-control mechanism was in place to prevent the corruption and decline of teaching and research: the dean. If deans heard of a classroom where the main focus was not on teaching students how to think and learn but on making them serve—directly serve—political and social ends, they could intervene to insist that classrooms were for education, not for faculty hobbyhorses or social activism. But deans became confused when they heard senior faculty loudly proclaim that everything was political. Not knowing how to respond when this view was advanced as au courant academic thought, they retreated into silence and allowed entire programs to slide into overt social activism. One purpose of this book is to stiffen their resistance by clarifying the logic of this claim. But deans will also have to regain the courage to correct situations that need correction. They must emerge from their intimidated state and begin once again to act as the quality control of the academy.

There is no doubt, however, that the road back to a functioning literature program on American college campuses will be long and hard. A whole generation of bright graduate students of literature (and therefore potential future literature professors) is looking at the present state of the field and many of the best of those students are deciding they do not see a productive life for themselves in the conditions that prevail. Too many of the most able are deciding to do something else with their lives. One of the saddest commentaries on the present state of affairs is that professors who have kept intact a sense of the power and variety of literature find it hardest to counsel them against that decision.

Notes

Introduction

1. The claims and counterclaims alluded to in this introduction are analyzed and documented in the chapters that follow. The particular contradiction noted at this point is pursued in Chap. 9.

2. A representative example of this ambiguous response is chronicled in Scott Heller's " 'Frame-Up' of Multicultural Movement Dissected by Scholars and Journalists," *Chronicle of Higher Education,* 27 November 1991, p. A15–A16. On one hand, the race-gender-class scholars who organized the conference that Heller reports on gave it the title: "The PC Frame-Up." But on the other, one of their number, Jon Wiener, said that "the uproar indicated that progressives had won significant victories on campuses."

3. The first full-length book to do so was Dinesh d'Souza's *Illiberal Education: The Politics of Race and Sex on Campus* (New York, 1991). Notable among those that followed are David Bromwich's *Politics by Other Means: Higher Education and Group Thinking* (New Haven, 1992) and Richard Bernstein's

Dictatorship of Virtue: Multiculturalism and the Battle for America's Future (New York, 1994).

4. For more on this point, see Chap. 2.

5. E.g., Frank Lentricchia, *Criticism and Social Change* (Chicago, 1983), p. 3: "I come down on the side of those who see our society as mainly unreasonable and that education should be one of the places where we can get involved in the process of transforming it."

6. See my *The Theory of Literary Criticism: A Logical Analysis* (Berkeley, 1974).

1   The Origins of Political Correctness

1. I am concerned here not with the origin of the term "political correctness" but, rather, with the phenomenon now associated with it. The term itself originated as part of the attempt to standardize thought and opinion according to the views of the party leadership following the successful Bolshevik Revolution.

2. Tacitus, *The Agricola and the Germania,* translation and introduction by H. Mattingly, revised by S. A. Hanford (Harmondsworth, 1970). The passages cited are from secs. 7, 8, 11, 19, and 26.

3. See Derek Freeman, *Margaret Mead and Samoa: The Making and Unmaking of an Anthropological Myth* (Cambridge, Mass., 1983).

4. John Searle, "The Storm over the University," *New York Review of Books,* 6 December 1990, p. 35.

5. See especially "Discours sur l'origine et les fondements de l'inégalité parmi les hommes" (A discourse upon the origin and foundation of inequality among mankind), in *Œuvres complètes de Jean-Jacques Rousseau,* ed. Bernard Gagnebin and Marcel Raymond, vol. 3 (Paris, 1964), pp. 111–237.

6. Rousseau, "Discours sur l'origine," p. 164.

7. Tacitus, *Germania,* sec. 44.

8. Gwyn Jones, *A History of the Vikings,* 2d ed. (Oxford, 1984), p. 183.

9. See, e.g., Simon Schama, *Citizens: A Chronicle of the French Revolution* (New York, 1989), p. 791: "Every atrocity the time could imagine was meted out to the defenseless population. Women were routinely raped, children killed, both mutilated."

10. The loss of life in some regions amounted to one-third of the population (Schama, *Citizens,* pp. 791–92).

11. See Robert Conquest, *The Great Terror: A Reassessment* (Oxford, 1990).

12. Rousseau, "Discours sur les sciences et les arts" (A discourse on the sciences and the arts), in *Œuvres complètes,* vol. 3, p. 7.

13. Terry Eagleton, *Literary Theory: An Introduction.* (Minneapolis, 1983), p. 25.

14. These are the words of Gerald Graff, who insists that this is the real point of deconstruction ("Toward Constructive Deconstruction: Reply to Champion," *Critical Review* 3 [1989] 90–92). Here Graff joins the long line of those who have undertaken to tell us what deconstruction really means, usually after the appearance of a highly critical account of what most other deconstructionists take it to mean.

15. See my *One Fairy Story Too Many: The Brothers Grimm and Their Tales* (Chicago, 1983).

16. Nicholas D. Kristof, "Stark Data on Women: 100 Million Are Missing," *New York Times,* 5 November 1991.

17. I consider this point in more detail in Chap. 4.

18. The claim by some feminists that this is a "rape culture" seems absurd when it is measured against the kinds of horrors that still occur outside the West— for example, the recent Serbian use of mass rape as a weapon of war. For a convincing demonstration of the fraudulence of the inflated statistics used by feminists to bolster this claim, see Christina Sommers, *Who Stole Feminism?* (New York, 1994), chap. 10, "Rape Research."

19. Annette Kolodny, "Among the Indians: The Uses of Captivity," *New York Times Book Review,* 31 January 1993, pp. 1, 26–29.

20. See David E. Stannard, *American Holocaust: Columbus and the Conquest of the New World* (Oxford, 1992), for this blinkered view of a beautiful civilization subjected to a genocidal holocaust by depraved Europeans. A useful corrective is Michael Berliner, "Man's Best Came with Columbus," *Los Angeles Times,* 30 December 1991.

21. For details, see two level-headed analyses that question the Goddess cult: Philip G. Davis, "The Goddess and the Academy," *Academic Questions* 6 (1993): 49–66; and Mary Lefkowitz, "The Twilight of the Goddess," *New Republic,* 3 August 1992, pp. 29–33. The most important academic proponent of the Goddess theory is Marija Gimbutas, for example, *The Goddesses and Gods of Old Europe* (London, 1982). A fuller discussion of the Goddess in the context of academic feminism is given in Chap. 3.

22. See Molefi Kete Asante, *The Afrocentric Idea* (Philadelphia, 1987), p. 65: "African society is essentially a society of harmonies." Johnnetta Cole, in her *Conversations: Straight Talk with America's Sister President* (New York, 1993), also gives us an idyllic picture of Africans before the Europeans, e.g., pp. 61 and 83.

23. This is the opinion of Fredric Jameson; see, e.g., his *Postmodernism: Or, the Cultural Logic of Late Capitalism* (Durham, N.C., 1991). For fuller discussion of his view, see Chap. 5, this vol.

24. A more detailed critique of these ideas and of the theory of cultural relativism is given in chap. 4.

25. Kolodny, "Among the Indians," p. 28.

26. Fredric Jameson, *The Ideologies of Theory: Essays, 1971–1986*, vol. 2, *Syntax of History* (Minneapolis, 1988), p. 189.

27. Robert Edgerton, *Sick Societies: Challenging the Myth of Primitive Harmony* (New York, 1992), p. 70.

2 The Diversity of Literature

1. Peter Washington, *Fraud: Literary Theory and the End of English* (London, 1989), p. 168. See also my review of *Fraud:* "Radical Literary Theory," *London Review of Books,* 8 February 1990, pp. 6–7.

2. Ruth Bottigheimer, *Grimms' Bad Girls and Bold Boys: The Moral and Social Vision of the Tales* (New Haven, 1987).

3. Some aspects of this argument were first set out in my *Theory of Literary Criticism,* chap. 3, "The Aims of the Study of Literature."

4. The painter's unhappy marriage complicates the picture: Is his unfaithful wife a psychological burden through which he excuses his failure or a further sign of the lack of any charismatic quality in his personality—or both?

5. This is Walther's "Owē war sint verswunden alliu mīniu jār." A convenient edition is *Walther von der Vogelweide—Gedichte,* trans. and with a commentary by Peter Wapnewski, 7th ed. (Frankfurt am Main, 1970).

6. This failure of criticism is now feeding back into literature itself, with disastrous results. Toni Morrison, for example, seems now to limit her writing to group grievances of race-gender-class issues, which results in a poverty of content that will make her work seem badly dated within a few decades and that will bring contempt on the Nobel committee that so foolishly allowed its mental horizons to be narrowed by the fads of our time. Morrison's critical writing follows the same path; see Heather Mac Donald, "Toni Morrison as Literary Critic," *Academic Questions* 7 (1974): 26–36, a devastating account of Morrison's "painfully bad critical prose." See also Bruce Bawer, "All That Jazz," *New Criterion* 10 (May 1992): 10–17: "Morrison doesn't flinch from employing the dreariest academic jargon of the day" (p. 16).

7. A case in point is Fredric Jameson; see below, Chap. 5.

8. See, e.g., Eagleton, *Literary Theory,* pp. 205, 209.

9. Eagleton, *Literary Theory,* p. 204; see also p. 197: "I began this book by arguing that literature did not exist."

10. Eagleton, *Literary Theory,* p. 213; see also p. 205: "My own view is that it is most useful to see 'literature' as a name which people give from time to time for different reasons to certain kinds of writing within a whole field of what Michel Foucault has called 'discursive practices', and that if anything is to be an object of study it is this whole field of practices rather than just those sometimes rather obscurely labelled literature." This is pure invention: there is nothing obscure about the word *literature,* nor is "from time to time" a justifiable qualification in view of the consistent use of the word to refer to a well-known body of writings.

11. It should be noted that there is another sense of the question What is literature? one that concerns the function of literature more than its definition. See my *Theory of Literary Criticism,* chap. 8, "The Function of Literature."

12. Ellis, *Theory of Literary Criticism,* chap. 2, "The Definition of Literature."

13. Eagleton, *Literary Theory,* p. 9

14. George Hunter, "The History of Styles as a Style of History," in *Addressing Frank Kermode: Essays in Criticism and Interpretation,* ed. Margaret Tudeau-Clayton and Martin Warner (London, 1991), p. 83.

15. This is not to say that some feminist critics do not sometimes read some texts appropriately; but to do so they have had to respond to what the text says, not measure it against race-gender-class expectations. That is, they have had to behave like critics, not feminists.

16. Gerald Graff, *Beyond the Culture Wars: How Teaching the Conflicts Can Revitalize American Education* (New York), pp. 103, 52.

17. Graff, *Beyond the Culture Wars,* p. 49.

18. Ibid., pp. 71, 47.

19. Alice Walker, *Living by the Word* (New York, 1986). The adoption provoked a controversy that is summarized in Nanette Asimov and Evelyn C. White, "State Reversal on 2 Stories by Alice Walker," *San Francisco Chronicle,* 12 March 1994. The previous December, the State Board had voted to remove the story from the test, but following protests about "political" motivation, that decision was reversed three months later. A common irony is present in this sequence of events: the protest about the removal of the story decried political motivation, but its inclusion had clearly been motivated by the politics of racial grievance in the first place.

20. For further discussion of this point, see my *Theory of Literary Criticism,* chap. 8.

21. Eagleton, *Literary Theory,* p. 200. One of the oddities of the present state of literary studies is that this now rather archaic Marxist language is repeated

by literary critics long after events in the real world have made it embarrassing to do so.

22. Peter Parrinder, " 'Secular Surrogates': Frank Kermode and the Idea of the Critic," in *Addressing Frank Kermode*, pp. 59, 61, 63, 66, 71–72.

23. Parrinder here separates interpretation from any concern with the content of what one is interpreting, needlessly, because interpretation is about diagnosing content. The real contrast should be between a concern for the unique content of each text and a rigid view of what is allowed to count as content before the text's character is known.

24. Frank Kermode, "The Men on the Dump: A Response," in *Addressing Frank Kermode*, p. 103.

3 Gender, Politics, and Criticism

1. Fredric Jameson, *The Political Unconscious: Narrative as a Socially Symbolic Act* (Ithaca, 1981), p. 20.

2. See my "Radical Literary Theory," *London Review of Books*, 8 February 1990, p. 7, for further treatment of this point.

3. Graff, *Beyond the Culture Wars*, p. 31.

4. Marilyn French, *The War Against Women* (New York, 1992); Catharine A. MacKinnon, *Toward a Feminist Theory of the State* (Cambridge, Mass., 1989), p. 174; Peggy McIntosh, *Interactive Phases of Curricular Re-vision: A Feminist Perspective*, Working Paper no. 124 of the Wellesley College Center for Research on Women (Wellesley, Mass., 1983). A recent article by Dennis Farney ("Blackboard Rumble: For Peggy McIntosh, 'Excellence' Can Be a Dangerous Concept," *Wall Street Journal*, 14 June 1994) documents well both the extent of McIntosh's influence and the nonsensical quality of her views.

5. Nan Robertson, *The Girls in the Balcony: Women, Men and the New York Times* (New York, 1992), p. 231.

6. French, *The War Against Women*, p. 16. French refers to this system as "institutionalized male supremacy" (p. 16), and she believes that it "began and spread as a war against women" (p. 14).

7. Sandra M. Gilbert and Susan Gubar, *The Madwoman in the Attic: The Woman Writer and the Nineteenth-Century Literary Imagination* (New Haven, 1979), p. 6.

8. Although feminists like Andrea Dworkin insist that our society is a "rape culture," it is clearly not in the same league as other areas of the world. Mass rape in Bosnia is one example. Rape is also used as political retribution in many countries. See, e.g., "Pressure Grows on the Moi Regime," *Guardian*

Weekly, 4 August 1991, p. 10, in which Victoria Brittain reports the rape of teenage girls by security forces in the aftermath of a prodemocracy rally in Nairobi; or Melissa Robertson's "Unveiled: Rape in Pakistan," *New Republic,* 9 March 1992, which tells of politically motivated rapes in a society where "a man can hurt his enemy most by raping his wife" (p. 11).

9. Fernand Braudel, *Civilization and Capitalism, 15th-18th Century,* vol. 1, *The Structures of Everyday Life,* translated from the French and revised by Sian Reynolds (New York, 1981), p. 90: "None of the royal families escaped the terrifying rate of infant mortality of the period." Braudel cites an enormous quantity of compelling evidence about the "precariousness and brevity of life" in those times.

10. The relevant data is available in a series of articles in the *Encyclopedia Britannica,* 15th ed. (Chicago, 1980). At the end of the eighteenth century, life expectancy in North America and northwestern Europe was 35 to 40 years (*s.v.* "Life-Span," Macropaedia, 10:913). By the eve of World War I, it was over 50 in the most advanced countries (*s.v.* "Population," 14:816). In the case of Italy, life expectancy for men remained within one year of that for women until the 1920s, when the figure for both reached 50. As longevity for both increased sharply in the next forty years, the gap widened, to 6.5 years by 1967 (*s.v.* "Italy," 9:1096). Life expectancy in the United States is nearly double that in many underdeveloped countries (*s.v.* "United States of America," 18:929). That of Tanzanians is now approximately 40 (*s.v.* "Tanzania," 17:1029).

11. Gilbert and Gubar, *Madwoman in the Attic,* pp. xi, xiii.

12. An example of the use of Desdemona to discuss the mistreatment of women in the sixteenth century, rather than to illuminate Shakespeare's *Othello,* is Lisa Jardine's " 'Why Should He Call Her Whore?' Defamation and Desdemona's Case," in *Addressing Frank Kermode,* pp. 124–53.

13. Philip Davis, "The Goddess and the Academy," *Academic Questions* 6 (1993): 49–66, and Mary Lefkowitz, "The Twilight of the Goddess."

14. Davis, "The Goddess and the Academy," pp. 50, 52.

15. Lefkowitz, "Twilight of the Goddess," p. 31.

16. Cheris Kramarae and Dale Spender, eds., *The Knowledge Explosion: Generations of Feminist Scholarship* (New York, 1992).

17. Marilyn J. Waring, "Economics," and Liz Stanley, "The Impact of Feminism on Sociology in the Last 20 Years," in *The Knowledge Explosion,* ed. Kramarae and Spender, pp. 305 and 257, respectively.

18. Shulamit Reinharz, "The Principles of Feminist Research," in *The Knowledge Explosion,* ed. Kramarae and Spender, p. 426.

19. Self-citations are ignored in this account.

20. Andrea Dworkin, *Intercourse* (New York, 1987).

21. See David Horowitz, "Cuss me Kate: The Lunacy of Catharine MacKinnon," *Heterodoxy* 2 (November 1993): 14–15.

22. Ronald M. Dworkin, "Women and Pornography," *New York Review of Books,* 21 October 1993, pp. 36–42.

23. Richard A. Posner, "Obsession," *New Republic,* 18 October 1993, pp. 31–36. For example, the book lacks "the careful distinctions, scrupulous weighing of evidence, and fair consideration of opposing views that one is entitled to expect in a work written by a professor at an eminent law school (Michigan) and published by a distinguished university press (Harvard)" (p. 31).

24. Anthony Daniels, "Feminism's Confused Fanatic," *Sunday Telegraph,* 29 May 1994, p. 9. Daniels goes on: "There is a good case to be made (whether one agrees with it or not) for the control of pornography. . . . Professor MacKinnon lacks the power to make such a case."

25. Elaine Showalter, ed., *The New Feminist Criticism: Essays on Women, Literature, and Theory* (New York, 1985); Gayle Greene and Coppélia Kahn, eds., *Making a Difference: Feminist Literary Criticism* (London, 1985).

26. Catharine Stimpson, "Feminist Criticism," in *Redrawing the Boundaries: The Transformation of English and American Literary Studies,* ed. Stephen Greenblatt and Giles Gunn (New York, 1992), p. 262.

27. The most prominent example of this turn is Carol Gilligan, *In a Different Voice: Psychological Theory and Women's Development* (Cambridge, Mass., 1982).

28. Peter Shaw, *The War Against the Intellect* (Iowa City, 1989), p. 85.

29. See Sommers, *Who Stole Feminism?* p. 67, citing a videotape of McIntosh expounding her system.

30. Dale Spender thinks that the difference can be found in women's lack of male arrogance; for Spender, women are "looking for an inclusive rather than an exclusive way of knowing" that avoids "replicating the mind-set of the male model—declaring that what one knows is all that there is to know." (Men, apparently, think they know everything.) "The Entry of Women to the Education of Men," in *The Knowledge Explosion,* ed. Kramarae and Spender, p. 241.

31. Sue Rosser, *Female-Friendly Science* (New York, 1990), pp. 60–61.

32. Ruth Bleier, ed., *Feminist Approaches to Science* (Elmsford, 1986), p. 16.

33. In the case of Carol Gilligan and Lyn Mikel Brown (*Meeting at the Crossroads: Women's Psychology and Girls' Development* [Cambridge, Mass., 1992]), women's ways of knowing are virtually equated with the counterculture values of the 1960s: to combat the influence of patriarchy, female students should do their own thing, mistrust anyone over thirty, discard their sexual

inhibitions, feel rather than think, do what feels good, and so on. See Barbara Rhoades Ellis's critique: "Big Girls Don't Cry," *Heterodoxy* 2 (October 1993): 8–10.

34. Helen Vendler, "Feminism and Literature," *New York Review of Books,* 31 May 1990, p. 23.

35. Sandra Harding, *The Science Question in Feminism* (Ithaca, 1986), p. 113. See also her *Whose Science? Whose Knowledge? Thinking from Women's Lives* (Ithaca, 1991).

36. Another staple of feminist writing on science is Donna Haraway's *Primate Visions: Gender, Race, and Nature in the World of Modern Science* (New York, 1989), which prompted Robin Dunbar ("The Apes as We Want to See Them," *New York Times Book Review,* 7 January 1990, p. 30) to comment, aptly, that "the less knowledgeable may greet it with enthusiasm" and "verbal complexity is too often a substitute for intellectual vacuity."

37. Paul R. Gross and Norman Levitt, *Higher Superstition: The Academic Left and Its Quarrels with Science* (Baltimore, 1994), p. 227.

38. Andrew Kadar, "The Sex-Bias Myth in Medicine," *Atlantic Monthly,* August 1994, pp. 66–70.

39. Kramarae and Spender, *The Knowledge Explosion,* p. 1.

40. Sandra M. Gilbert, "What Do Feminist Critics Want? A Postcard from the Volcano," in *The New Feminist Criticism,* p. 40.

41. Peggy McIntosh, "Warning: The New Scholarship on Women May Be Hazardous to Your Ego," *Women's Studies Quarterly* 10 (1982): 29–31.

42. Kramarae and Spender, *The Knowledge Explosion,* p. 335.

43. Sommers, *Who Stole Feminism?*; Elizabeth Fox-Genovese, *Feminism is NOT the Story of My Life* (New York, 1996); Daphne Patai and Noretta Koertge, *Professing Feminism: Cautionary Tales from the Strange World of Women's Studies* (New York, 1994).

44. Sommers, *Who Stole Feminism?* p. 160.

4 The Academic Politics of Race

1. Edward Said, *Culture and Imperialism* (New York, 1993), pp. 69–71.

2. Edward Said, *Orientalism* (New York, 1978), pp. 6, 123.

3. Stephen J. Greenblatt, *Renaissance Self-Fashioning: From More to Shakespeare* (Chicago, 1980), pp. 253, 174, 46.

4. Paul A. Cantor, "Stephen Greenblatt's New Historicist Vision," *Academic Questions* 6 (Fall 1993): 21.

5. For more on this point, see Chap. 9, this vol.

6. See Chap. 2, this vol.

7. An intriguing clash of politically correct values with the reality of cultural diversity was reported in Jack Foley, "Cockfighting Clash: Arrests Called Cultural Discrimination," *San Jose Mercury News,* 22 February 1993. A Filipino cockfighting enthusiast complained of "cultural discrimination" when animal rights activists filed charges against him.

8. See William Finnegan, *A Complicated War: The Harrowing of Mozambique* (Berkeley, 1992).

9. Barbara Crossette, "The Island that Fell from Grace," *New York Times Book Review,* 26 April 1992, p. 14, reviewing William McGowan's *Only Man Is Vile: The Tragedy of Sri Lanka* (New York, 1992).

10. See Thomas Sowell, *Preferential Policies: An International Perspective* (New York, 1990), pp. 76–89.

11. Jill Joliffe, "Behind the Timor Massacre," *Guardian Weekly,* 1 December 1991.

12. Michael Berliner, "Man's Best Came with Columbus," *Los Angeles Times,* 30 December 1991.

13. See, e.g., David Brion Davis, "Slaves in Islam," *New York Review of Books,* 11 October 1993, pp. 35–39.

14. Bernard Lewis, cited in Davis, "Slaves in Islam," p. 35.

15. *Encyclopaedia Britannica, s.v.* "Slavery, Serfdom, and Forced Labor," Macropaedia, 16:853–62.

16. "Alas, Slavery Lives," *Time,* 22 March 1993, p. 26.

17. B. J. Cutler, "Poor Kids Get Sold as Slaves," *San Jose Mercury News,* 4 October 1991.

18. *San Jose Mercury News,* 9 July 1991.

19. Dario Fernandez-Morera, "Anti-Americanisms Here and There," *Heterodoxy* 2 (February 1994): 14: "As in so many other fields of human endeavor, the Europeans and Americans just happened to be far better at this endeavor than anybody else."

20. See Richard Grenier, "The Greening of the Merciless Red Man," *Heterodoxy* 1 (October 1992): 8–9; also his "Indian Love Call," *Commentary* (March 1991): 46–50, a devastating critique of the romanticized picture of American Indians in the movie *Dancing with Wolves.*

21. J. H. Elliott, "The World after Columbus," *New York Review of Books,* 10 October 1991, p. 10.

22. I should note here that the term *Renaissance* is now considered too Eurocentric by many. The new politically correct term is "early modern European."

23. V. S. Naipaul, "Our Universal Civilization," *New York Review of Books,* 31 January 1991, pp. 22–25.

24. L. H. Gann, "African Reappraisals," *Heterodoxy* 2 (January 1994): 14–15.

25. See George B. N. Ayittey, *Africa Betrayed* (New York, 1992). This quotation is from the summary on the dust jacket.

26. See Chap. 1, this vol.

27. Edgerton, *Sick Societies*, chap. 6, "From Discontent to Rebellion."

28. Paul Sniderman and Thomas Piazza, *The Scar of Race* (Cambridge, Mass., 1993).

29. Arthur Schlesinger, Jr., *The Disuniting of America: Reflections on a Multicultural Society* (New York, 1992), pp. 126–29.

30. Johnnetta Cole, *Conversations: Straight Talk with America's Sister President* (New York, 1993), pp. 62, 177.

31. Henry Louis Gates, *Loose Canons: Notes on the Culture Wars* (New York, 1992), p. 35.

32. Mercifully, a realistic assessment of Said's writings has begun to emerge. Reviewing his "silly, vain, and meretricious" *Culture and Imperialism*, Rhoda Koenig writes: "One does not weep for Africans in bondage, but for academe, colonized by charlatans and sycophants who have put truth in chains" ("Limp Lit," *New York,* 1 March 1993, p. 119). Ernest Gellner, "The Mightier Pen? Edward Said and the Double Standards of Inside-out Colonialism" (*Times Literary Supplement,* 19 February 1993, p. 3–4), argues that Said's book is not a significant contribution to the discussion of colonialism. The *New Republic* ("Notebook" 14, March 1994, p. 8) goes further, but is not unfair, in calling Said "a faculty club revolutionary."

33. Mary Louise Pratt, *Imperial Eyes: Travel Writing and Transculturation* (London, 1992), pp. i, 4.

34. Pratt's book abounds in blatant double standards, however. For example, when white males look at a landscape with interest, they do so for Pratt with "imperial eyes" that seek to possess, but when women or black men do so, their perception is simply and genuinely appreciative. This difference of perception can be found only in Pratt's personal prejudices. See the review of *Imperial Eyes* by Douglas Fowler, *Heterodoxy* 1 (November 1992): 15.

35. "More Bias Found among Younger Whites, " *San Francisco Chronicle,* 12 June 1993.

36. Arch Puddington, "Black Anti-Semitism and How It Grows," *Commentary* (April 1993): 23.

37. For an incisive critique of Afrocentrism, see Mary Lefkowitz, *Not Out of Africa: How Afrocentrism Became an Excuse to Teach Myth as History* (New York, 1996).

38. Schlesinger, *Disuniting of America*, chap. 4.

5 *Class and Perfect Egalitarianism*

1. An amusing case is that of Sandra Bartky, who after years of using Marxist rhetoric suddenly, during a sharp exchange with Christina Sommers, objected to being linked to "moribund Marxist-Leninist rhetoric," as if to suggest that the collapse of Marxism had made the criticism, not the system, obsolete. Letter to the Editor, *Proceedings and Addresses of the American Philosophical Association* 65 (January 1992): 5.

2. Adolf Hitler, *Mein Kampf,* trans. Ralph Manheim (Boston, 1971), chap. 11, "Nation and Race." The German original is no longer available; it has been unlawful to publish it in Germany since 1955.

3. Race-gender-class scholars are often remarkably impervious to the notion that their political views may be related to such monstrosities as fascism. As an example, in response to my "The Origins of PC" (*Chronicle of Higher Education,* 15 January 1992, pp. B1–B2), Douglas Robinson (Letters to the Editor, 5 February) wrote that the alternative to political correctness was Nazi Germany, forgetting entirely that the essay he was ostensibly responding to had argued that cultural relativism was implicated in the rise of fascism in Germany.

4. Fredric Jameson, *The Ideologies of Theory: Essays, 1971–1986,* vol. 1, *Situations of Theory,* vol. 2, *Syntax of History* (Minneapolis, 1988); *Signatures of the Visible* (London, 1990); *Late Marxism: Adorno, or, the Persistence of the Dialectic* (London, 1990); *Postmodernism: Or, the Cultural Logic of Late Capitalism* (Durham, N.C., 1991). Jameson, *The Political Unconscious,* p. 20.

5. Ibid., p. 9.

6. Jameson, *The Ideologies of Theory,* vol. 2, pp. 188, 76; *Late Marxism,* p. 5.

7. Jameson, *The Ideologies of Theory,* vol. 2, pp. 207–08.

8. Jameson, *Late Marxism,* p. 250.

9. Jameson, *The Ideologies of Theory,* vol. 2, p. 189.

10. It is hard to avoid the thought that Marx's comment on the withering away of the state should have made it unnecessary for the world to endure the many decades of suffering by billions of people before it found out that Marxism was an unworkable political system. This was surely a sign of a broad streak of political naïveté in Marx.

11. See David Gordon, *Resurrecting Marx: The Analytical Marxists on Freedom, Exploitation, and Justice* (New Brunswick, 1990).

12. Jameson, *Late Marxism,* p. 5; *Postmodernism,* p. 49; *The Ideologies of Theory,* vol. 2, p. 207.

13. Jameson, *Signatures of the Visible,* p. 23.

14. Ibid., pp. 23–24.
15. Jameson, *The Ideologies of Theory*, vol. 2, p. 207.
16. Jameson, *Signatures of the Visible*, p. 37.
17. Jameson, *The Ideologies of Theory*, vol. 2, p. 208; *Postmodernism*, p. 417.
18. Jameson, *Late Marxism*, p. 250; *Postmodernism*, pp. 207, 335, 256, 258; *The Ideologies of Theory*, vol. 2, pp. 189, 203.
19. Dario Fernandez-Morera, "Materialist Discourse in Academia during the Age of Late Marxism," *Academic Questions* 4 (Spring 1991): 15–29.
20. Jameson, *Postmodernism*, pp. 335, 401, 25.
21. Jameson, *Late Marxism*, pp. 6, 3; *Postmodernism*, pp. xviii, 354.
22. Jameson, *Postmodernism*, pp. 401–02.
23. Ibid., pp. 257, 5.
24. Jameson, *Signatures of the Visible*, pp. 22, 32; *Late Marxism*, p. 248.
25. Jameson, *Signatures of the Visible*, p. 29.
26. Ibid.
27. Jameson, *Postmodernism*, p. 7. Jameson's incompetence regarding this painting does not stop here. He introduces it as "Van Gogh's well-known painting of the peasant shoes." Unfortunately for Jameson, it is well known that Van Gogh painted many pairs of shoes, and although he thinks he is continuing and modifying Heidegger's discussion of a Van Gogh shoes painting, he has the wrong one. His illustration (facing his p. 10) is not the one illustrated by Meyer Schapiro, who in a 1968 paper established (after corresponding with the philosopher) which of the shoes paintings Heidegger was talking about: "The Still Life as Personal Object: A Note on Heidegger and Van Gogh," reprinted in his *Theory and Philosophy of Art: Style, Artist and Society* (New York, 1994). In this paper Schapiro had already noted that Heidegger was clearly ignorant of the fact that these were Van Gogh's own boots; Jameson simply repeats Heidegger's mistake. I am indebted to John Hollander for drawing my attention to Schapiro's paper. Heidegger's discussion is in his *Der Ursprung des Kunstwerkes* (Frankfurt, 1950), which Jameson cites in the English translation ("The Origin of the Work of Art," in Albert Hofstadter and Richard Kuhns, eds., *Philosophies of Art and Beauty* [New York, 1964]).
28. Jameson, *Signatures of the Visible*, p. 31; *Postmodernism*, pp. 309, 44.
29. Jameson, *The Ideologies of Theory*, vol. 1, p. xxvii.
30. Jameson, *Postmodernism*, p. 1; *Late Marxism*, p. 249; *Postmodernism*, pp. 5, 45–46, ix.
31. See Chap. 3, this vol.
32. Jameson, *The Ideologies of Theory*, vol. 2, pp. 74, 73.
33. Second only to Jameson in influence among race-gender-class scholars is Terry Eagleton, and that too is disturbing. Eric Griffiths said recently that "a

Marxist could not but be ashamed of Terry Eagleton's productions—their disgraceful sloppiness in formulation, the abeyance in them of any sense of history more detailed than that of a 'quality' colour magazine, their self-publicizing, opportunism and political futility." "Dialectic without Detail," *Times Literary Supplement*, 28 June 1991, p. 7.

6   Activism and Knowledge

1. See Chap. 3, this vol.
2. See Barbara Rhoades Ellis' account of the conference, "Pod People Infest AAUW," *Heterodoxy* 1 (December 1992): 4–5. At last, the AAUW seems to recognize that McIntosh is a liability; see "AAUW Self-Defense," *National Review*, 26 September 1994, p. 2, where Anne Bryant, the executive director of AAUW, attempts to deny the degree of its involvement with McIntosh's ideas. In a reply in the same issue, Christina Hoff Sommers shows, however, that to do so Bryant has to misrepresent the facts.
3. Judith Lewis Herman, *Trauma and Recovery* (New York, 1992); Anne Campbell, *Men, Women, and Aggression* (New York, 1993); Susan Bordo, *Unbearable Weight: Feminism, Western Culture, and the Body* (Berkeley, 1993); Robbie F. Davis-Floyd, *Birth as an American Rite of Passage* (Berkeley, 1992); Sara Ruddick, "A New Birth of Birth," *New York Times Book Review,* 8 November 1992, p. 23.
4. See Chap. 3, this vol.
5. Phyllis Chesler, "The Shellshocked Woman," *New York Times Book Review,* 23 August 1992, pp. 11–12; Beryl Lieff Benderly, "The Perps Are Almost Always Male," *New York Times Book Review,* 20 June 1993, p. 10; Maud Ellmann, "Love Me Slender," *New York Times Book Review,* 26 September 1993, p. 14; and Ruddick, "A New Birth of Birth," p. 23. Ruddick assures us that "I share Ms. Davis-Floyd's suspicion of technocratic values, and can imagine the act of giving birth becoming an occasion for philosophic and political as well as personal transformation. And I admire, without qualification, the generous, critical, passionate spirit that animates this book." Many more such cases are cited in my "The Takeover of *The New York Times Book Review,*" *Heterodoxy* 2 (November 1993): 4, 5, 15.
6. See Kenneth Minogue, "Enlivening the Victims' Lives," *Times Literary Supplement,* 7 June 1991, p. 8: "Feminist Theory . . . does not really belong in the cool groves of academe. It is passionate and salvationist in a similar way to Marxism, new religious movements and occult enthusiasms: all of them know in advance not only the conclusions they will arrive at but the appropriate attitude towards those conclusions."

7. Myra Sadker and David Sadker, *Failing at Fairness* (New York, 1994).

8. Christina Hoff Sommers, however, has thrown considerable doubt on the existence of this drop in self-esteem in *Who Stole Feminism?* chap. 8.

9. For Susan Faludi, for example, all criticism of feminist thought is simply backlash: *Backlash: The Undeclared War against American Women* (New York, 1991).

10. An especially virulent example of this refusal to consider possible good faith in an intellectual opponent is former Harvard law professor Derrick Bell; see his *Faces at the Bottom of the Well: The Permanence of Racism* (New York, 1992). Bell sees racism everywhere and thinks blacks worse off now than at any time since the end of slavery. But even figures who cultivate a more moderate image, such as Cornel West, allow "the inference to stand that opposition to these policies [affirmative action] can be more or less legitimately perceived as racism," as Carol Ianonne puts it in her "Middle Man" (*National Review,* 19 July 1993, pp. 60–61), a review of West's *Race Matters* (Boston, 1993).

11. The most egregious example is still that of Stanley Fish, who, following the formation of a new chapter of the National Association of Scholars (NAS) at Duke University, said in a letter to the student newspaper (*The Chronicle,* 14 September 1990) that "the NAS is widely known to be racist, sexist, homophobic." Fish was trying to justify a letter he had written to the provost, Phillip Griffiths, in which he attempted to exclude the members of the organization from serving on key faculty committees, a letter Fish at first denied having written.

12. *MLA Newletter* (Summer 1991): 21; Peter Breuer, letter to the editor, *MLA Newsletter* (Fall 1991): 18.

13. See Linda Seebach, "Ground Rules Twist the Academic Game," *Los Angeles Daily News,* 18 February 1993; see also Sommers, *Who Stole Feminism?* chap. 5.

14. Caryn McTighe Musil, ed., *The Courage to Question: Women's Studies and Student Learning* (Washington, D.C., 1992); Musil, ed., *Students at the Center: Feminist Assessment* (Washington, D.C., 1992).

15. Musil, *Students at the Center,* p. 33.

16. Ibid., pp. 29–38.

17. Carolyn J. Mooney, "Review of Women's Studies Cites Personalized Learning as Strength," *Chronicle of Higher Education,* 10 March 1993, p. A15.

18. Denise K. Magner, "When Whites Teach Black Studies," *Chronicle of Higher Education,* 1 December 1993, pp. A19–A20. See also Magner's "White Professor Wins Discrimination Suit against Black College," *Chronicle of Higher Education,* 21 April 1993, p. A17, a report of the case of a white professor denied tenure at a historically black institution. Many black

students supported the professor, and the seniors voted to dedicate the 1993 college yearbook to him; here, as so often happens in matters of political correctness, students were more in touch with reality than were the professors and administrators.

19. See Sommers, *Who Stole Feminism?* pp. 36–37; and Ellis, "Pod People," p. 5.

20. John M. Ellis, *Against Deconstruction* (Princeton, 1988), p. 67.

21. Richard Levin, "Feminist Thematics and Shakespearean Tragedy," *PMLA* 103 (1988): 129.

22. *PMLA* 104 (1989): 77–78.

23. Arthur J. Weitzman, letter to the editor, *PMLA* 104 (1989): 357.

24. *PMLA* 104 (1989): 78–79.

25. Richard Wolin, ed., *The Heidegger Controversy* (New York, 1992); Thomas Sheehan, "A Normal Nazi," *New York Review of Books*, 14 January 1993, pp. 30–35.

26. An excellent account of this episode is David Lehman's *Signs of the Times: Deconstruction and the Fall of Paul de Man* (New York, 1991), especially chap. 9, "A Scandal in Academe." Lehman cuts through the special pleading of Derrida on behalf of de Man, neatly exposing double moral standards. Lehman leaves no doubt that this was shabby and dishonest behavior on Derrida's part.

27. *New York Review of Books*, 22 April 1993, a continuation of letters and replies printed in the 11 February, 4 March, and 25 March issues.

28. The multisignature letters were in *Proceedings and Addresses of the American Philosophical Association* 66 (January 1993): 97–108, following earlier exchanges in vols. 65 (January 1992): 92–99 and 65 (June 1992): 55–84. Sommers' reply was printed in the issue following the main body of letters, 66 (June 1993): 56–57.

29. Peter Washington, *Fraud, Literary Theory and the End of English* (London, 1989), p. 20. See also my review of *Fraud:* "Radical Literary Theory," *London Review of Books*, 8 February 1990, pp. 7–8.

7 Power, Objectivity, and PC Logic

1. See, e.g., Michel Foucault, *Power/Knowledge: Selected Essays and Interviews, 1972–77*, ed. Colin Gordon (New York, 1977). I am concerned here with the general shape of the idea that has entered into race-gender-class orthodoxy: power as the most important explanatory factor in human affairs. To examine the development of the idea and its use by Foucault in specific contexts— for example, in relation to sexuality or criminality—is beyond the scope of this book. The best general account of Foucault seems to me that by J. G.

Merquior, *Foucault* (Berkeley, 1985). See also James Miller, *The Passion of Michel Foucault* (New York, 1993). An uncommonly insightful short account is Mark Horowitz's review of Miller's *The Passion of Michel Foucault*, in *Heterodoxy* 1 (February 1993): 14–15.

2. Merquior, *Foucault*, p. 115.

3. This is essentially the stance of Michel Foucault in his *Surveiller et punir: Naissance de la prison* (Paris, 1975); translated by Alan Sheridan under the title *Discipline and Punish: The Birth of the Prison* (New York, 1977).

4. Thomas E. Wartenberg, ed., *Rethinking Power* (Albany, 1992).

5. See Chap. 3, this vol.

6. Ibid.

7. Merquior, *Foucault*, p. 117.

8. See, once more, Sniderman and Piazza, *The Scar of Race*.

9. See Jeremy L. Milk, "Inspiration or Hate-Monger?" *Chronicle of Higher Education*, 19 January 1994, pp. A33–A34. The fact that the *Chronicle of Higher Education* felt the need to keep an open mind in this title is itself remarkable.

10. See Mary Crystal Cage, "The Fiery Speeches Continue," *Chronicle of Higher Education*, 16 February 1994, pp. A41–A42.

11. Andrew Hacker, *Two Nations: Black and White, Separate, Hostile, Unequal* (New York, 1992).

12. See Linda Seebach, "Thwarting Attacks on the Constitution," *Los Angeles Daily News*, 11 March 1993.

13. Stanley Fish, *Doing What Comes Naturally: Change, Rhetoric, and the Practice of Theory in Literary and Legal Studies* (Durham, 1989).

14. Ibid., pp. 516 (here Fish borrows a phrase from Richard Rorty), 520.

15. Ibid., p. 11.

16. Ibid., pp. 345, 225.

17. An introduction is Mark Kelman's *A Guide to Critical Legal Studies* (Cambridge, Mass., 1987); Thomas S. Kuhn, *The Structure of Scientific Revolutions,* 2d ed. (Chicago, 1970).

18. Fish, *Doing What Comes Naturally*, pp. 520, 516.

19. Ibid., pp. 522, 521.

20. This is the view that words name the distinguishing characteristics of things; for a critique, see my *Language, Thought, and Logic* (Evanston, 1993).

8 Is Theory to Blame?

1. Erich Trunz, ed., *Goethes Werke,* Hamburger edition, 12th ed., 14 vols. (Munich, 1981), 13:317: "Und so kann man sagen, dass wir schon bei jedem

aufmerksamen Blick in die Welt theoretisieren"; and 12:432: "Das Höchste wäre zu begreifen, dass alles Faktische schon Theorie ist."

2. Ernst Cassirer, ed., *Immanuel Kants Werke*, 11 vols. (Berlin, 1912–23), vol. 3, *Kritik der reinen Vernunft*, p. 80: "Gedanken ohne Inhalt sind leer; Anschauungen ohne Begriffe sind blind."

3. See, e.g., René Wellek and Austin Warren, *Theory of Literature* (New Haven, 1949).

4. Guy Sircello, "The Poetry of Theory: Reflections on After the New Criticism," *Journal of Aesthetics and Art Criticism* 42 (1984): 387–96. The example is Frank Lentricchia's *After the New Criticism* (Chicago, 1980). Sircello confesses to inadequate knowledge of the field as a whole, and he does not grasp the fact that although Lentricchia's book is representative of the present state of the field, it is decidedly not "a good orientation to the whole field" (p. 387) in the sense of being a guide to its most distinguished and enduring work.

5. Inadequacies of this kind have led occasionally to the blanket claim that theory of criticism is not a useful activity. See W. J. T. Mitchell, ed., *Against Theory* (Chicago, 1985). Stanley Fish makes an argument for the irrelevance of theory a leading issue in his book *Doing What Comes Naturally,* but for reasons given in Chap. 7, it is logically unimportant in that context. An older version of this rejection of theory can be found in the critical pluralism that advocated an eclectic acceptance of all critical approaches, a view that precluded any analysis of their relative strengths and weaknesses. For arguments against this position, see my *Theory of Literary Criticism,* chap. 1.

6. A survey of the field and outline of an analysis of major issues is contained in my contribution ("Theory") to *The Princeton Encyclopedia of Poetry and Poetics,* ed. Alex Preminger and T. V. F. Brogan, 3d ed. (Princeton, 1993), pp. 1282–90. See also my *Theory of Literary Criticism* for further development of issues briefly raised here.

7. This debate began in earnest in 1946 with the essay "The Intentional Fallacy," by W. K. Wimsatt with Monroe C. Beardsley, republished in their collected theoretical essays, *The Verbal Icon: Studies in the Meaning of Poetry* (Lexington, Ky., 1954). Michel Foucault, "Qu'est-ce qu'un auteur?" *Bulletin de la Société française de Philosophie* 63 (1969): 73–104, appeared more than two decades later. An English version, "What Is an Author?" appeared in 1977 in *Language, Counter-Memory, and Practice: Selected Essays and Interviews,* trans. and ed. Donald Bouchard (Ithaca, 1977), pp. 113–38.

8. Ellis, *Against Deconstruction,* chap. 2.

9. Stephen J. Greenblatt, *Renaissance Self-Fashioning: From More to Shakespeare*

(Chicago, 1980), p. 4; and "Invisible Bullets: Renaissance Authority and Its Subversion," *Glyph* 8 (1981): 56.

10. "Is a New Historicist Free" (exchange of letters between Stephen Greenblatt and Paul Cantor), *Academic Questions* 7 (1994): 5–6.

11. See Paul Cantor's excellent discussion of this point in "Stephen Greenblatt's New Historicist Vision," *Academic Questions* 6 (1993): 21–36.

12. For details, see John M. Ellis and Evelyn W. Asher, "German Theory and Criticism: Twentieth Century to 1968," in *The Johns Hopkins Guide to Literary Theory and Criticism,* ed. Michael Groden and Martin Kreiswirth (Baltimore, 1994), pp. 348–52.

13. It is worth noting that the original proposal for the graduate program in the "History of Consciousness" at the Santa Cruz campus of the University of California was simply an exposition of Dilthey's *Geistesgeschichte.*

14. Edward Pechter, "The New Historicism and Its Discontents: Politicizing Renaissance Drama," *PMLA* 101 (1987): 299. Pechter continues: "When addressed to the left-liberal academic community, for whom the monarchy is an anachronism, feminism an article of faith, and colonialism a source of embarrassed guilt, these critical versions cannot help draining the plays of much of their potential to involve an audience."

15. Wimsatt, with Beardsley, *The Verbal Icon,* pp. 3–18.

16. These two contradictory viewpoints, which are both obsessed with male wrongdoing but which find it in diametrically opposed places, occur in the same anthology of feminist writing: Gayle Greene and Coppélia Kahn, eds., *Making a Difference: Feminist Literary Criticism* (London, 1985). The writers are Nelly Furman, "The Politics of Language: Beyond the Gender Principle," p. 71; and Sydney Janet Kaplan, "Varieties of Feminist Criticism," p. 41.

17. For an extended discussion of this strain in recent theory, see chap. 5 of my *Against Deconstruction.*

18. The number of race-gender-class scholars who have expressed this view is overwhelming. One example will suffice: Lorraine Code, *What Can She Know? Feminist Theory and the Construction of Knowledge* (Ithaca, 1991.)

19. Harry Levin, *Why Literary Criticism Is Not an Exact Science* (Cambridge, Mass., 1967).

20. Wimsatt, with Beardsley, *The Verbal Icon,* pp. 21–39.

21. Northrop Frye, *Anatomy of Criticism: Four Essays* (Princeton, 1957).

22. E.g., Claude Lévi-Strauss, *Anthropologie Structurale* (Paris, 1958).

23. Another strand of deconstructionist criticism suggests a different goal for criticism, however; it asserts that all texts undermine their surface meaning

and embrace the reverse of what they appear to say. Here, meaning has a much more determined shape, one knowable to readers if they will only read in a certain way. This strand is analyzed in my *Against Deconstruction,* chap. 3.

24. Leo Spitzer, *Linguistics and Literary History* (Princeton, 1948).

25. See the excellent discussion of Peirce's "Assault on Cartesianism," in W. B. Gallie, *Peirce and Pragmatism* (Harmondsworth, 1952), chap. 3.

26. Ibid., p. 35. See also the two aphorisms cited above, note 1.

27. Thomas S. Kuhn, *The Structure of Scientific Revolutions,* 2d ed. (Chicago, 1970).

28. Fish, *Doing What Comes Naturally,* pp. 345 and 487. Part of the blame here must go to Kuhn, who does not mention Peirce in the course of his book and appears not to have known the source of his own ideas.

29. Hayden White, *Metahistory: The Historical Imagination in Nineteenth-Century Europe* (Baltimore, 1973). White's position is developed in two further books: *Tropics of Discourse: Essays in Cultural Criticism* (Baltimore, 1978) and *The Content of the Form: Narrative Discourse and Historical Representation* (Baltimore, 1987).

30. This is the summary of Hans Kellner in his "Hayden White," in *The Johns Hopkins Guide to Literary Theory and Criticism,* ed. Michael Groden and Martin Kreiswirth (Baltimore, 1994), pp. 728–29.

31. White, *Metahistory,* p. 2.

32. E.g., E. H. Carr, *What Is History?* (New York, 1961).

33. Robert E. Spiller, "Literary History," in *The Aims and Methods of Scholarship in Modern Languages and Literatures,* ed. James Thorpe (New York, 1963), p. 53.

34. Kellner, "Hayden White," p. 728.

35. A typical instance here is the collection of essays *Aesthetics and Language,* ed. William Elton (Oxford, 1954).

36. See Northrop Frye, "Literary Criticism," in *The Aims and Methods of Scholarship in Modern Languages and Literatures,* ed. James Thorpe (New York, 1963), pp. 57–69.

37. A. J. Ayer, *Language, Truth, and Logic,* 2d ed. (London, 1946), chap. 6.

38. E.g., P. H. Nowell-Smith, *Ethics* (Harmondsworth, 1954).

39. This view is discussed in my *Theory of Literary Criticism,* a somewhat belated contribution to the second phase of literary theory. Its underlying logic is set out much more explicitly in *Language, Thought, and Logic.*

40. Barbara Herrnstein Smith's *Contingencies of Value: Alternative Perspectives for Critical Theory* (Cambridge, Mass., 1988) is the only sustained attempt to provide a theoretical basis for race-gender-class skepticism about evaluation.

Smith argues that "all value is radically contingent" (p. 30) and is therefore not an inherent quality of things; and that literary value is "relative," that is, "a changing function of multiple variables" (p. 11). Value, then, exists only in a particular situation for a particular set of people. Smith regards notions such as "the test of time" only as a surrogate for the illegitimate claim of universal value on the part of "those with cultural power" and believes that texts that survive this test do no more than "reflect and reinforce establishment ideologies" (p. 51). She also takes aim at those whom she calls "the custodians of the Western canon" for being unable to grasp the fact that Homer, Dante, and Shakespeare have value only for the "orthodoxly educated population of the West" and do not possess "transcendent universal value" (p. 53). For all her attempt at logical sophistication, Smith's argument thus descends into orthodox race-gender-class crudities and anti-Western animus. Her logic is not original: the attempt to veto all statements of value that are not statements of fact about the value of something in a particular situation is in fact logically identical with A. J. Ayer's logical positivism, and, like Ayer, she evades the crucial question of the use and function of general evaluative judgments. Nor is her logic truly supportive of the race-gender-class outlook she tries to bolster with it: her reduction of value to particular situations still could not prevent judgments about the relative universality of Western culture that would be based on the sheer number and variety of situations in which its influence is felt. The notion that Shakespeare will appeal only to one who is educated "orthodoxly" is particularly silly. Nor is Smith's position consistent with the highly negative attitude of race-gender-class critics to positivist logic. An excellent longer discussion of Smith's "hard-line utilitarianism" is Bromwich, *Politics by Other Means,* pp. 204–14.

41. Paul de Man, *The Resistance to Theory* (Minneapolis, 1986).

42. See my *Against Deconstruction* and Lehman's *Signs of the Times.*

43. In an interview on PBS's *McNeil-Lehrer Newshour* (19 June 1991), Fish said: "We have to realize that there are persons from outside the academy who are spearheading the attack on multiculturalism or political correctness, as it is sometimes called, organizations like the National Association of Scholars. . . . What this means is that much of the agitation occurring on campus has been produced by political, a political effort that originates off campus. . . . The two groups to whom the neo-conservatives address their complaints and their attacks first of all are alumni and second of all concerned communities around the various universities." Although his television audience was probably largely unaware that the National Association of Scholars (NAS) is an organization of academics—professors, college administrators, and graduate students—Fish himself knew it well; see above, Chap. 6, note 11. See

also Dorothy Rabinowitz, "Vive the Academic Resistance," *Wall Street Journal,* 13 November 1990.

44. See Scott Heller, "Changing Trends in Literary Scholarship Modify the Appearance of English Institute as It Celebrates 50th Meeting at Harvard," *Chronicle of Higher Education,* 11 September 1991, pp. A9–A10.

45. Two news items on the same page of the *Chronicle of Higher Education* (11 September 1991, p. A19) report opinions that the press is responsible for much of the political correctness controversy. The first cites Alan Wald's concern about impressions generated by "news organizations and conservative critics." The second announces that a special session of the next conference of the Modern Language Association of America is to be devoted to how the press covers new scholarship and speaks of "the tension between academics and journalists." The recently circulated manifesto of the Teachers for a Democratic Culture also attacks "media reports" and tells us that the "mainstream media have reported misinformed opinions as if they were established facts" (Scott Heller, "Scholars Form Group to Combat 'Malicious Distortions' by Conservatives," *Chronicle of Higher Education,* 18 September 1991, pp. A19–A20; Heller reports that the new group claims it has been "consistently misrepresented and unfairly attacked by conservative critics, journalists, and authors" [p. A19]). Although such claims are common, the distortions are rarely specified. The unbiased observer would in any case conclude that Stanley Fish, Catharine Stimpson, and others like them have had more than their share of access to the news media. Their image problem is due not to the public's being unaware of their opinions but to its knowledge of them.

46. Graff made this remark when interviewed by Denise Magner; see her "Gathering to Assess Battle against 'Political Correctness': Scholars Look for New Ways to Resist 'Illiberal Radicals,'" *Chronicle of Higher Education,* 30 October 1991, pp. A17–A19.

9 How Did It All Happen?

1. Three recent articles from the *Chronicle of Higher Education* show this pressure at work: Ivan Karp and Stephen D. Lavine, "Museums Must Take on New Roles in This Multicultural Society," 14 April 1993, pp. B3–B4: "The elite museum's theory of education, where high culture trickles down to the masses, is no longer unthinkingly accepted. . . . Museums are being asked to open up [to] . . . participation by previously marginalized groups"; Alan Wallach, "Revisionism Has Transformed Art History, but Not Museums," 22 January 1992, pp. B2–B3; and Lisa G. Corrin, "Do Museums Perpetuate

Cultural Bias?" 15 June 1994, p. B48: "Under enormous pressure, the museum community has been forced to consider the relation between what it does and the historical, political, and social context in which it operates." The Smithsonian has shown the kind of results these pressures will increasingly produce. According to William H. Truettner, a curator, an exhibit on the Wild West "relied heavily on the writings of the 'new' Western historians," and the accompanying texts "sought to explain the images on display as ideological constructions designed to justify national expansion" ("The West and the Heroic Ideal: Using Images to Interpret History," *Chronicle of Higher Education,* 20 November 1991). But the distinguished historian Daniel Boorstin saw it, rather, as "a perverse, historically inaccurate, destructive exhibit" (Kristin Huckshorn, "Wild West Tamed in Reinterpreted Art," *San Jose Mercury News,* 22 May 1991). Two more examples of the new Smithsonian style are noted in a recent *Wall Street Journal* editorial ("War and the Smithsonian," 29 August 1994). A television special informed viewers that cannibalism in a New Guinea tribe was "a well-functioning example of how a complete criminal justice system works"; and a proposed script for an exhibit centering on the *Enola Gay* (the plane that bombed Hiroshima) was to read: "For most Americans, this war . . . was a war of vengeance. For most Japanese, it was a war to defend their unique culture against Western imperialism." (After much public criticism, the exhibition was canceled.) It is interesting to observe that ideological obsession here goes hand in hand with moral obtuseness and serious ignorance of history—all at the nation's most important museum of American culture and history.

2. This is also Camille Paglia's impression, to judge from her "The Nursery-School Campus: The Corrupting of the Humanities in the U.S.," *Times Literary Supplement,* 22 May 1992, p. 19.

3. W. K. Wimsatt, "Battering the Object: The Ontological Approach," in *Contemporary Criticism,* ed. Malcolm Bradbury and David Palmer (London, 1971), p. 65.

4. See Adam Begley's "The I's Have It: Duke's Moi Critics Expose Themselves," *Lingua Franca* 4 (March-April 1994): 54–59.

5. Elaine Marks, "President's Column," *MLA Newsletter,* Spring 1993, pp. 2–3.

6. Stanley Fish, "Why Literary Criticism Is Like Virtue," *London Review of Books,* 10 June 1993, p. 11. See also Dinesh D'Souza, "Pied Pipers of Relativism Reverse Course," *Wall Street Journal,* 27 July 1993.

7. Steven Watts, "Academe's Leftists Are Something of a Fraud," *Chronicle of Higher Education,* 29 April 1992, p. A40. See also Paglia ("The Nursery-School Campus"), who also insists that "they are not radicals at all. . . . They are people without deep beliefs."

8. For example, in the literature department at the University of California, Santa Cruz, a bitter conflict has broken out between two factions that are roughly equal in size. The conflict is not about the value of race-gender-class perspectives, for both sides share that orientation; it is over a difference in the interpretation of the new creed. The older group uses race-gender-class to do new readings of classic texts; these are the literary radicals, who may denounce the canonical authors in ritual fashion but still keep writing about them. In the other group are the real radicals. Their position on race, gender, and class is no literary-critical pose, and so they actually read and teach the literature of the downtrodden ("World Literature" is the technical term here). In their favor, it must be said that they can recognize something phony when they see it, but even so, it is chilling to come face to face with a race-gender-class group that really means what it says and accepts the grim consequences.

9. Barbara Herrnstein Smith, "Hirsch, Literacy, and the National Culture," in *The Politics of Liberal Education,* ed. Darryl J. Gless and Barbara Herrnstein Smith (Durham, 1992), p. 89.

10. See also Allan Bloom, *The Closing of the American Mind* (New York, 1987), p. 159.

11. On the more general question of the dangers posed by the intellectual ambitions of the intelligentsia, see Gary Saul Morson, "What Is the Intelligentsia? An Old Russian Question," *Academic Questions* 6 (1993): 20–38.

12. It is, of course, neither, for Marx, not Derrida, is responsible for this train of thought. In a forthcoming book, Dario Fernandez-Morera points out that this allegedly deconstructive technique is only the standard dialectical materialist reduction of motivation, known to academicians and students in the formerly communist countries of eastern Europe by the derogatory shorthand "diamat." It is ironic that this elderly reductionist habit is now seen as avant-garde thought by campus radicals in the West.

13. Many colleagues seem to me to be blind to this connection. When I ask them how they think affirmative action has affected the department, they understand the issue I am raising to be the quality of the new minority and female faculty and students but never the content of the curriculum or the intellectual climate of the department.

14. Sowell, *Preferential Policies,* pp. 76–87.

15. Helen Vendler, "Feminism and Literature," *New York Review of Books,* 30 May 1990, pp. 19–25.

16. John Le Carré, *Smiley's People* (London, 1979), p. 67.

17. For example, when Rebecca Sinkler, the partisan feminist editor of the *New York Times Book Review,* gave the book to her old friend and former teacher

Nina Auerbach for a predictable trashing (12 June 1994), the malice and dishonesty of Auerbach's review was so obvious (e.g., "Christina Hoff Sommers is a wallflower at feminist conferences. In revenge, she attends them obsessively, writes down all the stupid things she hears, and has now spewed them back") that it provoked not just a storm of protest but a response almost without precedent. A whole series of columns in other newspapers commented on this unethical behavior by Sinkler and Auerbach: the *New York Daily News* (12 June), *Washington Post* (14 June), *New York Post* (14 June), *Worcester Telegram and Gazette* (14 June and 16 June), and *Boston Globe* (16 June).

18. See above, Chap. 1.

19. Carolyn J. Mooney, "Study Finds Professors Are Still Teaching the Classics, Sometimes in New Ways," *Chronicle of Higher Education*, 6 November 1991, pp. A1–A2.

20. Peter Shaw, "The Modern Language Association Is Misleading the Public," *Chronicle of Higher Education*, 27 November 1991, p. B3, and Will Morissey, Norman Fruman, and Thomas Short, "Ideology and Literary Studies," pt. 2, "The MLA's Deceptive Survey," *Academic Questions* 6 (1993): 46–58. See also the subsequent correspondence in the *Chronicle of Higher Education*, 18 December 1991 and 8 January 1992; and John Sutherland, "The Annual MLA Disaster," *London Review of Books*, 16 December 1993, pp. 11–12.

21. See Clint Bolick's review of Guinier's *The Tyranny of the Majority* (New York, 1994), in *The Defender* 1 (May 1994): 12–13.

22. See my review of *Conversations: Straight Talk with America's Sister President*, by Johnnetta Cole (New York, 1993), in *Heterodoxy* 1 (March 1993): 15.

23. Gregory S. Jay, "The First Round in the Culture Wars," *Chronicle of Higher Education*, 26 February 1992.

24. See Chap. 6, this vol.

25. As Carol Iannone aptly observed, this is a mythical center: "PC with a Human Face," *Commentary* 95 (June 1993): 44–48. It is inhabited either by people who are really in favor of race-gender-class but are scared of looking like radicals or by people who are really against race-gender-class but are scared of being labeled right-wing. There are two positions here, not three.

26. See the interesting article by John Leo, "The Professors of Dogmatism," *U.S. News and World Report*, 18 January 1993, p. 25, on the 1992 annual MLA conference, at which Stimpson was still insisting that PC "doesn't actually exist."

27. See, on Paglia, the "Reductio ad Absurdum" column, *Heterodoxy* 1 (May 1992): 3; on Parks, "LSU's War against Men," *Heterodoxy* 1 (June 1992): 4–5; on Gribben, Richard Bernstein, *Dictatorship of Virtue*, chap. 9.

28. See the account of this phenomenon in Sommers, *Who Stole Feminism?* chap. 5, "The Feminist Classroom."

29. Graff uses a personal anecdote to prove his point: he tells us that as a student he listened at ten o'clock to a lecturer who took a New Critical approach to Milton, then at eleven went to a class where New Critical theories were said to have no applicability to Milton. That is what I, too, remember from my student days, and how interesting it was. But Graff? "I hardly focused at the time on the fact that my two teachers were in disagreement. . . . Since no one was asking me to think about the relationship between the two courses, I did not" (*Beyond the Culture Wars,* p. 108.) This is an astonishing admission. The only thing that this anecdote suggests is a remarkable lack of intellectual curiosity on Graff's part at the time.

30. See also Stephen Burd's "Defiant Conservative Relishes the NEH Fights to Come," *Chronicle of Higher Education,* 29 June 1994, p. A25, a profile of Peter Shaw, member of the National Council on the Humanities. When asked to comment on Shaw's views for this profile, Graff responded: "Peter Shaw is an ignoramus."

31. Graff, *Beyond the Culture Wars,* p. 169.

32. Ibid., p. 100. Graff's attempt to attack economists from his new position on the radical left is equally embarrassing, but his silliest assertion is the claim that Fredric Jameson is "not as far as he may seem from Orwell" (p. 159). A man who must persuade himself that an unreconstructed apologist for Stalin and Mao is not far from Orwell is clearly under strain.

33. For an account of an effort that is already under way in California, see Joye Mercer, "Assault on Affirmative Action," *Chronicle of Higher Education,* 16 March 1994, p. A25.

Index